African American Biographies

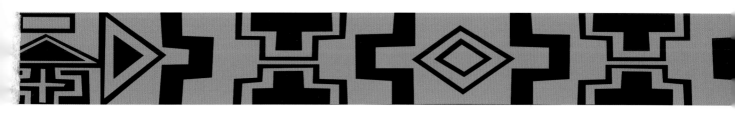

Volume 4

Edwards, Herman—Greener, Richard

an imprint of

■SCHOLASTIC

www.scholastic.com/librarypublishing

First published 2006 by Grolier,
an imprint of Scholastic Library Publishing,
Old Sherman Turnpike
Danbury, Connecticut 06816

© 2006 The Brown Reference Group plc

Set ISBN 978-0-7172-6090-4
Volume ISBN 978-0-7172-6094-2

Library of Congress Cataloging-in-Publication Data
African American biographies.
    p. cm.
    Includes index.
    Contents: v.1. Aaliyah–Blyden, Edward W.—v.2. Bond, Horace
Mann–Clarke, John Henrik—v.3. Cleaver, Eldridge–Edmonds, Kenneth
"Babyface"—v.4. Edwards, Herman–Greener, Richard —v.5. Greenfield,
Elizabeth–Jacobs, Harriet—v.6. Jakes, T. D.–Loury, Glenn C.—v.7. Love,
Nat–Oliver, Joe "King"—v.8. O'Neal, Shaquille–Satcher, David—v.9.
Savage, Augusta–Tyson, Cicely—v.10. Tyson, Mike–Zollar, Doris
    ISBN 978-0-7172-6090-4
    I. African Americans—Biography—Juvenile literature. I.
        Scholastic Library Publishing

E185.96.A439 2006
920'.009296073–dc22
[B]

                        2005050391

For information address the publisher:
Grolier, Scholastic Library Publishing,
Old Sherman Turnpike,
Danbury, Connecticut 06816

FOR THE BROWN REFERENCE GROUP PLC

Project Editors: Sally MacEachern, Aruna Vasudevan
Design: Q2A Solutions
Picture Researcher: Laila Torsun
Index: Kay Ollerenshaw
Design Manager: Lynne Ross
Production Director: Alastair Gourlay
Senior Managing Editor: Tim Cooke
Editorial Director: Lindsey Lowe

Academic consultants:

        Molefi Kete Asante, Professor,
            Department of African American
            Studies, Temple University
        Mario J. Azevedo, Chair and Frank Porter
            Graham Professor, Department of Africana
            Studies, University of North Carolina at
            Charlotte
        Scott M. Lacy, University of California Faculty
            Fellow, Department of Black Studies,
            University of California
        Mawusi Renee Simmons, Development
            Consultant and Museum Docent, University
            of Pennsylvania Museum Philadelphia,
            Pennsylvania

Printed and bound in Singapore

ABOUT THIS SET

This is one of a set of 10 books about the African Americans who have helped shape the past of the United States and who play a vital part in the nation's life today. Some were leaders of the abolitionist movement against slavery in the latter half of the 19th century; others excelled in their fields despite being born into slavery themselves. The abolition of slavery after the Civil War (1861–1865) did not mark the end of the prejudice that prevented most black Americans from fulfilling their potential, however. During the first half of the 20th century the African Americans who made their names in the arts, entertainment, sports, academia, or business remained exceptions who reached prominence as the result of a determined struggle to overcome discrimination and disadvantage.

The civil rights advances of the 1950s and 1960s removed legal and institutional barriers to African American achievement, but pioneers in many fields still faced greater difficulties than their white peers. By the start of the 21st century, however, black Americans had become prominent in all fields of endeavor, from space exploration to government.

This set contains biographies of more than a thousand of the many African Americans who have made a mark. Some are household names; others are largely—and unjustly—overlooked or forgotten. Their entries explain not only what they achieved, but also why it was important. Every entry has a box of key dates for quick reference. Longer entries also include boxes on the people who inspired great African Americans or people they themselves have influenced in turn. Most entries have a "See also" feature that refers you to related articles elsewhere in the set. If you want to find out more about an individual there are suggested books and Web sites. Addresses may change, however, and the accuracy of information on sites may vary.

Throughout the set are a number of guidepost articles. They provide an overview of particular aspects of African American experience, such as the civil rights movement or the Harlem Renaissance of the 1920s, and help place the individuals featured in the biographies in a wider context.

The biographies are arranged alphabetically, mostly by last name but also by stage name. Each volume contains an index that covers the whole set and will help you locate entries easily.

CONTENTS

EDWARDS, Herman
Football Player, Coach

Herman Edwards was an outstanding football player who became a distinguished coach when he retired from playing in the National Football League (NFL).

Herman Edwards was born in New Jersey in 1954 and raised in Seaside, California. He went to Monterey High School and the University of California, Berkeley. There he played cornerback for the Golden Bears in 1972 and 1974, and set a team record with four interceptions in one game. He played the 1973 season with Monterey Peninsula Junior College and his senior season at San Diego State, where he obtained a BA in criminal justice.

From NFL player to coach

From 1977 to 1985 Edwards played in the NFL for the Philadelphia Eagles, making 33 career interceptions, the third-highest in the team's history. He split his final season in 1986 between the Los Angeles Rams and the Atlanta Falcons.

After retiring, Edwards became defensive back coach at San Jose State (1987–1989) and then moved to the Kansas City Chiefs, where he worked first in their Minority Fellowship program and then as defensive back coach.

In 1996 Edwards was appointed assistant head coach/defensive backfield coach of the Tampa Bay Buccaneers. Under him the Bucs finished in the top ten in pass defense in four of the next five seasons and in 1998 and 1999 had the NFL's second-ranked pass defense.

In January 2001 Edwards became the New York Jets' 13th full-time head coach. He quickly instilled in the team his philosophy and discipline, and the benefits were immediate. That season they went 7–1 on the road, their best away record ever, and reached the playoffs for the first time since 1998. The following year they won the highly

▲ *Herman Edwards flashes a smile during a 2003 game against the Jacksonville Jaguars at Giants Stadium. The Jets won 13–10.*

competitive AFC East and made back-to-back postseason appearances for the first time since 1985–1986. In his fourth season Edwards guided the Jets to the third-best winning percentage in their history (.547) and reached his own 30-win mark with the club in 53 games, one more than record-holder Joe Walton. Edwards is the only coach to have led the Green and White to winning seasons in three of his first four years.

Further reading: Goodman, Michael E. *The History of the New York Jets.* Mankato, MN: Creative Education, 2005.
http://www.newyorkjets.com/coaches/index.php?coaches_id=3 (Jets coaches' roster).

KEY DATES	
1954	Born in Monmouth, New Jersey, on April 27.
1977	Plays in the NFL with the Philadelphia Eagles.
1986	Retires from playing football.
1989	Joins the Kansas City Chiefs.
1996	Becomes assistant head coach of the Tampa Bay Buccaneers.
2001	Appointed head coach of the New York Jets.

ELDER, Clarence L.
Engineer, Inventor

Clarence L. Elder is a leading inventor and entrepreneur. The company he founded after leaving college in the 1950s is now an international leader in the field of electronic engineering. Its most profitable and widely used product, the Occustat system, makes a significant contribution to energy conservation in the United States and abroad.

Early life

Elder was born in Georgia in 1935. He studied electronics at Morgan State College (now Morgan State University) in Baltimore, Maryland. Not long after he graduated in 1956, Elder set up his own company, Elder Systems, Inc., in Baltimore. His business grew steadily, and in 1969 he won an award at the New York International Patent Exposition for outstanding achievement in the field of electronics.

Heating patent

Elder made his mark in 1975, when he patented a method of monitoring and regulating the heat in buildings—U.S. patent number 4,000,400. (A patent is the grant of a property right to the inventor, issued by the U.S. Patent and Trademark Office. It protects the invention for 20 years from the date of registration.)

Elder's invention—known as the Occustat system—works in conjunction with air-conditioning to regulate the temperature in a room according to the number of people who are in it. The more crowded the room, the less heat it requires; the fewer people it contains, the warmer it needs to be for comfort. When the room is empty, the heating or air-conditioning is reduced to minimum levels.

Occustat works by means of a beam of light across the doors that monitors comings and goings and adjusts the heating level accordingly. The invention is a major energy conserver that has saved the companies and schools that use it up to 30 percent on power bills.

Elder describes the system in his related patent documents: "The present invention relates to controlling the environment for comfort and for economy and also to register an accurate count of persons entering and leaving a space such as a room or building with means to control the illumination and temperature modification of the building to reduce costs by reducing the illumination and modifying the temperature, either heating or cooling, to more economical levels when the space is unoccupied."

Lighting

A variant form of the same system is now also used to control lighting: When Occustat-wired rooms are empty, the lights go out automatically and remain off until the next person enters them. This, too, has been a major economy for the firms, educational establishments, and even domestic residences that use the system.

Elder's inventions have provided the impetus for further developments in what has become known as Smart Room technology, which uses sensors, cameras, and computers to respond to the words, movements, and gestures of the inhabitants of the room.

Building on success

By the end of the 20th century, Elder and his associates owned 12 U.S. and foreign patents, trademarks, and copyrights. They include an electronically controlled noncapsizable ship container, and a sweepstakes programmer. Elder himself largely avoids publicity, preferring his work to speak for him.

Educators hope that the success of engineers like Elder will inspire young black students to take up engineering. According to a 2000 statement from a White House advisory group, although African Americans made up a quarter of the total workforce in the United States, only 5.9% of black workers were engineers.

KEY DATES	
1935	Born in Georgia.
1956	Graduates from Morgan State College, Baltimore, Maryland.
1975	Patents Occustat temperature-and light-regulating system.

Further reading: Aaseng, Nathan. *Black Inventors*. New York, NY: Facts on File, 1997.
Sullivan, Otha Richard, and Jim Haskins. *African American Inventors*. Hoboken, NJ: John Wiley & Sons, 1998.
http://web.mit.edu/invent/iow/elder.html (Inventor of the Week).
http://www.eepatents.com/patents/4000400.pdf (Description of patent 4,000,400).

ELDER, Lee
Golfer

Lee Elder became the first African American to play in the Masters Tournament in 1975 and the first to be included on the U.S. Ryder Cup team in 1979.

Robert Lee Elder was born in 1934. When he was nine, his father was killed while serving in the Army during World War II (1939–1945). His mother died three months later, apparently of grief. Left to fend for himself, Elder earned money by caddying at the all-white Tennison Park Golf Club in Dallas, Texas. He taught himself to play and was soon traveling the country playing for money. By 1967 he had earned enough to enroll in the Professional Golfers' Association of America (PGA) Tour's qualifying school.

Struggling with the establishment

Elder made the grade; but the professional golf circuit was white-dominated, and Elder experienced numerous humiliations. In 1968, for example, he and fellow African American pros were refused entry to the Pensacola Country Club, Florida, and had to change in the parking lot. Six years later he returned to the course to win the Monsanto Open in a playoff against Scotland's Peter Oosterhuis.

That victory qualified Elder for the Masters at Augusta, Georgia. In theory the Masters had been open to black golfers since 1960, but none had ever been invited despite mounting pressure on the organizers from Congress. Elder made history in 1975 by stepping out onto the course. He later recalled, "I didn't realize how important it was at the time, because all I really wanted so badly to do was play in the tournament." Despite huge media attention, Elder shot a respectable 74 in the first round, but after a 78 on the second day he missed the cut, the score that would have enabled him to continue playing the final two days, by four strokes.

▲ *Lee Elder displays the winner's trophy at the 1974 Monsanto Open in Pensacola, Florida.*

Elder played in five more Masters tournaments. In 1979 he became the first black man to play on the U.S. team in the biannual competition between the United States and Europe for the Ryder Cup. In addition to Pensacola Elder won another three PGA Tour events. By the time he retired from top-level competition in 1984, he had earned over $1 million in prize money. Elder joined the Senior PGA Tour that year, finishing second on the earnings list. When he finally quit playing, he worked to promote golf among ethnic minority youth.

See also: Color Bar and Professional Sports

Further reading: McDaniel, Pete. *Uneven Lies: The Heroic Story of African-Americans in Golf.* Greenwich, CT: American Golfer, 2000.
http://www.afrogolf.com/leeelder.html (Photos and stats).

KEY DATES	
1934	Born in Dallas, Texas, on July 14.
1959	Turns pro.
1967	Joins PGA tour.
1975	Plays in first Masters tournament.
1979	Selected for the U.S. Ryder Cup team.
1984	Retires to Senior Circuit.

ELDERS, Joycelyn
Public Health Advocate

A distinguished physician and public health advocate, Joycelyn Elders was the first African American to be appointed to the post of surgeon general advising the government on the nation's health care. Her forthright opinions on controversial issues such as contraception, teenage pregnancy, and universal health care brought criticism from conservatives, while her courage and determination in tackling serious national problems attracted the admiration of many others.

Born Minnie Lee Jones in Schaal, Arkansas, on August 13, 1933, she changed her name to Minnie Joycelyn Lee while in college; Elders is the name she took after her second marriage in 1960.

▼ *Joycelyn Elders testifies at her confirmation hearing for the post of surgeon general in Washington, D.C., on July 23, 1993.*

From sharecropper's daughter…

Elders was brought up in a poor sharecropping, or farming, community in southwestern Arkansas. She and her seven brothers and sisters were raised in a three-room shack with no running water, and all were expected to work in the cotton fields during planting and harvest time rather than attending school. Schaal, like many black communities in Arkansas, had few health facilities. Elders's mother gave birth without medical help, while one of her bothers had to travel 13 miles (21km) on a mule to see a physician after suffering a ruptured appendix.

At age 15 Elders won a church scholarship to attend Philander Smith College, an all-black institution in Little Rock, Arkansas. Her father opposed her enrollment; but she was supported by her mother and grandmother, who did extra farm work to pay for her bus fare into town. In college Elders was inspired to become a doctor after hearing a speech given by Edith Irby Jones (*see box on p. 8*), the first African American to study at the University of Arkansas's College of Medicine (UAMS).

After graduating with a BA in 1952, Elders joined the Army, serving in the Women's Medical Specialist Corps. It was not until 1956 that she was able to enroll at UAMS. Despite the recent end of segregation in public education, Elders—one of only three African Americans in a class of 100—still faced discrimination from students and teaching staff. Despite such difficulties, she received her MD (doctor of medicine) in 1960 and her MS in biochemistry in 1967. She joined the faculty staff of UAMS in 1971.

… to surgeon general

In her clinical practice and research Elders specialized in pediatrics—the branch of medicine concerned with childhood health—in which she rapidly established herself as a leading expert. Her high profile brought her to the attention of Arkansas governor Bill Clinton, who in 1986 appointed her director of the state's Department of Health. Elders believed passionately that government had an important role to play in protecting citizens' health, and that it had a duty to directly assist people whenever it was in their interest for it to do so. Among her many achievements in Arkansas were a tenfold increase in the number of early childhood screenings, a doubling of childhood vaccinations, and a massive extension in the funding of rural health care.

INFLUENCES AND INSPIRATION

Elders dates her ambition to become a medical doctor to an encounter with Edith Irby Jones at age 16. Until then she had hoped to become, at best, a laboratory technician. Jones's inspirational example, however, showed Elders that she could achieve much more.

Jones was born in Hot Springs, Arkansas, in 1927. Like Elders, she was the daughter of a sharecropper. Like Elders, too, she was able to overcome the inequalities of the educational system through a combination of her own ability and determination and the support of her family and community. In 1948, after winning a scholarship to the historically black Knoxville College in Tennessee, she won a place at the University of Arkansas College of Medicine—the first African American to do so. During her studies she had to eat in a different dining room from her white colleagues and sleep in different lodgings. Having received her MD in 1952, Jones went on to establish successful practices, first in Hot Springs and later in downtown Houston, Texas. Throughout her career she fought for better health care for the poor and minorities, and campaigned for civil rights in the wider community. In 1985 Jones was elected the first woman president of the Black National Medical Association.

Elders paid special attention to the sexual health of Arkansas's young people. At the time she took office, some 20 percent of pregnancies within the state were among teenagers—a figure that was much higher than the national average—while the incidence of sexually transmitted diseases (STDs), including HIV, was rising rapidly. In order to educate young people about the dangers of STDs and how to protect themselves against disease and unwanted pregnancies, Elders established 18 school-based clinics that gave advice about contraception.

While many people welcomed Elders's work, it attracted criticism from conservative and religious groups, who argued that by educating young people about sex, she was encouraging them to have sex. Elders insisted that she was enabling teenagers to make informed decisions about their lives and about managing their own bodies.

Criticism sharpened when, in 1993, the newly elected President Clinton nominated Elders to the office of surgeon general—the leading government spokesperson and adviser on national health issues. Despite intense opposition, the Senate confirmed Elders in the position.

As surgeon general Elders continued to address many of the issues she had tackled in Arkansas such as teenage pregnancy, AIDS, and drug and alcohol abuse. She was also closely associated with Clinton's plan to introduce universal health care, which, he proposed, would ensure every citizen the right to free medical treatment. The proposal was vehemently opposed by Republicans, who argued that income taxes would have to rise in order to pay for it. In her new role Elders soon found herself under attack from her opponents, particularly over issues relating to children's and young adults' sexual health.

On World AIDS Day, 1994, during an address given to the United Nations, Elders was asked whether she thought masturbation should be promoted as a way of encouraging young people to avoid risky sexual activities. Her unguarded response that it was a "part of human sexuality and a part of something that should perhaps be taught" caused uproar in the national media and led Clinton to ask for her resignation.

Elders returned to her research and teaching at UAMS. She continued to speak out on public-health issues, giving lectures and appearing on television. She believes that she still has an important role to play in encouraging debate about health matters that are all too often avoided as "embarrassing" or too "sensitive." Only in this way, she believes, can positive change be achieved.

KEY DATES

1933   Born in Schaal, Arkansas, on August 13.

1986   Appointed director of the Arkansas Department of Health.

1993   Confirmed as the 16th surgeon general of the United States on September 7.

1994   Resigns as surgeon general.

Further reading: Elders, Joycelyn M. *Joycelyn Elders, M.D.: From Sharecropper's Daughter to Surgeon General of the United States of America*. New York, NY: Quill, 1997. www.peacehost.net/PacifistNation/EldersJocelyn.htm (Informative article on Elders).

ELDRIDGE, Elleanor
Entrepreneur, Writer

A hard-working businesswoman and an astute real-estate entrepreneur, Elleanor Eldridge also wrote one of the few known narratives of the life of an early 19th-century free black woman.

Early life

The daughter of Hannah and Robin Eldridge, Elleanor was born in Warwick, Rhode Island, in 1785, the youngest of nine children. Hannah, who was part Native American, died when Eldridge was 10 years old. Soon after she went to work for one of her mother's former employers and her namesake, Elleanor Baker, where she learned math, spinning, and weaving. From age 15 Eldridge worked as a dairywoman for Captain Benjamin Greene, becoming known for her quality cheeses. She remained with his family for nearly 12 years.

Real estate ventures

After Greene's death in 1812 Eldridge left Rhode Island and went to live in Adams, Massachusetts, with her oldest sister. There she helped establish a business weaving, nursing, laundering, and making soap. Eventually Eldridge made enough money to buy a plot of land, on which she built a house that she rented out.

Returning to Rhode Island three years later, Eldridge set up business as a house painter and decorator in Providence. After seven years she was able to use the profits to buy another piece of land and build a house for herself and a renter. Before long Eldridge had bought another two lots of land and a house in Warwick.

Illness and loss

In 1831 disaster struck. Eldridge became ill with typhus fever and left the state to recover. While she was away a rumor circulated that she had died, and an unscrupulous creditor conspired with the sheriff and the auctioneer to sell off her properties.

On her return Eldridge found that her properties, which together were worth more than $4,000, had been auctioned illegally to pay a $240 debt. In addition, the two wings of her first house, which she had built herself, had been pulled down, and all the families who had been renting from her had been compelled to leave their homes at a single week's notice, being forced to take shelter in barns, outhouses, and even in the woods.

KEY DATES	
1785	Born in Warwick, Rhode Island, on March 26.
1815	Starts house painting and decorating business.
1831	Law officials illegally sell her properties.
1837	Buys back property in out-of-court settlement.
1838	Publishes *The Memoirs of Elleanor Eldridge*.
1865	Dies at about this time.

With the support of friends, and after representing herself in court in 1837, Eldridge was eventually able to buy back what was rightfully hers. However, she had to raise $2,700 to do so, as the purchaser kept raising the amount he required.

Writer

In 1838, with the help of editor and abolitionist Frances H. Green (1805–1878), Eldridge published a memoir of her life to raise funds to offset the amount she had borrowed to regain her property. The memoir, which included poetry and testimonials of support from friends, employers, and business colleagues, gives a clear indication of the esteem, respect, and love she came to enjoy in Rhode Island, despite the actions of a small group of dishonest men.

According to the memoirs "The whole affair … was a wanton outrage upon the simplest and most evident principles of justice. But the subject of this wrong, or rather of this accumulation of wrongs, was a woman, and therefore weak—a COLORED WOMAN—and therefore contemptible. No MAN ever would have been treated so; and if A WHITE WOMAN had been the subject of such wrongs, the whole town—nay, the whole country, would have been indignant: and the actors would have been held up to the contempt they deserve!"

Little more is known about Eldridge after the publication of her memoirs. It is thought that she died in 1865 at age 80.

Further reading: Clark Hine, Darlene, and Kathleen Thompson. *A Shining Thread of Hope.* New York, NY: Broadway, 1999.
http://docsouth.unc.edu/neh/eldridge/eldridge.html
(Transcribed text of *The Memoirs of Elleanor Eldridge*).

ELDRIDGE, Roy
Musician

Roy Eldridge was one of jazz's greatest trumpeters. During the swing period of the 1930s he was regarded as one of the best solo players of the time. His music formed a bridge between the pioneering style of Louis Armstrong and the more modern jazz of Dizzy Gillespie.

David Roy Eldridge was born on January 29, 1911, in Pittsburgh, Pennsylvania, and learned the trumpet from his older brother Joe. They played together in small bands around the city. At age 16 Eldridge turned professional, touring the Midwest with bands.

In 1930 Eldridge moved to New York City, where he played with Cecil Scott, Elmer Snowden, and Charles Johnson, among others. While there he acquired the nickname "Little Jazz" because of his height. After a return to Pittsburgh he moved back to New York in 1935, where he recorded the first of his solos with Teddy Hill, bringing him wider popular recognition.

The following year he formed his own eight-piece band with his brother Joe at the Three Deuces in Chicago. As a bandleader Eldridge recorded more solo records, including "After You've Gone" and "Wabash Stomp." But the band did not make much money, and in 1941 Eldridge accepted an offer to join Gene Krupa's band.

Eldridge was one of the first African Americans to join a white band, and he suffered many racist attacks as they toured across the country. He came close to a nervous breakdown as a result. When Krupa's band broke up in 1943, Eldridge went freelance. A spell with Artie Shaw's band in 1944 ended after yet more racial abuse on tour.

Another attempt at starting his own band failed, and after a brief reunion with Krupa in 1949 Eldridge began a long association with Norman Granz's Jazz at the Philharmonic. By the late 1940s he was beginning to feel

▲ *Roy Eldridge was an exuberant player who enjoyed improvising in jam sessions.*

his jazz-playing was old-fashioned, and in 1950 he moved to Paris, France, where he was feted by the French public and made some of his finest recordings.

On his return to the United States in April 1951, Eldridge continued to work with small bands, toured, appeared at festivals, and recorded several highly regarded albums. In 1961 he starred on the television show *After Hours*. During the 1960s he played with many of jazz's greats, including Ella Fitzgerald and Count Basie. From 1970 to 1980, when he had a stroke, he led a jazz band at Ryan's nightclub in New York. Eldridge died in 1989.

See also: Armstrong, Louis; Basie, Count; Fitzgerald, Ella; Gillespie, Dizzy; Johnson, Charles

Further reading: Chilton, John. *Roy Eldridge: Little Jazz Giant.* New York, NY: Continuum International Publishing Group, 2003.
www2.worldbook.com/features/aamusic/html/eldridge.htm
(Brief biography).

KEY DATES	
1911	Born in Pittsburgh, Pennsylvania, on January 29.
1927	Starts to play trumpet and drums professionally.
1936	Forms own eight-piece band.
1941	Joins Gene Krupa's band.
1950	Visits Paris, France.
1989	Dies in Valley Stream, New York, on February 26.

ELLINGTON, Duke
Composer, Pianist, Bandleader

The most influential composer in 20th-century jazz, the legendary Duke Ellington composed and performed about 2,000 big-band style jazz pieces. He also wrote classical orchestral, chamber, and solo-piano works.

The "Duke"

Edward Kennedy Ellington was born into a middle-class family in Washington, D.C., on April 29, 1899. Ellington's parents, James and Daisy, taught him to be proud of his race and to believe that he could achieve his dreams. Ellington's pride in himself emerged in everything that he did, and he was nicknamed "Duke" by his classmates.

Ellington began taking piano lessons at age seven, but it was not until he was in his early teens that he developed a real interest in music. Ellington was a talented artist and was studying commercial art when he started to take notice of the ragtime music played by local pianists in Washington and also in Philadelphia, where he spent holidays with his mother. He later credited the pianist Harvey Brooks, who had a "tremendous left

▼ *Duke Ellington worked with Billy Strayhorn on the composition of the score to Otto Preminger's movie* **Anatomy of a Murder** *(1959).*

hand," with making him want to excel at the piano. By the time Ellington was 15, he was composing his own work. He began to perform with other local young musicians, such as the drummer Sonny Greer, saxophonist Otto "Toby" Hardwick, and trumpeter Arthur Whetsol. In 1917, three months before graduating, Ellington dropped out of school to concentrate on his professional music career. He married Edna Thompson a year later, and the couple had a son.

The road to success

Ellington's good looks, easy style, and talent made him popular with audiences. He increasingly performed with Greer, Hardwick, Whetsol, and the banjoist Elmer Snowden: These men formed the core of Ellington's first great bands. In 1923 the group, now called the Washingtonians, moved to New York, where they played at Harlem's Exclusive Club, the Hollywood (later the Kentucky Club), and Ciros. Within two years the Washingtonians had been renamed the Duke Ellington Orchestra and were 11-musicians strong.

In the fall of 1927 the Duke Ellington Orchestra began a long-term gig at the Cotton Club, the most prominent nightclub in the Harlem area of New York City. The venue was racially segregated: Only whites were admitted as customers, but all of the waiters and most of the entertainers were African American. The club was able to transmit live radio broadcasts, and it was through these transmissions that Ellington became famous to people not just in America but also across the world. One of the reasons for his growing popularity was the new sounds he and his now 14-strong band created. Employing musicians with unique sounds such as trombonist Lawrence Brown,

<hr>

INFLUENCES AND INSPIRATION

Duke Ellington had a gift for blending simple blues and the emotion of gospel music together with sophisticated musical styles. His music attracted fans from all over the world.

Ellington was among the first people to focus on musical form and composition in jazz. This influenced musicians such as Thelonious Monk, who developed a band style built around the original piano mannerisms that evolved from Ellington.

Composer Cecil Taylor paid tribute to the influence that Duke had on him when he commented that Ellington had showed him how it was possible to "incorporate all kinds of music and other influences as part of my life as an American Negro. Everything Duke lived is in his music."

Ellington's image as a reserved, intelligent, and serious composer also influenced singer and guitarist B. B. King as a child: King went on to model his stage performance on the Duke. He also wanted his band to reflect the big-band sound of Ellington and Count Basie.

<hr>

alto saxophonist Johnny Hodges, and clarinetist Barney Bigard, Ellington combined improvised solos with written arrangements in a way that had never been equaled.

Mass appeal

Unlike many of the other bands at the time, the Ellington Orchestra was able to make the change from the jazz sounds of the 1920s to the swing music of the 1930s. Their song "It Don't Mean a Thing (If It Ain't Got That Swing)" came to define the era. It was this ability to adapt with the times that kept Ellington a major force in jazz music up until his death.

In 1930 Ellington and his orchestra played in the Amos 'n' Andy film *Check and Double Check*, making the first of what would be many movie appearances. A year later Ellington and his band left the Cotton Club. They began to tour Europe in 1933. For the next 40 years Ellington had an almost constant touring schedule, which was broken only by engagements at clubs in New York, Chicago, Los Angeles, London, and Paris.

In early 1939 Ellington hired Billy Strayhorn, a young composer, arranger, and pianist. Ellington's musical partnership with Strayhorn is considered one of the most important in American music. Strayhorn composed and cowrote some of the most famous pieces of music associated with Ellington, including "Take the 'A' Train." Ellington referred to Strayhorn as "my right arm, my left arm, all the eyes in the back of my head, my brainwaves in his head and his in mine."

In 1943 Ellington became the first African American bandleader to perform at New York's legendary Carnegie Hall. The program included one of Ellington's longest and most ambitious pieces of music, "Black, Brown, and Beige: A Tone Parallel to the History of the American Negro," written in celebration of his African American heritage.

It was the first of a series of suites or instrumental compositions made up of a series of sections.

In 1959 Ellington's soundtrack for the movie *Anatomy of a Murder* was the first commissioned from an African American composer for a major Hollywood film; it won three Grammy Awards. He was also nominated for an Oscar for his next score, *Paris Blues* (1961).

Religion was important to Ellington, and he began composing what he referred to as "sacred concerts." His work "In the Beginning, God" won a 1966 Grammy Award for best original jazz composition.

Ellington always believed in African American equality. During the 1960s he played benefit concerts for the NAACP and donated money to the civil rights movement. In 1963, the 100th anniversary of the Emancipation Proclamation that ended slavery, Ellington produced a composition to mark the celebrations. The climax of "My People" was two pieces, "King Fit the Battle of Alabama," a celebration of the civil rights struggle in Birmingham, Alabama, led by Martin Luther King, Jr., and "What Color Is Virtue?"

Ellington received many honors and awards, including the Presidential Medal of Freedom in 1969. In 1973 he was diagnosed with lung cancer. Even after being hospitalized, he continued to compose. He died in New York in 1974: More than 10,000 people attended his funeral.

<hr>

See also: Basie, Count; Bigard, Barney; Brown, Lawrence; Hodges, Johnny; King, B. B.; Monk, Thelonious; Strayhorn, Billy

<hr>

Further reading: Hasse, John Edward. *Beyond Category: The Life and Genius of Duke Ellington*. New York, NY: Da Capo Press, 1995.
Ellington, Duke. *Music Is My Mistress*. New York, NY: Da Capo Press, 1976.
www.dukeellington.com (Official site).

ELLIOTT, Robert Brown
Attorney, Politician

Robert Brown Elliott was a brilliant politician, attorney, and military officer, and the first black commanding general of South Carolina's National Guard during the Reconstruction period after the Civil War (1861–1865).

Also known as R. B. Elliott, he was thought to have been born of Jamaican parents in Liverpool, England, in 1842. After attending High Holborn Academy in London, he graduated from Eton College in 1859 and went on to study law. Elliott then served in the Royal Navy, arriving in Boston, Massachusetts, on a navy ship shortly after the Civil War.

In 1867 Elliott moved to South Carolina, where he was admitted to the bar, established a law practice, and worked as an editor on the *Charleston Leader.* After becoming active in the state Republican Party, he served in the 1868 South Carolina constitutional convention and won a seat in the lower house of the state legislature.

From 1869 until 1871 Elliott held the office of assistant adjutant general, making him the first black commanding general of the S.C. National Guard. Part of this role included the formation of a state militia (often called the black militia) to protect citizens from the Ku Klux Klan.

Brilliant orator

The enfranchisement of millions of African American voters after the Civil War resulted in several blacks being elected to Congress for the first time. One was Elliott, who was elected as a Republican in 1871. That same year he delivered his most famous speech, in favor of a bill that went on to become the Civil Rights Act of 1875, which legislated against racial discrimination in public buildings. Following the speech, Elliott's Democratic opponents were so angry that they "denied his authorship … upon the general principle that the Negro, of himself, could

▲ *Robert Brown Elliot in 1874, when he resigned from Congress to return to South Carolina.*

accomplish nothing of literary excellence." Elliott served in Congress until 1874, when he resigned to return to South Carolina to fight political corruption and serve as speaker of the lower house. He was elected state attorney general in 1876 but was forced out of office after just a year.

In 1877 Elliott moved to New Orleans, resumed law practice, and continued to give lectures and addresses. His practice was boycotted by whites because of his earlier political activism, and Elliott died in poverty in 1884.

See also: Emancipation and Reconstruction

Further reading: Lamson, Peggy. *The Glorious Failure: Black Congressman Robert Brown Elliott and the Reconstruction in South Carolina.* New York, NY: Norton, 1973.
http://www.wallbuilders.com/resources/
search/detail.php?ResourceID=34 (Article detailing Elliott's celebrated civil rights speech of 1871).

KEY DATES	
1842	Probably born in Liverpool, England, on August 11.
1868	Elected to South Carolina legislature.
1869	Appointed first black commanding general of South Carolina National Guard.
1871	Becomes U.S. congressman.
1884	Dies in New Orleans, Louisiana, on August 9.

ELLISON, Ralph
Writer

Ralph Ellison is chiefly famous for his only complete novel, *Invisible Man* (1952). When it won the National Book Award in 1953, making Ellison the first African American to receive the honor, it instantly propelled him from an unknown writer to a prominent and influential national figure.

Ralph Waldo Ellison was born in Oklahoma City, Oklahoma, on March 1, 1914. His father, Lewis, named his son after the famous essayist and poet Ralph Waldo Emerson (1803–1882). Lewis made a living selling ice and coal; he died in an accident when Ralph was three years

old. His mother, Ida, was forced to take a number of jobs, including that of a maid, to support her two young children.

Ellison attended segregated public schools, where he excelled in music. In 1933 he enrolled at Tuskegee Institute in Alabama to study music on a state scholarship. Many southern states awarded such scholarships to black students to discourage them from applying to white universities. Because there was no money for his travel, Ellison had to hitch a ride on a train to get to Tuskegee. In his third year (1936) Ellison's scholarship was terminated. He decided to seek work in New York for the summer and planned to return to Tuskegee to complete his degree in the fall. At this point he was chiefly interested in music, literature, and sculpture.

▼ *Ralph Ellison in 1964 when he was elected to the National Institute of Arts and Letters; in 1967 he became vice president.*

A change of plan

In New York Ellison met some of the writers who had made their names during the 1920s flowering of creative talent known as the Harlem Renaissance. They included Langston Hughes and Arna Bontemps, who introduced him to novelist Richard Wright. As a result, Ellison's life changed drastically; he never returned to Tuskegee. Instead he began reading such celebrated writers as Ernest Hemingway and T. S. Eliot, whose poem "The Waste Land" helped him see a connection between music—jazz in particular—and literature. He was also influenced by Wright's work (*see box*).

Two years later in 1938, at Wright's urging, Ellison became involved in the Federal Writers' Project in New York. The project had developed in response to the Great Depression as part of President Franklin D. Roosevelt's New Deal to provide employment. The Writers' Project provided work for unemployed writers by getting them to prepare state guidebooks, write historical pamphlets, and record the points of interest of each state that was participating. Ellison interviewed elderly African Americans and built up a collection of folklore and oral histories. As a result he learned a great deal about the culture of black people and their traditions, much of which was later reflected in his writings.

In September 1938 Ellison married Rose Aramita Poindexter, a dancer and actress; they divorced in 1945. In 1946 he married Fanny McConnell; the couple remained together until Ellison's death.

INFLUENCES AND INSPIRATION

Ralph Ellison was influenced by the works and ideas of a number of writers, including T. S. Eliot, Ralph Waldo Emerson, Mark Twain, Henry David Thoreau, and Fyodor Dostoyevsky. However, the man who influenced him most was his early mentor, Richard Wright. Wright was a member of the Communist Party, and his political views radicalized Ellison, although he never felt comfortable with the rigid doctrine of the Communist Party. Wright's writing also influenced Ellison, in particular his highly acclaimed protest novel *Native Son* (1940) and his nonfiction collaboration with photographer Edwin Rosskam, *Twelve Million Black Voices: A Folk History of the Negro in the U.S.* (1941). Ellison thought that this work was even more powerful than *Native Son*.

A writing career

Ellison started his writing career with reviews, essays, and short stories, some of which were published in magazines like *New Challenges* and *Masses*. His first short story, "Slick Gonna Learn," was published in 1939.

The friendship between Ellison and Wright began to sour as Wright accused his protégé of imitating his writing. Eventually the two parted ways. Ellison became more intensively dedicated to his literary work, and in 1940–1941 he published two essays with African American folklore themes. In 1943 Ellison received a contract for a manuscript based on a character in his short story "Flying Home," but was drafted into military service in World War II (1939–1945), serving in the merchant marines.

The Invisible Man

On his return to the United States in 1945, Ellison changed the direction of his manuscript. The first part was published in 1947 in *Horizon* as "Invisible Man." The completed novel was published seven years later, in 1952. It tells the story of an unnamed boy who grew up in the South, was expelled from a black college, and ended up in New York. Despite his efforts to find his place in society, the naive and idealistic central character's identity as a human being remains "invisible" to both the white community, who cannot see beyond his blackness, and his fellow blacks.

Invisible Man made Ellison's reputation as one of the greatest writers of the 20th century. The book remained on the bestseller list for 16 weeks after its publication. In 1953 it earned Ellison the National Book Award for Fiction and the Russwarm Award. In 1965, 200 literary critics declared the book "the most distinguished American novel written since World War II."

After the *Invisible Man*

In 1964 Ellison published *Shadow and Act*, a collection of political, social, and critical essays, followed by another collection of essays, *Going to the Territory*, in 1987.

Ellison was fellow of the American Academy in Rome from 1955 to 1957. On his return to the United States he held several visiting professorships, including the Albert Schweitzer Professor in the Humanities at New York University. He received the Medal of Freedom in 1969 and the National Medal of Arts in 1985.

Ellison spent 40 years working on a huge multivolume novel, some chapters of which were published from 1960 onward. In 1967 a house fire destroyed over 350 pages of manuscript, and the novel was unfinished when Ellison died of cancer in 1994. It was not until 1999 that his long-awaited second novel was published under the editorship of John Callahan, a professor at Lewis and Clark College and Ellison's literary executor. *Juneteenth* was a 368-page condensation of over 2,000 pages of manuscript.

See also: Bontemps, Arna; Harlem Renaissance; Hughes, Langston; Wright, Richard

Further reading: Jackson, Lawrence. *Ralph Ellison: Emergence of Genius.* Hoboken, NJ: John Wiley & Sons, 2002. http://www.centerx.gseis.ucla.edu/weblio/ellison.html (UCLA site on Ellison).

KEY DATES

1914	Born in Oklahoma City, Oklahoma, on March 1.
1933	Becomes a student at Tuskegee Institute.
1938	Joins the Federal Writers' Project.
1952	Publishes novel *Invisible Man*.
1967	Fire destroys part of his second novel.
1994	Dies in New York City on April 16.
1999	Second novel, *Juneteenth*, is published.

EMANCIPATION AND RECONSTRUCTION

In the context of U.S. history, emancipation refers to the freeing of African Americans from slavery. Reconstruction is the name given to the postwar period from 1865 to 1877, when legislation was passed to enfranchise former slaves in the South.

In 1862 President Abraham Lincoln issued the Emancipation Proclamation during the Civil War (1861–1865). It proposed to free all slaves in Confederate states that had not surrendered before January 1, 1863. It affected at least four million slaves in the South and, in effect, made the conflict a war about slavery. In December 1865, following the end of the war, the Thirteenth Amendment to the Constitution declared slavery illegal throughout the United States.

The process of Reconstruction was intended to help the freed African Americans by helping them become independent of their former owners and self-supporting. Reconstruction was, however, highly controversial and its achievements somewhat limited. Its brief existence—it lasted only 12 years—ended amid political machinations in Washington, D.C.

Background

Emancipation was the culmination of decades of opposition to slavery. Tensions between the Northern states, where slavery was abolished, and the South, where slavery was the basis of the economy, were a contributing factor in 1861 to the secession of the Confederate states from the Union. The resulting civil war, however, did not begin as a war about slavery. Lincoln, despite being perceived in the South as opposed to slavery, insisted that he fought the war to preserve the Union and put down the rebellion of the South, not to liberate the slaves.

By the middle of 1862, however, there were good reasons for Lincoln to revise his intention. Northern morale had been weakened by Confederate military successes. Confederate success was in large part thanks to the slave labor that kept the economy working while white Southerners were freed for military service. Meanwhile, the Union needed a new source of recruits and was eager to prevent Great Britain from recognizing the Confederate government.

Five days after the Union victory at the battle of Antietam (Sharpsburg) on September 17, 1862, Lincoln issued the Emancipation Proclamation (*see box on p. 19*). It was an ultimatum to the Confederate states that, if they did not surrender by January 1, 1863, their slaves would be declared free.

Confederate president Jefferson Davis rejected the proclamation as an atttempt to get the Southern slaves to rise up against the government. He said that it was "the most execrable measure recorded in the history of guilty man." In the North, while most abolitionists welcomed the proclamation, some objected that Lincoln had based it on military necessity—he called it "an act of justice, warranted by the Constitution upon military necessity"—rather than moral grounds. It was therefore limited in its scope; it would only apply to territory still under Confederate control as it was captured by the Union armies. It did not affect the 800,000 slaves held in Union states

KEY DATES	
1831	American Anti-Slavery Society founded.
1861	Fort Sumter is attacked in April; Civil War begins; in May General Butler refuses to return escaped "contrabands" to slavery; in August General Fremont orders emancipation of slaves in Missouri; Lincoln countermands him; First Confiscation Act frees captured slaves used by Confederate Army.
1862	In April Congress provides funds for compensated emancipation; border states spurn the proposal; in May General Hunter's order abolishing slavery in South Carolina, Georgia, and Florida is revoked by Lincoln; Lincoln issues Preliminary Emancipation Proclamation after Battle of Antietam on September 22.
1863	Emancipation Proclamation takes effect on January 1.
1865	Thirteenth Amendment to the Constitution enacted.
1868	Fourteenth and Fifteenth Amendments to the Constitution.
1877	End of Reconstruction; Union troops pulled out of the South.

President Abraham Lincoln (center) with Major Allan Pinkerton (left) and General John A. McClernand at Antietam, Maryland, in 1862.

along the Confederate border or in Confederate territory already captured by the Union.

When no Confederate states surrendered by January 1, 1863, a revised Emancipation Proclamation came into effect. By linking the Northern cause with the abolition of slavery, Lincoln both reinvigorated the North and ensured that no European nations would recognize the Confederate government. That was important, because both France and Great Britain had considered recognizing the Confederacy in order to gain access to its vast supplies of cotton, on which their industry had depended. The Proclamation had other immediate advantages for the North. It declared that freed slaves would now be accepted into the Union Army and Navy; previously the army had turned away black volunteers. Free

blacks and former slaves eagerly joined up: A total of 180,000 served in the Union military between 1863 and 1865. The Confederacy, meanwhile, maintained its bar on recruiting African Americans.

Despite the limited scope of the Emancipation Proclamation, it was a turning point. It made the war a campaign against slavery and clearly indicated that a Northern victory would bring its elimination. Lincoln later called the Emancipation Proclamation "the central act of my administration and the greatest event of the nineteenth century."

Constitutional amendments

Following the end of the conflict so-called "radical" Republicans in Congress orchestrated the passage of several measures designed to prevent any return to slavery in the South and to assist freed African American men and women. The measures included three amendments to the Constitution. The Thirteenth Amendment (1865) completed

the promise of emancipation by abolishing slavery on U.S. soil. The Fourteenth Amendment (1866) made African Americans U.S. citizens, while the Fifteenth Amendment (1868) gave African American men the right to vote. Two further pieces of legislation addressed the position of African Americans. In 1867 the Freedmen's Bureau was established to help newly freed slaves to adjust to their freedom through property acquisition, schooling, health care, and integration of their families into society. In 1875 the Civil Rights Bill was promulgated with the aim of ending discrimination in public facilities.

In 1867 and 1868 Congress passed a series of Reconstruction Acts that divided the South into five military districts, each controlled by the Union Army, which was to oversee elections in which all freedmen could vote. Ratification of the amendments to the Constitution was a term of readmission of the Southern states to the Union. Arkansas, North Carolina, South Carolina, Louisiana, Alabama, and Florida were readmitted in 1868; Virginia, Mississippi, Texas, and Georgia were readmitted in 1870.

Political progress

The seven years of Reconstruction had beneficial effects for many African Americans. Many voted for the first time; some also became office holders. Few of these office holders were former slaves, however: Most came from the class of free blacks that had always existed in the South.

Between 1868 and 1895 African Americans gained 23 seats in the U.S. House of Representatives. There were two black senators from Mississippi, the first ever in the U.S. Senate (Hiram Revels in 1870 and Bruce K. Blanche from 1875 to 1881). John R. Lynch served as house speaker in the Mississippi legislature and then as a member of the U.S. House of Representatives for two terms between 1873 and 1883.

Similar gains, mostly on the local and state level, occurred in other Southern states. In many counties black (male) voters outnumbered white (male) voters, as was the case in South Carolina, Georgia, Florida, Alabama, Mississippi, and Louisiana. This gave newly enfranchised African American voters significant political power. Most supported

In 1863 thousands of African Americans flooded into Washington, D.C. To house them a camp called Freeman's Village was set up across the Potomac River in Arlington, Virginia.

the Republican Party; the Democratic Party was perceived as the party of slave owners and slavery. The Republican Party, which had previously been only a Northern party, now organized throughout the South. Black voters provided 80 percent of its support as it gained political power across the South.

Improved conditions
Political representation was accompanied by other improvements in African American life. Literacy rates rose dramatically with increased education, from 18.6 percent in 1870 to 30 percent in 1880 and 42.9 percent in 1890. Even though many former slaves remained on the plantations as sharecroppers, often living in conditions of great poverty, many others became wage earners for the first time, acquired property, worshiped freely in their churches, and

reunited with their families or started new families whose marriages were recognized by the state and the nation.

Weaknesses of Reconstruction
Despite the advances achieved, Reconstruction was weaker than it appeared. The changes it brought in the South were dependent on continued military occupation. The changes were greatly resented by Southerners, largely on racist grounds but also because they perceived Reconstruction as an attempt by the North to force them to become "Yankees." In their eyes, the supporters of Reconstruction became two hated stereotypes: carpetbaggers were Northerners who had come South after the war to try to influence its development, while scalawags were Southern supporters of the Republican Party.

Southern resistance to Reconstruction had violent

TURNING POINT

At the outbreak of the Civil War in 1861 President Abraham Lincoln's sole objective was to save the Union. He once said: "If I could save the Union without freeing the slaves, I would do it; if I could save it by freeing some and leaving others alone, I would also do it. What I do about slavery and the colored race, I do because I believe it helps save the Union." When

Lincoln made his Emancipation Proclamation on September 22, 1862, therefore, his main motivation was military rather than ideological. His chief purpose was to demoralize the South. He knew that the proclamation would create consternation and encourage many slaves to run away, as fugitive laws would no longer be enforced anywhere.

The Emancipation Proclamation was received with joy and jubilation among slaves, abolitionists, and most Northerners. A black preacher of the time wrote: "The effect of this announcement was startling beyond description, and the scene was wild and grand. Joy and gladness exhausted all forms of expression, from shouts of praise to sobs and tears."

expression in the activities of the Ku Klux Klan, a white supremacist organization formed in 1865 by veterans of the Confederate Army. The Klan launched a campaign of violent intimidation intended to prevent blacks from voting. Under Grand Wizard Nathan Bedford, it lynched some 3,500 African Americans between 1866 and 1875. By the middle of the 1870s such intimidation had succeeded in reducing Republican support in the South. Democrats had regained control of all but three Southern states.

Reconstruction was also weakened by a lack of political will in Washington, D.C. In 1865, after the assassination of Abraham Lincoln, the presidency had passed to Vice President Andrew Johnson, a Democrat from Tennessee who, although committed to the Union, was not hostile to slavery itself. Soon after coming to office, Johnson rescinded an order made during the war by Union general William T. Sherman that set out to provide every freedman with 40 acres of land and a mule. Johnson went on to resist Congress's

attempts to pass legislation on behalf of black Americans. The clash between the president and the Congress came to a head in 1868, when Johnson avoided impeachment by only one vote.

End of Reconstruction

Johnson's successor, Ulysses S. Grant, was more committed to upholding the rights of Southern blacks. He used federal troops to combat the activities of the Ku Klux Klan, for example. The end of Grant's second term in 1876, however, brought a presidential election whose result led to an abrupt end of Reconstruction.

Victory in the election was disputed by Democrat Samuel Tilden and Republican Rutherford B. Hayes. After months of wrangling the Democrats, who now dominated the House of Representatives, agreed to allow Hayes to take office in return for a Republican promise to withdraw the last federal troops from the South. The Tilden–Hayes Compromise of February 26, 1877, marked the end of Reconstruction.

The effort of Southern whites to continue racial segregation at led to the introduction of Jim Crow laws. By 1890 legislation had resulted in the complete separation of facilities throughout the South and the introduction of obstacles to the voting rights of African Americans through measures such as literacy tests, poll taxes, and grandfather clauses. Without federal troops to oversee the polls, intimidation increased. Thus, the Democrats were once again in control of the South and it was not until almost one hundred years later that the civil rights of African Americans and other minorities were restored and enforced.

See also: Blanche, Bruce K.; Discrimination; Lynch, John R.; Political Representation; Revels, Hiram; Slavery

---

Further reading: DuBois, W. E. B. *Black Reconstruction in America, 1860-1880*. New York, NY: Free Press, 1998. Franklin, John Hope, and Alfred A. Moss, Jr. *From Slavery to Freedom*. New York, NY: McGraw-Hill, 1994.

EMEAGWALI, Philip
Scientist

Philip Emeagwali is recognized as one of the fathers of the Internet, and ranks alongside computer pioneers such as Tim Berners-Lee (1955–), inventor of the World Wide Web, and Vint Cerf (1943–), developer of the first commercial email service.

Early years in Africa
The eldest of nine children, Emeagwali was born in Nigeria in 1954. In 1967 the Nigerian province of Biafra, which was inhabited mainly by the Igbo people, declared its independence from the central government. At the age

▼ *Philip Emeagwali's achievements have made him one of the most respected authorities on the potential of new technology.*

of only 14 Emeagwali was conscripted as a soldier with the rebel forces. As the civil war escalated and acts of genocide were committed against members of the Igbo, Emeagwali's family fled to England. By the time Biafra was forced to surrender in 1970, between 500,000 and several million people had died.

A successful exile
In England Emeagwali studied at home with the help of his father, who regularly made him do a hundred math problems an hour. In later life, when people hailed him as a genius, Philip would say: "Every one of us has the power to be a genius. I was not born a genius; it was nurtured in me by my father."

On the strength of this tough training, Emeagwali won a scholarship to Oregon State University and immigrated to the United States in 1974. After receiving a bachelor's degree in math he moved to George Washington University in Washington, D.C., where he completed two masters degrees—one in civil and environmental engineering, the other in ocean, coastal, and marine engineering. He also earned a master's degree in mathematics from the University of Maryland, and later attended graduate school at the University of Michigan.

Ahead of his time
Emeagwali's first job was as a civil engineer in Michigan, where he worked on the construction of highways and dams. But he was not content with his day job, and spent his spare time working on new ideas. One of these, inspired by a 1922 work of science fiction, involved linking 64,000 computers worldwide in order to forecast global weather. He approached experts and potential backers, but they all rejected his scheme—which he named the HyperBall—as impossible. Undeterred, Emeagwali wrote a detailed proposal that described the use of 64 binary thousand (65,536) processors to perform the world's fastest computation. However, the idea had not yet found its time.

Success at last
It was not until 1987 that Emeagwali's scheme bore fruit. Scientists at the National Laboratory at Los Alamos, Texas, tried and failed to program the center's 65,536 processors to simulate nuclear explosions. They invited suggestions

INFLUENCES AND INSPIRATION

Emeagwali is an inspiration to many young people, particularly in Africa. His name has been immortalized in ballads and every week about 10,000 African students use his Web site to complete their school homework.

For his part Emeagwali says: "I'm a black scientist and an African scientist. So when I became prominent, I tried to use that voice." He particularly deplores the "brain drain" from the developing world to the West, saying that "if the Internet and telecommunications break down the barriers of space and time, it means somebody in Africa or India could be employed in the United States or Canada."

The United Nations has inducted him into its Gallery of Prominent Refugees in recognition of his journey from a refugee camp to respected computer and internet guru.

Emeagwali believes that a wealthy person should use his or her fortune to benefit others. But he does not believe in giving money away. He has created "Africa One," a communication design that will bring fiber optics technology to 41 points on Africa's shoreline. He believes that Africans have the ability to make their nations wealthy, but that they need communications and a change in world attitudes.

from outsiders and accepted Emeagwali's proposals: He successfully reprogrammed all of their computers remotely from Michigan. As a result he became known as "the Bill Gates of Africa."

The Connection Machine

Next Emeagwali applied his expertise with computers to determine how and where oil flows underground. The apparatus he constructed for this purpose, known as the Connection Machine, enabled drillers and prospectors to save millions of dollars by concentrating their efforts in the most likely areas—previously vast sums had been squandered on speculative test wells that turned up nothing. Emeagwali's invention also led to the discovery of significant deposits in geological formations that had never previously been considered as potential sites for exploration.

The Connection Machine was the fastest computer of its time, a machine of remarkable power that was capable of 3.1 billion calculations per second. It won Emeagwali the 1989 International Gordon Bell Prize, awarded by the Institute of Electrical and Electronics

Engineers and widely regarded as the computer science equivalent of the Nobel Prize.

Emeagwali-designed computers have since been used to forecast the weather, to monitor blood flow in the human heart, to calculate the movement of buried nuclear waste, to track the spread of AIDS, and to determine the long-term effect of gases in the air.

Honors and awards

In 1991 Emeagwali was named Scientist of the Year by the National Society of Black Engineers. Two years later America's National Technical Association (ANTA) awarded him the title of Computer Scientist of the Year, and he was Nigerian Achiever of the Year in 1994. His wife, Dale Emeagwali, is a professor at Morgan State University in Baltimore and was ANTA's Scientist of the Year in 1996.

Emeagwali heads a consulting firm in Washington, D.C., which is used by a wide range of organizations from the United Nations to telecommunications companies. He believes that within the next hundred years computers at each node of the Internet will be so much faster and more intelligent than they are today that the World Wide Web will be rendered obsolete. He also believes that bionic implants will rewire human brains into computers, thus enabling email to be sent and received telepathically. He cheerfully admits that this sounds like science fiction, but, with his track record, few people dismiss his views as far-fetched.

KEY DATES	
1954	Born in Akure, Nigeria, on August 23.
1968	Fights in Nigerian civil war.
1974	Immigrates to United States.
1987	Creates world's most powerful computer.
1989	Wins International Gordon Bell Prize.

Further reading: Henderson, Susan K. *African-American Inventors III: Patricia Bath, Philip Emeagwali, Henry Sampson, Valerie Thomas, Peter Tolliver.* Mankato, MN: Capstone Press, 1998. http://www.emeagwali.com/index1.shtml (Corporate site).

EQUIANO, Olaudah

Writer, Abolitionist

Olaudah Equiano is best known as the author of *The Interesting Narrative of the Life of Olaudah Equiano, or Gustavus Vassa the African*, published in 1789—a richly detailed autobiographical account of his life as a slave and an important document in the early abolitionist movement.

A mysterious beginning

In his work Equiano claimed that he was born in about 1745 in what is now Nigeria, and that he was seized by white slave traders and transported to the Bahamas. A recent scholar has argued, however, that evidence suggests that Equiano was born into slavery on a plantation in South Carolina, and that he drew on the accounts of fellow slaves for his descriptions of Africa and slave ships. He did this to make his own story—and the case against slavery—more persuasive. The truth, however, remains uncertain.

Buying freedom

At age 11 Equiano was sold to a British naval officer, who educated him and took him on numerous voyages. The officer also gave Equiano a new name, Gustavus Vassa, after the first Swedish king. The boy learned to read and write when he was sent to school in London, England,

▼ *Frontispiece and title page from* **The Interesting Narrative of the Life of Olaudah Equiano,** *which was published in 1789.*

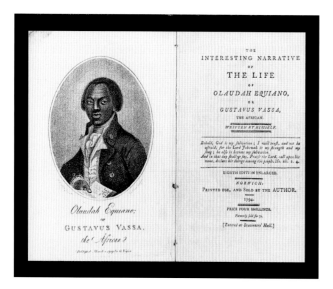

KEY DATES

1745   Born in Essaka, Nigeria, or South Carolina.

1766   Buys his freedom

1789   Publishes his autobiography, *The Interesting Narrative of the Life of Olaudah Equiano.*

1797   Dies in London, England, on March 31.

between sea voyages. Later Equiano was sold to a plantation owner on the island of Montserrat, where he worked as an overseer. By careful saving he was able to buy his freedom in 1766 and returned to London that year.

For a while Equiano made his living working on board British naval ships. In 1773 he even went on an expedition to the North Pole to find out whether there was a northwest passage from Britain to Asia. It was at about this time that Equiano converted to Christianity and first became involved in the English antislavery movement.

The interesting narrative

In 1789, with the help of English abolitionists such as John Wesley, Equiano published his memoirs and went on a nationwide lecture tour to publicize both them and the antislavery cause. Unlike most other previous "slave narratives," *The Interesting Narrative* was written down by its author rather than being dictated to a white secretary. Thus the book, as well as being a powerful plea for an end to the slave trade, was also a challenge to the widespread European belief that Africans were less intelligent and less civilized than white people.

Equiano's work was a huge success and was translated into Dutch, German, and Russian. It made him rich enough to marry a white Englishwoman in 1792 and settle in the English town of Soham. The couple had two daughters. Equiano died in 1797.

See also: Slavery

Further reading: Sollors, Werner (ed.). *The Interesting Narrative of the Life of Olaudah Equiano, or Gustavus Vassa, the African.* New York, NY: Norton Critical Editions, 2001.
http://www.brycchancarey.com/equiano/index.htm
(Biography including passages from Equiano's work).

ERVING, Julius
Basketball Player

By the time Julius Erving retired from professional basketball, he had scored over 30,000 career points, becoming one of only three basketball players in history to achieve such a total.

Erving was born in 1950 in East Meadow, New York. When he was three, his father left home, leaving his mother to raise the family. Erving showed early promise in basketball, joining a Salvation Army team and averaging 11 points per game by age 10.

School legend

At Roosevelt High School, New York, Erving's promise turned into an exceptional talent. His teammates called him "the Doctor" then "Dr. J." because of his skill, and his coach pushed him to play for the University of Massachusetts—he joined the university in 1968. At UMass he became an on-court legend, drawing capacity crowds to see a player who averaged 20 points and 20 rebounds per game, one of only six players in National Collegiate Athletic Association (NCAA) history to do so. With an athletic, often airborne style that dominated the hoop and other players, Erving was a top scorer, twice hitting 37 points in a game.

A pro career was beckoning, and in 1971 Erving joined the Virginia Squires of the American Basketball Association (ABA). In his first season Erving was voted Rookie of the Year, and by 1972 he headed the ABA's scoring rankings with an average 31.9 points. Erving left the Squires in 1973 following a wrangle over his contract and joined the ABA New York Nets. He maintained his position at the top of the league's scoring and was named MVP in 1974 and 1976. He also made ABA First Team All-Star from 1973 through 1976.

▲ *Julius Erving joined the Philadelphia 76ers in 1976, retiring after the 1986–1987 season.*

Erving left the ABA for the National Basketball Association (NBA) in 1976, joining the Philadelphia 76ers. Highlights of his 11-year NBA career included being named to the NBA 35th Anniversary All-Star Team in 1980 and pushing the 76ers to the 1983 NBA championship title.

Erving retired after the 1986–1987 season. He was an on-air personality for NBC Sports and served several major corporations in management positions. In 1993 he was elected to the Basketball Hall of Fame. In 1997 he became executive vice president for the Orlando Magic.

Further reading: Macht, Norman. *Julius Erving* (NBA Legends) New York, NY: Chelsea House Publications, 1994. http://www.hoophall.com/halloffamers/Erving.htm (Statistics and biography).

KEY DATES

1950 Born in East Meadow, New York, on February 22.

1964 Begins playing for the Roosevelt High School basketball team.

1968 Begins playing for the University of Massachusetts team.

1971 Turns pro and joins the ABA Virginia Squires.

1987 Retires from professional basketball.

1993 Elected to the Basketball Hall of Fame.

ESTEBAN
Explorer

Variously known to history as Estevanico, "Black Stephen," and "Stephen the Moor," Estebán was the first African to explore North America. His story, reported in several 16th-century Spanish chronicles, is obscured by a great deal of hearsay and exaggeration, but it is nonetheless clear that he was a courageous, enterprising, and resourceful figure.

From Morocco to Florida

Estebán was born in the seaport of Azemmour in Morocco in about 1503. Azemmour was captured by the Portuguese in 1513, and the young Estebán was sold into slavery in the early 1520s. He eventually became the servant of a Spanish aristocrat, Andrés de Dorantes. At this time Spain was sending numerous expeditions to the "New World" of the Americas in order to found new colonies and to exploit the continent's great natural wealth. In 1527 Dorantes sailed as commander of a company of infantry in Pánfilo de Narváez's expedition to conquer the lands stretching west from Florida along the Gulf of Mexico. Dorantes took Estebán with him on the mission; they landed in Florida on April 12, 1528.

Upon arrival the Spanish faced destructive hurricanes and repeated attacks from indigenous Americans living in the region. Narváez and his men built small rafts to sail across the Gulf of Mexico; three of them sank and most of the Spanish force, including Narváez, drowned. The 80 or so survivors, who included Dorantes and Estebán, landed at Galveston Island off the coast of Texas. Most of the group died during the long, bitter winter that followed; by 1533 only Estebán, Dorantes, and two other men, Cabeza de Vaca and Alonso Castillo Maldonado, were still alive, struggling to survive.

Proving his worth

By 1535 Estebán spoke several Native American languages and was considered to be a shaman or medicine man after he removed an arrow from a Native American, saving his life. Estebán's brown skin and tall stature, together with his possession of a medicine rattle decorated with owl feathers, which was a gift from a friendly chief, added to his reputation as a healer. With the aid of Native Americans the men traveled westward through what is now Texas and then on to Mexico, which was already part of the Spanish empire. During their long journey the party relied heavily

KEY DATES

1503   Born in Azemmour, Morocco, at about this time.

1520s   Sold into slavery during the 1520–1521 drought, when the Portuguese conquerors fell on hard times.

1527   Sets out on expedition to Florida as the slave of Andrés de Dorantes.

1536   Reaches Mexico City after years of hardship and captivity.

1539   Killed at Hawikuh, in present-day New Mexico.

on Estebán's skills as a negotiator and linguist. Finally, in July 1536 the men reached Mexico City, where they were welcomed by Viceroy Antonio de Mendoza. Impressed by their adventures, Mendoza invited the men to lead a fresh expedition northward, this time to discover the "Seven Cities of Cíbola." Estebán and the others had heard much about the seven cities during their long travels: It was rumored to possess astonishing riches and to be located somewhere north of the Sonoran Mountains. In the end the viceroy appointed a Spanish monk, Fray Marcos de Niza, as the expedition's nominal leader, and Estebán accompanied him as his guide and interpreter.

A new expedition

The expedition set out in 1539, but Niza soon became annoyed with the welcome Estebán received from the local people. Niza ordered Estebán to go ahead and send runners back to report on his progress. Estebán took about four weeks to reach the pueblo (village) of Hawikuh, whose impressive, multistoried mud buildings seemed to confirm that Estebán had indeed discovered the fabled "Seven Cities." The local Zuni people were mistrustful of the newcomers, however. Some reports state that they were suspicious of Estebán because they thought that he was a spy, others believed that the owl feathers on Estebán's rattle were unlucky. The Zuni imprisoned the group, and Estebán was reported to have been killed while trying to escape.

Further reading: Arrington, Carolyn. *Black Explorer in Spanish Texas: Estevanico.* Austin, TX: Eakin Press, 1986.
http://www.estevanico.org (Estavanico Society site).

EUROPE, James Reese

Conductor, Composer

James Reese Europe holds an important place in the history of American music; he was hailed during his lifetime as "the world's greatest exponent of syncopation" for his sophisticated ragtime. To music historians he was a transitional figure between ragtime and jazz.

Europe was born into a musical family in 1881; both his brother and sister became outstanding musicians. The family moved to Washington, D.C., where Europe received his first formal music education in violin and piano. He moved to New York in 1903, working in nightclubs and studying with composer Harry T. Burleigh. By 1907 he was music director of the Broadway musical *The Shoo-fly Regiment*. In 1909 Europe cofounded the Clef Club, a

▼ *James Reese Europe (left) was asked by his commander to form a military band. As director of the Hellfighters, he went to France in 1918.*

pioneering black musicians' union, and became conductor of the Clef Club Orchestra. Europe conducted the orchestra in the historic "Concert of Negro Music" at Carnegie Hall in 1912, which catapulted Europe and his orchestra into the limelight and brought them to the attention of a white audience; they played again at Carnegie Hall in 1913 and 1914 as the National Negro Symphony Orchestra. From 1914 Europe collaborated with the dancers Vernon and Irene Castle, and was instrumental in developing the foxtrot; he also received a recording contract from the Victor Talking Machine Company.

During World War I (1914–1918) Europe joined the Army and led the 369th U.S. Infantry Regiment Band, the Hellfighters. The band went to France in late 1918 and played a large part in spreading the American music that the recording company Pathé promoted as jazz. After the war the Hellfighters were welcomed back to the United States in February 1919 with great honors and set out on a tour of the country. At a concert in Boston Europe was stabbed to death by one of his band members, who was angered by Europe's strict direction. Europe was buried with military honors at Arlington Cemetery.

Europe composed over 100 small pieces, including "Castle House Rag," "Castle Walk," "On Patrol in No Man's Land," and "All of No Man's Land Is Ours." Europe, like Burleigh, believed that American Negro folk song played an important part in giving American music a distinctive voice, and that popular music expression had a high musical value.

KEY DATES	
1881	Born in Mobile, Alabama, on February 22.
1912	Gives first concert at Carnegie Hall, New York, on May 2.
1918	Becomes leader of the Hellfighters during World War I.
1919	Dies in Boston, Massachusetts, on May 9.

See also: Burleigh, Harry T.

Further reading: Badger, Reid. A *Life in Ragtime: A Biography of James Reese Europe*. New York, NY: Oxford University Press, 1995.
http://www.jass.com/Others/europe.html (Biography).

EVANS, Lee
Athlete

Runner Lee Evans won two gold medals at the 1968 Olympic Games in Mexico City. His victories set records that would stand for more than 20 years, but Evans had almost boycotted the games to protest human rights violations both in the United States and abroad.

Road to the Olympics

Lee Edward Evans was born in Madera, California, on February 25, 1947. His talent as a track star was obvious from an early age. He was undefeated at his school, Overfelt High in San Jose, California, and improved his 440-yard time from 48.2 in 1964 to 46.9 in 1965.

After graduating from high school, Evans went to San Jose State University, where he was coached by Hall of Famer Bud Winter. In 1966 Evans won the Amateur Athletic Union (AAU) 440-yard championship; later that year he was a member of the 4 x 400-meter relay team that was the first in history to break three minutes.

In 1967, after people refused to rent accommodations to black students at the university, Evans helped set up the Olympic Project for Human Rights (OPHR), which advocated boycotting the 1968 Olympic Games. Evans later commented that although the OPHR members wanted to attend the games, they also wanted to draw attention to human rights abuses. In 1968 Evans set an unofficial world record for the 400 meters of 44 seconds in the Olympic trials. He went on to win the gold medal with a time of 43.86 seconds. The record stood until 1988, when Butch Reynolds beat it by 0.57 seconds. In the relay final Evans ran the anchor leg for the U.S. team, which also included Vince Matthews, Ron Freeman, and Larry James. They won the gold in a time of 2 minutes, 56.2 seconds, a record that remained unbroken for 24 years. Evans was unable to

▲ *Lee Evans (middle), Larry James, and Ron Freeman all wore black berets at the 1968 Mexico Olympics to show their support for the black power movement.*

defend his 400-meter title at the 1972 Olympics in Munich, West Germany; he had to withdraw from the event because of a pulled hamstring.

In 1973 Evans turned professional. Two years later he went to work overseas directing the national track-and-field programs of Nigeria and Saudi Arabia. Evans also trained athletes in 18 countries over the next two decades. In 2002 Evans joined the University of Washington to coach the male and female sprinters and their relay teams.

See also: Political Movements; Reynolds, Butch

Further reading: Bass, Amy. *Not the Triumph but the Struggle: The 1968 Olympics and the Making of the Black Athlete.* Minneapolis, MN: University of Minnesota Press, 2004.
http://vm.mtsac.edu/relays/HallFame/Evans.html
(Career stats and brief biography).

KEY DATES	
1947	Born in Madera, California, on February 25.
1966	Wins AAU 440-yard championship.
1968	Wins two gold medals at Mexico Olympics.
1972	Prevented from competing in Munich Olympic Games owing to injury.
1975	Coaches overseas until 1997.
2002	Takes up coaching post at University of Washington.

EVANS, Mari
Writer

While she is most closely associated with the writers of the black arts movement of the 1960s and 1970s, Mari Evans has had a long and distinguished career as a writer, teacher, and academic. In addition to her forceful, direct poetry, she has written a number of books for children, as well as plays and essays.

Poetry

Evans was born on July 16, 1923, in Toledo, Ohio. She was raised in a traditional family and studied at the University of Toledo. She has taught in schools and universities across the Midwest and East, including Indiana University, Purdue, and Spelman College.

During the 1960s Evans became an activist in the civil rights movement and began to write poetry that promoted black empowerment. Her first collection of poetry, *Where Is All the Music?*, was published in 1968. Three other critically acclaimed collections have followed: *I Am a Black Woman* (1970), *Nightstar: 1973–1978* (1981), and *A Dark and Splendid Mass* (1992).

Like other African American poets of the 1960s and 1970s, Evans wrote her poetry solely for a black audience. She used the colloquial language of black Americans, distilling its rhythms and idioms to create her beautifully crafted verse. One of her most famous poems of this time is "I am a black woman," in which an African American "Everywoman" asserts her sense of self-esteem and empowerment: "I am a black woman / tall as a cypress / strong / beyond all definition...."

Children's writer

In her writing for children, Evans also addresses black issues and needs. *In Singing Black: Alternative Nursery Rhymes for Children* (1978), she creates poems for very young African American children that, unlike the nursery rhymes of white Western tradition, encourage them to feel positive about their skin color and heritage. Her other books for children include *Rap Stories* (1974), *Jim Flying High* (1979), and *Dear Corinne, Tell Somebody! Love, Annie: A Book about Secrets* (1999).

Other works

Evans is also an accomplished jazz musician and composer who says her first love has always been music. In 1979 she used her musical and writing skills to create a musical adaptation of Zora Neale Hurston's 1937 novel *Their Eyes Were Watching God,* which includes 20 jazz-based songs.

Evans has also written numerous articles and edited a number of books, including the important critical anthology of 15 postwar African American women writers *Black Women Writers (1950–1980): A Critical Evaluation* (1984). It was the first comprehensive study of the black women writers who came to prominence between the 1950s and 1980s.

Awards

Evans's work has been included in more than 400 anthologies and textbooks. She has received many honors and awards, including the Indiana University Writers' Conference award, the Black Academy of Arts and Letters' first annual poetry award, and fellowships from Yaddo, an artists' community in Saratoga Springs, New York, and the National Endowment for the Arts. In 1997 Evans was one of 12 writers honored by the Ugandan and Ghanaian governments when their photographs were included on a set of postage stamps. In 1998 Evans was inducted into the National Literary Hall of Fame for Writers of African Descent. In 2005 Evans published a collection of critical essays, *Clarity as Concept: A Poet's Perspective.*

KEY DATES

1923	Born in Toledo, Ohio, on July 16.
1970	Publishes her collection *I Am a Black Woman.*
1978	Publishes *In Singing Black: Alternative Nursery Rhymes for Children.*
1992	Publishes *A Dark and Splendid Mass.*
1998	Inducted into the National Literary Hall of Fame for Writers of African Descent.

See also: Civil Rights; Hurston, Zora Neale

Further reading: Nielsen, Aldon Lynn, and Albert Gelpi (eds.). *Black Chant: Languages of African-American Postmodernism.* (Cambridge Studies in American Literature & Culture). New York, NY: Cambridge University Press, 1997.
www.math.buffalo.edu/~sww/poetry/evans_mari.html (Biography plus samples of Evans's work).

EVANTI, Lillian
Opera Singer

Lillian Evanti was the first African American opera singer to gain an international reputation. Her pioneering career made her an inspirational figure for later generations of professional black singers, including Marian Anderson and Mattiwilda Dobbs

"Madame Evanti"

Evanti was born Annie Wilson Lillian Evans on August 12, 1890, in Washington, D.C. Both of her parents, Anne Brooks and Bruce Evans, were teachers. Evans showed her talent for singing early, performing at a charity concert at age four. She went on to attend some of the most prestigious black educational institutions in Washington—Armstrong Manual Training School, Miner Normal School, and finally Howard University School of Music, from which she graduated in 1917.

While at Howard, Evans was coached by Professor Roy Wilfred Tibbs, who later became her husband. With Tibbs's encouragement Evans continued to train as an opera

▼ *Lillian Evanti played Violetta in the National Negro Opera Company's production of* **La Traviata** *in 1943.*

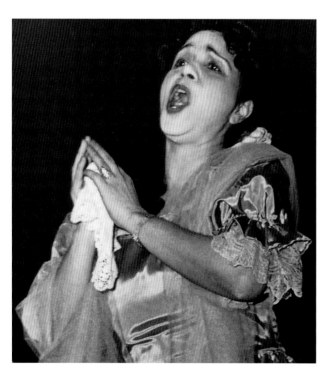

KEY DATES	
1890	Born in Washington, D.C., on August 12.
1925	Makes her professional debut in Nice, France.
1941	Cofounds the National Negro Opera Company (NNOC).
1943	Sings the role of Violetta in the NNOC's production of *La Traviata* until 1944.
1967	Dies in Washington, D.C., on December 6.

singer; she even took an exotic-sounding stage name, Madame Lillian Evanti, which combined her family name with her married name. Her career was hampered by the fact that U.S. opera companies refused to employ African American singers and musicians, however, and in order to pursue her career, Evanti moved to Europe, arriving in Paris, France, in 1924. She made her professional debut at the Casino Theater in Nice in 1925, singing the title role in the opera *Lakmé*.

"Madame Evanti" returned to Washington, D.C., seven years later, giving a recital at the Belasco Theater, one of the few stages in the city where African Americans could perform for integregated audiences. Evanti's home in Washington's Shaw District became an important meeting place for leading black artists and writers of the day. By 1934 she was a huge success and was invited to sing at the White House by President Franklin D. Roosevelt.

In 1941 Evanti cofounded the National Negro Opera Company (NNOC) with musician and educator Mary Dawson (1894–1962). Evanti wanted to create a place where black American opera singers could study and perform. Evanti sang one of her most celebrated roles, Violetta, in the 1943–1944 NNOC production of *La Traviata* (A Woman Gone Astray). Evanti later toured in the United States, South America, and Europe. She died in 1967.

See also: Anderson, Marian; Dobbs, Mattiwilda

Further reading: Southern, Eileen. *The Music of Black Americans: A History.* New York, NY: W. W. Norton & Company, 1997.
www.aaregistry.com/african_american_history/
1069/Lillian_E_Evanti_a_magnificent_voice (Short biography).

EVERS, Medgar
Civil Rights Activist

Known by many in the civil rights movement as the "Man in Mississippi," Medgar Evers was one of the most respected figures in the struggle for civil rights in the 1950s and early 1960s. He became one of the first martyrs of the movement when he was assassinated in 1963 by a white supremacist. His death propelled the civil rights struggle into the hearts and minds of Americans and the world. As Evers himself once said, "You can kill a man but you can't kill an idea."

Early life

Medgar Wiley Evers was born on July 2, 1925, in Decatur, Mississippi. He was the third of four children. In the years after his birth Mississippi was a region filled with racism toward blacks, and Evers was deeply affected by the discrimination he experienced himself and witnessed against others. Evers earned a high school diploma before joining the Army in 1943. He fought in World War II (1939–1945), seeing action in France and Germany. He left the Army in 1946 and returned to the United States to study business administration at Alcorn Agricultural and Mechanical College, Mississippi.

Evers was very active in college life, earning him a place in the *Who's Who in American Colleges*. In his senior year he met and married Myrlie Beasley. He graduated with a BA in 1952.

Civil rights activities

After college Evers worked as an insurance salesman in Philadelphia, Mississippi, where he helped organize the activities of the National Association for the Advancement of Colored People (NAACP). He once explained the guiding principle of his work by saying, "The gifts of God should be enjoyed by all citizens in Mississippi."

Following the U.S. Supreme Court case of *Brown v. Board of Education* in 1954, which ended segregation in schools, Evers quit his insurance job and attempted to enroll in the University of Mississippi Law School. When his application was refused, he moved to Jackson, the state capital, and became Mississippi's first field secretary for the NAACP. He worked to recruit members and register African American voters. He also investigated crimes against blacks, such as the lynching of 14-year-old Emmett Till (1941–1955), who was killed for speaking to a white

▼ *The death of Medgar Evers in 1963 spurred other civil rights leaders to fight for equality all the harder.*

KEY DATES

1925 Born in Decatur, Mississippi, on July 2.

1943 Joins the Army.

1951 Marries Myrlie Beasley.

1954 Becomes the first field secretary for the Mississippi branch of the NAACP.

1963 Shot by a waiting assassin on June 12 as he returns home from an NAACP meeting.

1994 Evers's assassin is finally convicted of murder after a third trial; he is sentenced to life imprisonment.

INFLUENCES AND INSPIRATION

The death of Medgar Evers sent a shock wave across the civil rights movement and the African American community. The effect Evers's martyrdom had on galvanizing support for the civil rights movement from both blacks and whites is impossible to quantify. However, his death did inspire two of the people closest to him to take his place in the struggle for equality.

Evers's wife, Myrlie, stayed in Mississippi until the failure of Beckwith's second trial. She then took her three children to California to build a new life. She never forgot that her husband's assassin had escaped justice. She searched tirelessly for new evidence, and her work was eventually rewarded when Beckwith was convicted in 1994.

Myrlie Evers-Williams (she married activist Walter Williams in 1975) is known not just for pursuing justice for her husband but also for achievements in her own right. A graduate of Pomona College in California, she was the first African American woman to be named to the Los Angeles Board of Public Works in 1988. In 1995 Evers-Williams, who by then had moved to Oregon, became the first woman chair of the NAACP.

J. Charles Evers (1922–) was Medgar Evers's older brother. Along with Medgar, Charles worked for the NAACP in Philadelphia, Mississippi, during the 1950s. While Medgar decided to make civil rights his full-time occupation in 1954, Charles remained working for the family

insurance business. In 1957 he moved to Chicago, where he became a successful real-estate agent and nightclub owner. He even worked as a DJ.

Following the killing of his brother, Charles moved back to Mississippi and took up Medgar's post as Mississippi field secretary for the NAACP. The move sparked Charles's political ambitions. In 1969 he was elected mayor of Fayette, Mississippi, becoming the first African American mayor in a racially mixed Southern town since the end of the Civil War (1861–1865).

In 1971 Charles stood for the governorship of Mississippi on an independent ticket. He failed to win office, but was reelected as mayor in 1973. In 1978 he made a failed bid to become a senator.

woman. In 1955 Evers organized a boycott of gas stations that did not allow blacks to use their restrooms. He also became well-known for his success in getting the first African American admitted to the University of Mississippi.

Death threats
Soon Evers became a target of hate among Mississippi's white population. He and his family were first threatened with death in 1955. Their house in Jackson was firebombed in May 1963. A month later, on June 12, 1963, Evers was shot in the back outside his house as he returned from a NAACP meeting. He was taken to a hospital, where he died 50 minutes later. Evers was buried with full military honors in Arlington National Cemetery in Virginia. Thousands of African Americans attended his funeral. The NAACP awarded Evers the Spingarn Medal after his death.

Fight for justice
The police found the fingerprints of white supremacist Byron De La Beckwith (1921–2001) on the rifle that was used to shoot Evers. Beckwith was charged with murder. However, all-white juries in two trials failed to reach a verdict, and Beckwith walked free in 1964. In 1989

evidence came to light that white supremacists had helped Beckwith's defense team screen the jurors in the original trials. An investigation was launched but found no evidence of jury tampering. However, investigators also found previously unknown witnesses to the crime. When their evidence was put before a racially mixed jury in a third trial in 1994, Beckwith was convicted at last and given a life sentence. He died in jail. In 1996 Hollywood made a movie of Myrlie's struggle for justice and the final trial, *Ghosts of Mississippi*.

See also: Civil Rights; Evers–Williams, Myrlie; National Organizations

Further reading: Brown, Jennie. *Medgar Evers*. Los Angeles, CA: Melrose Square Publishing Co., 1994.
Nossiter, Adam. *Of Long Memory: Mississippi and the Murder of Medgar Evers*. New York, NY: Da Capo Press, 2002.
Vollers, Maryanne. *Ghosts of Mississippi: The Murder of Medgar Evers, the Trials of Byron De La Beckwith, and the Haunting of the New South*. Boston, MA: Little, Brown, 1996.
http://www.africawithin.com/bios/medgar_evers.htm (Biography).

EVERS-WILLIAMS, Myrlie
Civil Rights Activist

Myrlie Evers-Williams is a civil rights activist, community leader, and successful businesswoman. Married first to the civil rights leader Medgar Evers, who was assassinated in 1963, and then to activist Walter Williams in 1975, Evers-Williams fought for more than 30 years to bring her first husband's killer to justice.

Myrlie Louise Beasley was born in Vicksburg, Mississippi, in 1933. Raised by her grandmother and her aunt following her parents' separation, Evers-Williams lived a sheltered childhood. Inspired by her guardians, both of whom were schoolteachers, she enrolled at Alcorn A&M College, Mississippi, in 1950. On her first day she met upperclassman Medgar Evers, and the couple married on Christmas Eve of the following year.

Civil rights activism

Already active in the National Association for the Advancement of Colored People (NAACP), Medgar Evers was named Mississippi state field secretary in 1954; he established an NAACP office in Jackson with his wife as secretary. The couple became well-known activists in the years that followed, organizing demonstrations, boycotts, and voter registration drives. Their high-profile status, however, also put them and their three children in danger. In 1955 the Evers family began receiving death threats from white supremacists: Medgar took to wearing disguises around town and changing his route home. In the early hours of the morning on June 12, 1963, however, Myrlie opened the door to find her fatally injured husband lying on the porch: He had been shot by a sniper.

Although segregationist and white supremacist Byron De La Beckwith was arrested and his fingerprints were found on the rifle that killed Medgar Evers, two all-white juries failed to convict him.

▲ *Myrlie Evers-Williams at the funeral of her husband on June 15, 1963.*

Evers-Williams moved to Claremont, California, and cowrote a book about her husband, *For Us, the Living* (1967). In 1968 she graduated with a BA in sociology and went to work for Claremont College. In 1988 she became the first black American woman appointed to the Los Angeles Board of Public Works. All the while she fought to bring Beckwith to justice: He was finally found guilty of murder in 1994 and sentenced to life in prison. A year later Evers-Williams became the first woman to chair the NAACP (until 1998). She published her memoirs in 1999.

See also: Civil Rights; Evers, Medgar

Further reading: Evers-Williams, Myrlie, and Melinda Blau. *Watch Me Fly: What I Learned on the Way to Becoming the Woman I Was Meant to Be.* New York, NY: Little Brown, 1999.

KEY DATES	
1933	Born in Vicksburg, Mississippi, on March 17.
1963	Medgar Evers is shot dead on June 12.
1963	Writes *For Us, the Living*.
1994	Byron De La Beckwith found guilty of Evers's murder.
1995	Becomes chair of the board of the NAACP.

EWING, Patrick
Basketball Player

Patrick Ewing enjoyed a successful career with the New York Knicks between 1985 and 2000. He was named one of the 50 greatest players in the history of the National Basketball Association (NBA) in 1996.

Patrick Aloysius Ewing was born on August 5, 1962, in Kingston, Jamaica. As a child he played mainly cricket and soccer; it was only after his family moved to Cambridge, Massachusetts, in 1975 that he took up basketball. By the time Ewing was playing for Rindge and Latin High School, he was 7 feet (2.1m) tall and had developed an astonishing flair for the game. He drove the team to three consecutive state championship wins. His talent brought him to the attention of collegiate teams, and in 1982 he chose to attend Georgetown University, whose basketball coach was John Thompson, a former Boston Celtics player.

Under Thompson's guidance Ewing brought an electrifying performance to the collegiate game. In 1984 he led Georgetown to the National Collegiate Athletic Association (NCAA) championship. That same year he was named the NCAA Tournament Most Valuable Player (MVP) and was a member of the gold-medal-winning U.S. team at the Los Angeles Olympic Games. In 1985 Ewing joined the New York Knicks. Despite being new to the professional game, he was offered a $1.7 million deal, such was the enthusiasm to sign him up.

Knicks career

Ewing's first season with the Knicks lived up to expectations. He achieved a league-leading points and rebounds total for a first-year player, and earned the Rookie of the Year award. Ewing developed an all-round skill on offense and defense despite the fact that injuries plagued him for his first two years with the Knicks. His presence helped the team win the NBA Atlantic Division in 1989. In 1992 Ewing played in his second Olympic Games, this time in Barcelona, Spain, where once again the U.S. team took gold.

In the 1993–1994 season Ewing surpassed Walt Frazier to become the Knicks' all-time leading scorer. He led the team to the NBA Finals. However, despite blocking 30 shots from the Houston Rockets, he was unable to help the Knicks to victory. Over the following four seasons Ewing averaged no fewer than 20.8 points per season, but toward the end of his Knicks career he was again troubled by persistent injuries. In 2000 Ewing finally left New York and

▲ *Patrick Ewing was an NBA All-Star 11 times and twice played for the U.S. team in the Olympic Games.*

played for one season each with the Seattle Supersonics and the Orlando Magic before retiring in 2002. He then joined the Washington Wizards as an assistant coach.

KEY DATES	
1962	Born in Kingston, Jamaica, on August 5.
1975	Moves to Cambridge, Massachusetts, and begins playing basketball.
1982	Joins the Georgetown University team.
1984	Wins an Olympic gold medal in Los Angeles.
1985	Signs with the New York Knicks.
1992	Wins a second Olympic gold medal in Barcelona.
2000	Leaves the Knicks and retires two years later.

See also: Frazier, Walt; Thompson, John

Further reading: Weiner, Paul, *Patrick Ewing* (Basketball Legends). New York, NY: Chelsea House Publications, 1995.
http://www.nba.com/playerfile/patrick_ewing/bio.html
(Extensive background information on Ewing).

FARD, Wallace. D.
Religious Leader, Activist

Wallace D. Fard was the founder of the Temple of Islam, a Black Muslim religious movement that later became known as the Nation of Islam (NOI).

Fard's origins are a mystery. Some sources place his birth in 1871, some in 1877, and others in 1891, and his place of birth ranges from New Zealand, Britain, and the West Indies to California. He is generally believed to have been of Arab descent. Fard was known by many different names, including Wali Fard, W. D. Farad, Wali Farad, Wallace Delaney Fard, Wali Fard Muhammad, Wallace Fard Muhammad, and Wallace D. Fard.

The Temple of Islam

In the summer of 1930 a peddler named Wallace D. Fard appeared in the Paradise Valley area of Detroit, Michigan, an area predominantly inhabited by African Americans who had moved from the South to the industrial North during the Great Migration. He sold bric-a-brac door-to-door while telling his customers stories about Africa. The stories were popular and he began to speak to groups of people in their homes. Gradually Fard's talks became more political and religious, and he started to teach from the Koran, saying that Islam was the only true religion. As his following grew, Fard gave his talks in local halls.

On July 4, 1930, Fard announced the formation of the Temple of Islam, which later became Temple No. 1 of the Nation of Islam. Fard claimed that a mad black scientist named Yakub created white people 6,000 years ago as a curse and test for more advanced black races. Fard declared that he had been sent by Allah to reclaim his people, the tribe of Shabazz, who had been kidnapped and sent to America in chains.

Some of his followers believed that Fard was the reincarnation of religious leader Noble Drew Ali; others called him the "Master," the "Prophet," or "God-in-Person." Nation of Islam theology states, "We believe that Allah (God) appeared in the Person of Master W. Fard Muhammad, July 1930; the long-awaited 'Messiah' of the Christians and the 'Mahdi' of the Muslims."

Elijah Poole

In 1931 Elijah Poole, who had moved to Detroit in the late 1920s, attended a Temple of Islam service. He approached Fard, who renamed Poole Elijah Muhammad and declared that he was the supreme minister of Islam.

▲ *Heavyweight boxing champion and NOI follower Muhammad Ali holds up photographs of Wallace Fard (left) and Elijah Muhammad.*

Fard and his followers soon ran into trouble with the white authorities. Some people believed that the NOI was a cult and rumors circulated that it allowed ritual killings and supported voodoo. After Fard was arrested three times he left Michigan in 1933 for Chicago. He was arrested there for disorderly conduct in September 1933 and disappeared without a trace in 1934.

Elijah Muhammad declared that Fard was not a prophet but God and that Muhammad was his messenger. He assumed the leadership of the Nation of Islam in 1934. The movement celebrates Savior's Day on February 26 to commemorate Fard's birthday.

KEY DATES	
1871	Born in 1871, 1877, or 1891.
1930	Forms Temple of Islam in Detroit on July 4.
1931	Meets Elijah Poole, whom he renames Muhammad.
1933	Moves to Chicago.
1934	Disappears in Chicago.

See also: Ali, Noble Drew; Great Migration; Muhammad, Elijah

Further reading: http://www.noi.org/ (Official Nation of Islam site).
http://www.metrotimes.com/editorial/story.asp?id=4650 (Article on Fard from *Metro Times*, Detroit)

FARMER, James
Founder of Congress of Racial Equality

James Farmer was one of the main leaders of the civil rights movement, along with Martin Luther King, Jr., Whitney Young, and Roy Wilkins.

Early life

Born in Marshall, Texas, in 1920, James Leonard Farmer, Jr., was brought up in an environment that valued education and religion. His father was one of only 25 African Americans in the South to hold a PhD. Farmer was himself an exceptional student and skipped several grades in elementary school. At age 14 he began studying at Wiley College in Marshall, where his father taught.

In 1938 Farmer went on to the School of Religion at Howard University, Washington, D.C. He graduated with a degree in divinity in 1941, the same year that the United States entered World War II (1939–1945). Farmer was exempt from the draft because of his degree.

He objected to the war, particularly because of segregation in the armed forces. He also refused to preach to segregated congregations in Methodist churches. He became the secretary for race relations for the Fellowship of Reconciliation (FOR) in Chicago, a pacifist organization that sought to change racial attitudes.

CORE

In 1942 Farmer and a group of University of Chicago students founded the Congress of Racial Equality (CORE). Influenced by Mahatma Gandhi (1869–1948), who was using passive resistance to achieve independence in India at the time; Farmer believed that nonviolent protest was the best means to fight inequality in the United States.

Farmer initially recruited CORE members at FOR meetings while traveling with field secretary Bayard Rustin. Just a few years after its founding, CORE had 60,000 members in 70 chapters across the country.

KEY DATES	
1920	Born in Marshall, Texas, on January 20.
1942	Helps found CORE.
1968	Runs for Congress on Republican ticket.
1998	Awarded Medal of Freedom by President Clinton.
1999	Dies in Fredericksburg, Virginia, on July 9.

▲ *James Farmer received the Medal of Freedom from President Bill Clinton in 1998.*

Farmer became the national director of CORE in 1953, and he propelled the organization to the forefront of the civil rights movement. Farmer was often arrested, and in 1963 he was hunted by state troopers in Plaquemine, Louisiana. His life was saved by a funeral director who made him pretend to be dead in the back of a hearse.

In the late 1960s Farmer left CORE and began to lecture on civil rights at Lincoln University, Pennsylvania. He also ran for Congress as a Republican in 1968 but was defeated by Democrat Shirley Chisholm. He served as assistant secretary of Health, Education, and Welfare in the first Nixon administration before retiring in 1971. A diabetes sufferer, Farmer lost his sight and both his legs through the disease in old age. He died in 1999.

See also: Chisholm, Shirley; King, Martin Luther, Jr.; Rustin, Bayard; Wilkins, Roy; Young, Whitney M., Jr.

Further reading: Farmer, James. *Lay Bare the Heart.* New York, NY: New American Library Trade, 1991.
http://www.medaloffreedom.com/JamesFarmer.htm (Biography).

FARRAKHAN, Louis
Religious Leader

Louis Eugene Walcott, now known as the Honorable Louis Abdul Farrakhan, is leader of the political and religious group the Nation of Islam (NOI). He is often criticized for his comments about American racism. However, the head of the Congress of National Black Churches, African Methodist Episcopal bishop John Hurst Adams, once said of him, "Farrakhan is tapping deep feelings based on four hundred years of racism, and speaks for many more blacks than just his followers."

Born on May 11, 1933, in the West Indian community in the Roxbury section of Boston, Massachusetts, Walcott was raised with his brother Alvin by his mother. She came from the Caribbean island of St. Kitts and ran a highly disciplined and spiritual household. His father, a New York cab driver, was not involved in his upbringing.

Music career
Walcott displayed musical talent from an early age. He was an accomplished violinist, performing by age 13 with the Boston College Orchestra and the Boston Civic Symphony. At age 14 Walcott won the *Ted Mack Amateur Hour*, a popular radio talent show on which he was one of the first African Americans to appear.

Walcott also excelled both academically and as a high school track star. He attended Winston Salem Teacher's College in North Carolina on a track scholarship in the fall of 1950. There he continued playing the violin and formed a calypso band. In 1953 Walcott married his childhood sweetheart, now known as Mother Khadijah Farrakhan. They have nine children, 23 grandchildren, and four great-grandchildren.

In the 1950s Walcott became famous as the Charmer, a leading calypso singer in the United States. He had started in this profession in 1949 at age 16. According to biographer Arthur Magida, he became inspired by seeing the great New York calypso band of Gerald Clark (1899–1977). In 2000 a compact disk was issued that includes all 12 of Farrakhan's recordings as the Charmer.

A change in direction
Walcott went to Chicago in February 1955 as part of the *Calypso Follies* show at the Blue Angel nightclub. He became interested in the Nation of Islam when he attended a lecture by Elijah Muhammad, leader and founding member of the Nation of Islam. He abandoned his career as a calypso singer when NOI's charismatic minister Malcolm X told the New York temple that all Muslims would have to get out of show business or get out of the Nation of Islam. While most musicians left the organization, the then named Louis X remained. He was later named Louis Farrakhan by Elijah Muhammad. In 1956 Farrakhan became a minister himself, head of the NOI's Temple Number 11 in Boston.

In 1965, following the assassination of Malcolm X, Elijah Muhammad appointed Farrakhan to Temple Number 7 in New York City. This had been X's previous position before he left the NOI in 1964. Farrakhan began to work tirelessly to restore the image of the Nation of Islam, his work made all the harder after three African American

▼ *Louis Farrakhan's impassioned speeches have made him a popular, although highly controversial, figure.*

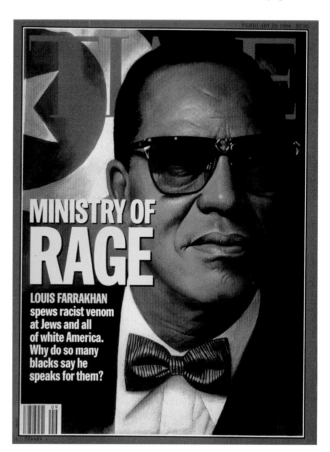

INFLUENCES AND INSPIRATION

Louis Farrakhan has been referred to, quoted, and sampled on many hip-hop projects, and has had both a direct and indirect influence on the genre. He is revered among many artists and audiences of the spoken word. For example, the hip-hop group Public Enemy, which can be credited with providing some of the foundation for the genre, has acknowledged that they were influenced, by, among other people, Muhammad Ali (also a prominent Nation of Islam member) and Louis Farrakhan. Farrakhan has been embraced as a respected elder and leader across the hip-hop community.

Rap and hip-hop are not new phenomena to the Nation of Islam. The Five Percenters, a 1964 offshoot of the NOI started by Clarence 13X, have been involved in the development of hip-hop since the late 1970s.

Farrakhan has addressed at least three major "Hip-Hop Summits" sponsored by mogul Russell Simmons in New York and Los Angeles. Each time he brought a tough message to audiences that included the likes of P. Diddy, Sistah Souljah of Public Enemy, and Snoop Dogg.

On June 13, 2001, at the first summit, Farrakhan challenged the leaders of the hip-hop community to accept the responsibility of leadership. "One rap song from you is worth more than a thousand of my speeches," he told the crowd at the summit. "You are the new leadership."

In February of 2002 at a summit sponsored by Simmons, Farrakhan urged the community to come closer to God and recognize the power of words. He made a call for the hip-hop community to use its influence and become peacemakers for society. He argued that in order to establish peace, hip-hoppers have to take steps toward being at peace with themselves and to become more spiritually grounded.

He also urged the rappers present never to be afraid of speaking the truth. As they become closer to God and more spiritually connected, he urged them, they would feel less fear and experience a greater sense of security.

KEY DATES

1933   Born in Boston, Massachusetts, on May 11.

1950   Begins to perform as a calypso singer.

1955   Meets Elijah Muhammad, the leader of the Nation of Islam, in Chicago.

1956   Becomes minister of Temple Number 11 in Boston.

1965   Appointed to Temple Number 7 in New York City after the assassination of Malcolm X.

1978   Disagrees with the direction of the Nation of Islam's leadership; forms a new organization and becomes its global leader.

1995   Million Man March takes place in Washington, D.C., on October 17.

Controversy

Farrakhan is considered highly controversial because of his views about whites, black empowerment, and the Israel–Palestine conflict. He calls for separatism between whites and blacks, and asserts black racial supremacy, appealing to the anger many black people feel toward whites. Farrakhan has made efforts to improve the conditions of persecuted people around the world. He advocates community and family stability, healthy living, economic development, and personal responsibility. In 1995 he orchestrated with other leaders the Million Man March—a call for a million "sober, disciplined, committed, dedicated, inspired black men" to meet in Washington, D.C. The event was a staggering success. He also encourages positive messages in rap and hip-hop.

See also: Ali, Muhammad; Combs, Sean; Malcolm X; Muhammad, Elijah; Political Movements; Simmons, Russell; Snoop Dogg

Further reading: Alexander, Amy (ed.). *The Farrakhan Factor: African-American Writers on Leadership, Nationhood, and Minister Louis Farrakhan.* New York, NY: Grove Press, 1999. www.noi.org (Nation of Islam site).

Muslims were convicted of killing Malcolm X. In 1975 Elijah Muhammad died, and his son Warith Deen Mohammed (1933–) took over. Mohammed changed the name and doctrine of his father's organization. Farrakhan disliked the changes and formed another Nation of Islam in 1978, with himself as worldwide leader.

FATHER Divine
Religious Leader

Father Divine was the name given to a charismatic preacher who may have been named George Baker. He founded the Peace Mission, a religious movement that was influential during the Great Depression of the 1930s.

Baker was born in about 1877, probably in Georgia. Nothing is known of his early life, but he began preaching in the South from about 1900. In 1915 Baker moved to Sayville, New York, and set up a mission. From his base there he became a successful businessman: His main interests were in property, but he also owned restaurants and grocery stores. He continued preaching and became known as Major M. J. Divine and later as Father Divine.

The Peace Mission
The Peace Mission attracted a large following, mainly but not exclusively among African Americans—the exact numbers are unknown, but they were probably in the tens of thousands. At the height of the movement there were 178 centers, or "heavens" as they were known, most in New York and Philadelphia. As the Peace Mission spread, it sometimes used whites to buy property on its behalf in segregated areas.

Father Divine's teachings were not connected to any particular religious church or group and were aimed at ending poverty and racial discrimination. He encouraged his followers to ignore race and promoted equality between men and women. As a result, a large proportion of his followers were women.

Father Divine was forced to relocate his mission to Harlem in 1933 and nine years later to Philadelphia; but far from weakening the Mission's appeal, the moves helped attract an even larger following among the inhabitants of the urban ghettos of the Northeast.

The Peace Mission offered members low-cost food and shelter at a time of great need. In return it demanded

▲ *Father Divine in 1953; his followers believed he was the incarnation of God.*

morality, celibacy, acts of charity, the surrender of personal property, and the observance of racial equality. In 1946 Father Divine married a white Canadian, Edna Rose Ritchings (Mother Divine). In 1954 he was given an estate in Philadelphia, which became his home until his death in 1965. His wife succeeded to the leadership. As Father Divine's health failed, Mission membership dropped. Today Father Divine's International Peace Mission Movement still exists but has a dwindling membership.

See also: Religion and African Americans

Further reading: Harris, Sara, with Harriet Crittenden. *Father Divine, Holy Husband.* Garden City, NY: Macmillan, 1971.
http://religiousmovements.lib.virginia.edu/nrms/Fatherd.html (Father Divine and the Peace Mission).

KEY DATES	
1877	Born near Savannah, Georgia, at about this time.
1900	Becomes a preacher.
1915	Sets up a mission in Sayville, New York.
1965	Dies in Lower Merion Township, Pennsylvania, on September 10.

FAUSET, Crystal
Politician

Crystal Bird Fauset was the first African American woman to be elected to any state legislature. A gifted public speaker, she specialized in race relations and did much to champion women and African Americans.

Born on June 27, 1893, in Princess Anne, Maryland, Fauset was one of the youngest in a family of nine. Orphaned at age six, she was raised by her aunt in Boston, Massachusetts. She attended integrated schools and graduated from the Boston Normal School in 1914. After teaching briefly, in 1918 she became the national secretary for young African American girls of the YMCA (Young Women's Christian Association). She traveled across the country studying the situation of African Americans and speaking in public.

In 1927 the American Friends Service Committee (AFRS) asked Fauset to lecture on African American aspirations. Following her graduation with a BS from Teachers College, Columbia University, in 1931, she became a social worker and administrator for African American affairs at the New York and Philadelphia YMCAs.

▼ *Crystal Fauset in about 1941, when she was special consultant on Negro Affairs.*

From Democrat to Republican

In the 1930s the economic inequality and hardship of the Great Depression prompted Fauset to join the Democratic Party so that she could play an active role in helping redress the situation. In 1935 she became director of Colored Women's Activities for the Democratic National Committee. Her success led to the Democrats asking her to run for the Pennsylvania House of Representatives in 1938 in a largely white district. Fauset won, gaining many of the female votes. She only served a year before resigning to become assistant state director of the education and recreation program of the WPA (Works Project Administration) set up by President Franklin D. Roosevelt to employ people on relief on useful projects.

First Lady Eleanor Roosevelt helped Fauset to her next post as special consultant on Negro Affairs in the Office of Civilian Defense, a post she held between 1941 and 1944. However, Fauset felt that the Democrats were not doing enough to help African Americans, and in 1945 she switched her support to the Republican Party.

In 1945 Fauset helped found the United Nations Council of Philadelphia and began traveling extensively. After attending independence celebrations in India and several African nations, Fauset became increasingly critical of the failure of her own country to address race problems. She died in Philadelphia in 1965 after a heart attack, a few months before the Voting Rights Act was passed—a cause to which she had devoted much of her life.

Further reading: Bogin, Ruth. "Crystal Dreda Bird Fauset" in *Notable American Women—The Modern Period.* Cambridge, MA: Harvard University Press, 1980.
http://www.aaregistry.com/african_american_history/562/A_political_first_Crystal_B_Fauset (Biography).

FAUSET, Jessie Redmon
Writer, Critic

Jessie Redmon Fauset is probably best known for her role as a writer and a mentor of other young writers during the Harlem Renaissance, the black arts movement that took place in New York City in the 1920s.

Early life
Born in Camden County, New Jersey, in 1882, Fauset was the seventh child of Redmon and Annie Seamon Fauset. Her father was a Presbyterian minister, and her family was part of well-to-do Philadelphia society, cultured but neither rich nor poor.

▼ *Jessie Redmon Fauset's writing dealt with interracial relationships and the color bar.*

Fauset attended the prestigious Philadelphia High School for Girls. She won a scholarship to Cornell University, New York, becoming the first African American woman to study there; she graduated in 1905.

From Washington to New York
In 1906 Fauset went to teach Latin and French at M Street High School in Washington, D.C. She spent 13 years teaching at various schools in the area. While teaching, she contributed to *Crisis*, the magazine of the National Association for the Advancement of Colored People (NAACP). The editor of *Crisis*, W. E. B. DuBois, persuaded Fauset to move to New York and become the magazine's literary editor. Later she became contributing editor.

While at the magazine Fauset supported young black writers, encouraging and promoting Jean Toomer, Langston Hughes, and Countee Cullen, among others. Fauset herself also contributed essays, mainly biographies of prominent African Americans. In 1932 she explained, "It is urgent that ambitious Negro youth be able to read of the achievements of their race."

Writing
Fauset's first novel, *There Is Confusion*, was published in 1924. She wrote three more, including *Comedy American Style* (1933), which is probably her best known. Fauset married in 1929 but moved in with her brother following her husband's death in 1958. She died in 1961.

KEY DATES	
1882	Born in Camden Country, New Jersey, on April 27.
1905	Graduates from Cornell University.
1924	Publishes first novel, *There Is Confusion*.
1961	Dies in Philadelphia, Pennsylvania, on April 30.

See also: Cullen, Countee; DuBois, W. E. B; Harlem Renaissance; Hughes, Langston; Johnson, Charles; Locke, Alain; Toomer, Jean

Further reading: Sylvander, Carolyn W. *Jessie Redmon Fauset: Black American Writer*. Troy, NY: Whitston Publishing Co.,1981.
http://www.nku.edu/~diesmanj/fauset.html (Poems by Fauset).

FETCHIT, Stepin
Actor

In the opinion of many film critics comedy actor Stepin Fetchit was the first black movie star. Nonetheless, he was derided and for a time ostracized by African Americans for his portrayal of characters that many believed promoted an offensive racial stereotype.

Born Lincoln Theodore Monroe Andrew Perry in 1902, he attended a Catholic boarding school until age 12. He ran away to tour the South with minstrel shows and carnivals as a vaudeville singer, dancer, and comic. In partnership with Ed Lee he became part of an act called *Step 'n' Fetchit: Two Dancing Fools from Dixie.* When he went solo in the early 1920s, he retained Stepin Fetchit as his stage name.

▼ *Stepin Fetchit was the first African American movie star. He was elevated to the Black Filmmakers Hall of Fame in 1978.*

KEY DATES	
1902	Born in Key West, Florida, on May 30.
1914	Leaves home to join the vaudeville circuit.
1927	Makes film debut as Highpockets in *In Old Kentucky.*
1947	Declares bankruptcy.
1985	Dies in Woodland Hills, California, on November 19.

Comedy relief

On moving to Hollywood in the late 1920s, Stepin Fetchit found he was most often employed as what many directors saw as a movie's black comedy relief. Tall and lanky, with a slow way of speaking and a perpetually bemused and sad-looking demeanor, Stepin Fetchit soon shot to fame in a succession of roles as lazy, shiftless, dimwitted farmhands, slaves, and servants who seldom missed an opportunity to bow and fawn around their white bosses.

Despite these limited roles, few could deny Stepin Fetchit's ability as a performer nor his remarkable comic timing. Both black and white audiences found him hysterically funny, and he made a huge impact. He was the most celebrated black actor in Hollywood during the 1930s and sometimes shared top billing with his white costars. Stepin Fetchit appeared in more than 40 films in 50 years, making his debut in *In Old Kentucky* (1927).

Decline

Stepin Fetchit was the first African American actor to become a millionaire, owning 12 cars and employing a staff of 16 Chinese servants. However, he squandered his fortune and was forced to declare bankruptcy in 1947.

Despite playing negative stereotypes of blacks, Stepin Fetchit received many awards, including the Special Image Award from the National Association for the Advancement of Colored People (NAACP) in 1976; and despite his critics, he undoubtedly paved the way for later black actors. Stepin Fetchit converted to Islam in the late 1960s and died of pneumonia in 1985.

Further reading: Watkins, Mel. *Stepin Fetchit: The Life and Times of Lincoln Perry.* New York, NY: Pantheon, 2005.
http://www.africanamericans.com/StepinFetchit.htm (Biography and filmography).

FIELDS, Mary
Pioneer

Also known as "Black Mary" or "Stagecoach Mary," Mary Fields was born a slave in Hickman County, Tennessee, in 1832. She was orphaned at an early age, and following the Emancipation Proclamation in 1863 she moved to Mississippi. There she is said to have worked as a chambermaid on the legendary steamboat *Robert E. Lee* during the late 1860s and early 1870s.

Church worker

Fields eventually moved to Toledo, Ohio, in 1884, where she befriended Mother Superior Amadeus of the Catholic Ursuline Sisters. She began to work in the convent as a handywoman, doing such chores as washing clothes, raising chickens, cooking, and gardening.

Amadeus had opened a girls' school for Blackfoot Indians in Cascade, Montana, where the Jesuit order had established a mission. When the nun fell sick in 1885, Fields traveled to Cascade, about 600 miles (965km) north of Helena, the state capital, to help her. She took care of Amadeus and decided to stay at the new mission, helping build the Convent of St. Peter.

At 6 feet (1.82m) tall and weighing 200 pounds (90kg), Fields became the talk of the town. She drank in saloons, smoked cigars, and was frequently involved in altercations and brawls with men, some of whom she beat mercilessly. Her revolver around her waist at all times, the bad-tempered Fields was feared by many people. Indeed, at one point she challenged a man to a gun duel. Fields's bad reputation reached Bishop Brondell, the first Catholic bishop of Montana, who recommended that Sister Amadeus dismiss her.

On the open road

Fields was fired, but Sister Amadeus helped her start a restaurant in Cascade. The restaurant failed, however, because Fields allowed too many customers to pay on credit, and her establishment did not enjoy a reputation for good food. Again with Sister Amadeus's assistance Fields went on to become a delivery driver for the U.S. Postal Service. Fields traveled in her coach, pulled by her mule Moses, back and forth between Cascade and Helena. She made this journey regularly for eight years. Dressed like a man, smoking heavily, and drinking in saloons whenever she could, Fields never missed a single delivery. Legend has it that she braved the elements as well as animals (she was once surrounded by wolves), drunken cowboys, and bandits, to the extent that many people did not know and did not believe she was a woman. When she retired at age 70 in 1903, Fields settled in Cascade and opened a laundry business, while also babysitting for a little extra money.

Later life

In Cascade at the start of the 20th century, Fields was the only African American in town, but she became endeared to its citizens, especially once her temper had changed for the better. In fact, she became so popular that the town mayor allowed her to drink and smoke with men in the saloons, something no other woman in Cascade was allowed to do. She was known for her love for the town's baseball team, becoming their biggest fan. She would bring flowers to the players.

When Fields's laundry was destroyed by fire in 1912, the townspeople collected contributions and helped her rebuild it. Old and ill, Fields died from liver failure in Cascade in 1914 and was buried in the Hillside Cemetery. She was fondly remembered for her generosity. She fed the hungry, helped build the Catholic convent and church, and was an extremely dependable courier. The legends of her adventures in the Wild West have made her one of the most unusual African American women. Although living in a white environment, she was loved and respected. While she was alive, the whole town honored her whenever she declared her birthday, which varied each year since no one knew her actual birth date.

Further reading: Miller, Robert H. *The Story of Stagecoach Mary Fields*. Englewood Cliff, NJ: Silver Burdett Press, 1995. http://www.cascademontana.com/mary.htm (Biography of historical figures from Cascade, Montana). www.lkwdpl.org/wihohio/fiel-mar.htm (Biography).

KEY DATES	
1832	Born in Virginia.
1884	Moves to Toledo, Ohio.
1885	Settles in Cascade, Montana; helps build the Convent of St. Peter.
1914	Dies in Cascade.

50 CENT
Musician

Originally known as much for his violent past as his music, the rapper 50 Cent has risen to become one the world's biggest music stars.

Early life

The hip-hop star who would become known as 50 Cent was born Curtis Jackson III, in 1976. Even by the standards of Jamaica, Queens, the New York City neighborhood in which he grew up, 50 Cent's childhood was turbulent. His father had been absent since his birth, and his mother, a local drug dealer, was killed when he was eight years old. 50 Cent was brought up by his grandparents. He began dealing drugs himself while he was still a child, an existence that soon brought him into conflict with the law.

Road to rap

50 Cent's first involvement in music came in 1996, when he met Jam Master Jay (1966–2003) of the legendary hip-hop group Run-DMC, who encouraged him to start rapping. 50 Cent soon signed with Columbia Records, for whom he recorded 36 tracks that were intended to provide

▼ *Rapper 50 Cent decided to give up crime and pursue a music career after the birth of his son.*

the material for his debut album, *Power of the Dollar*. A single from the prospective album, "How to Rob" (2000), caused considerable controversy for his attacks on big-name hip-hop stars such as Jay-Z and Ghostface Killah.

Shortly after the single's release 50 Cent almost died when he was ambushed and shot nine times in Queens. The incident was violent enough to scare off Columbia Records, who shelved *Power of the Dollar*. However, the incident only added to 50 Cent's reputation in the macho world of gangsta rap and hip-hop. For the next two years 50 Cent concentrated on building an underground following by recording tracks for amateur mix-tapes. These recordings brought him to the attention of rapper Eminem, who landed 50 Cent a record contract.

After appearing on the soundtrack to the Eminem movie *8 Mile*, 50 Cent recorded his official debut album, *Get Rich or Die Tryin'*. The album, released in February 2003, reached No. 1 on the *Billboard* chart and sold more than 800,000 copies in just five days. Later that year the album *Beg for Mercy* from G-Unit, a rap collective fronted by 50 Cent, debuted at No. 2 on the chart.

Relations within G-Unit became strained in early 2005, when tension grew between 50 Cent and his protégé, Game. The rivalry led to a shooting incident between factions linked to the two rappers. At the same time, 50 Cent's fortunes hit a new high. In March he became the first solo artist to be featured on three singles in the Top 5 of the *Billboard* chart. In the same month his second album, *The Massacre*, topped the album charts.

> **KEY DATES**
>
> **1976** Born in Queens, New York, on July 6.
>
> **2000** Is shot nine times while sitting in the passenger seat of a car in Jamaica, Queens, on May 24.
>
> **2003** Debut album for a major label, *Get Rich or Die Tryin'*, is released in February.

See also: Jay–Z

Further reading: Cepeda, Raquel (ed.). *And It Don't Stop: The Best American Hip-Hop Journalism of the Last 25 Years*. New York, NY: Faber & Faber, 2004.
www.50cent.com (Official site).

FISHBURNE, Lawrence
Actor, Writer, Director

Critically acclaimed actor, playwright, screenwriter, director, and producer Lawrence Fishburne is celebrated for his distinguished and weighty performances.

Fishburne was born in Georgia in 1961. Following his parents' divorce, he moved with his mother to Brooklyn, New York. There he showed an early aptitude for drama, winning his first TV role at age 10 in the series *One Life to Live*. Four years later he made his film debut in *Cornbread, Earl and Me*. In 1979, after lying about his age, he was cast as Clean, a member of a torpedo boat crew in Francis Ford Coppola's classic war movie *Apocalypse Now*.

Although at first he was mostly cast in minor supporting roles, Fishburne steadily built his reputation, appearing in two additional Coppola films, *Rumble Fish* (1983) and *The Cotton Club* (1984), and Steven Spielberg's *The Color Purple* (1985), and giving highly praised performances in Spike Lee's *School Daze* (1986) and Abel Ferrara's *King of New York* (1990).

National and international fame

Fishburne appeared regularly as Cowboy Curtis on the CBS TV show *Pee-wee's Playhouse*, where he met future film director John Singleton. Playing Furious Styles in Singleton's debut picture, *Boyz N the Hood* (1991), brought Fishburne widespread recognition, as did a Tony Award for the Broadway play *Two Trains Running* (1992). However, Fishburne gained international fame as Ike Turner in the Tina Turner biographical movie *What's Love Got to Do with It* (1993), for which he received an Oscar nomination.

Fully established as a versatile actor, in 1995 Fishburne became the first African American to appear in the title role of Shakespeare's play *Othello* on screen; he also delivered a multiaward-nominated performance in *The Tuskegee*

▲ *Lawrence Fishburne attends the 2005 screening of* **Assault on Precinct 13.**

Airmen. Fishburne starred in and produced *Always Outnumbered* (1998) and the HBO series *Miss Evers' Boys*, for which he won an NAACP Image Award. As Morpheus, a key role in the *Matrix* (1999) and its sequels *Matrix: Reloaded* and *Matrix: Revolutions* (both 2003), Fishburne attained superstar status. Performances in *Mystic River* (2003) and *Assault on Precinct 13* (2005), together with his work for UNICEF, have served to foster his standing as one of Hollywood's most charismatic actors.

See also: Lee, Spike; Singleton, John; Turner, Ike; Turner, Tina

Further reading: Halliwell, Leslie. *Halliwell's Who's Who in the Movies*. New York, NY: HarperResource, 2003.
http://www.imdb.com/name/nm0000401/ (Internet Movie Database entry).

KEY DATES

1961	Born in Augusta, Georgia, on July 30.
1975	Film debut in *Cornbread, Earl and Me*.
1992	Wins Tony Award for his Broadway debut in *Two Trains Running*.
1993	Oscar nomination for his role as Ike Turner in *What's Love Got to Do with It*.
1996	Appointed National Ambassador for U.S. Fund for UNICEF (United Nations Children's Fund).

FISHER, Rudolph
Physician, Writer

One of the key figures of the Harlem Renaissance, Rudolph Fisher combined successes in both medical and literary fields during his short but prolific career.

Rudolph John Chauncey Fisher was born on May 9, 1897, in Washington, D.C., and raised in Providence, Rhode Island. A talented student, he graduated with a BA from Brown University in 1919, having studied both English and biology. Fisher obtained a master's degree in biology the following year, and in 1920 he returned to Washington to start a medical degree at Howard University.

Fisher graduated in 1924 with the highest honors and interned at Freedman's Hospital in Washington. The same year he married Jane Ryder, a teacher, with whom he had one son.

Fisher moved to New York in 1925, where he soon established himself as a talented physician. Specializing in bacteriology, pathology, and roentgenology—the use of X-rays—he studied for two years at the national Research Council of Columbia University's College of Physicians and Surgeons. His first short story, "The City of Refuge," was published in the *Atlantic Monthly* in 1925.

▼ *Rudolph Fisher's promising career as a writer and physician was cut short when he developed cancer as a result of working with high doses of radiation.*

Fisher, unlike many other African American writers, was published in mainstream magazines such as *Atlantic Monthly* and *McClure's*, as well as in African American publications such as *Crisis* and *Opportunity*. His first novel, *The Walls of Jericho* (1928), dealt with the tensions among the different social classes of Harlem society. The novel won praise for its refusal to make the African American inhabitants of Harlem seem exotic.

After its publication, Fisher consolidated his two careers. In 1929 he was appointed superintendent of the International Hospital on Seventh Avenue, a position he held until 1932. Between 1930 and 1934 he worked as a roentgenologist while serving on the literature committee of the 135th Street Young Men's Christian Association.

Fisher published his second novel, *The Conjure-Man Dies: A Mystery Tale of Dark Harlem*, in 1932. Widely recognized as the first black detective novel, it again portrayed Harlem society but within the structure of a mystery. Fisher was prolific: In less than a decade he published 15 short stories, two novels, six book reviews, magazine features, and a play, as well as medical articles.

Fisher developed intestinal cancer and, despite surgery, died on December 26, 1934, at age 37.

KEY DATES	
1897	Born in Washington, D.C., on May 9.
1919	Graduates with BA from Brown University.
1920	Receives MA in biology from Brown University.
1924	Graduates from Howard University Medical School.
1925	Moves to New York; starts medical career and publishes first short story.
1928	Publishes first novel, *The Walls of Jericho*.
1934	Dies in New York City on December 26.

See also: Harlem Renaissance

Further reading: McCluskey, John A., Jr. (ed.) *The City of Refuge: The Collected Stories of Rudolph Fisher*. Columbia, MO: University of Missouri Press, 1991.
http://www.dclibrary.org/blkren/bios/fisherr.html (Biography and links to Harlem Renaissance).

FITZGERALD, Ella
Singer, Songwriter

Ella Fitzgerald is known throughout the world as the "First Lady of Jazz" and is arguably the most famous female vocalist of the 20th century. A versatile and talented singer, performing in both jazz and popular musical styles, Fitzgerald is most recognized for her "scat" singing. This is a technique in which a jazz singer improvises and enhances a melody by singing nonsense syllables as if his or her voice was a horn or other instrument. Fitzgerald is often credited for her mastery of "scat" and her transformation of the technique into an art form.

Early life
Ella Jane Fitzgerald was born in Newport News, Virginia, in 1918. When she was a young child she moved with her mother to Yonkers, New York. Fitzgerald attended public schools, where she excelled as a student. She was given private piano lessons, and became an eager dancer. During a difficult period as a teenager, Fitzgerald got into trouble and spent time at a reform school.

In 1934, at age 16, Fitzgerald embarked on her career as a singer when she won the Apollo Theater's Amateur Night Contest in Harlem. The next year she won a contest at the Harlem Opera House, where she then performed for a week with the Tiny Bradshaw Band.

In 1936 Fitzgerald made her first recording, "Love and Kisses." Soon afterward she began experimenting with the bebop jazz style and "scat" singing in her rendition of the song "If You Can't Sing It, You Have to Swing It."

First hit
While performing at the Harlem Opera House, Fitzgerald was heard by drummer and bandleader Chick Webb. Although he was reluctant to have a female in his band, Webb hired Fitzgerald as his featured singer. She performed regularly with the Chick Webb Orchestra at Harlem's Savoy Ballroom. In 1938 her recording of "A-Tisket, A-Tasket" with the Chick Webb Orchestra was released, sold a million copies, and remained on the music charts for 17 weeks. Fitzgerald's fashioning of this children's nursery rhyme into a song became a jazz classic and one of her most remembered performances.

In 1939, when Webb died, Fitzgerald took over the band, which became known as Ella Fitzgerald and Her Famous Orchestra, until it disbanded in 1941.

During the 1940s and 1950s Fitzgerald performed as a solo artist, singing and recording popular songs. In 1946 she toured with Dizzy Gillespie's band. During this time, she joined Norman Granz' Jazz at the Philharmonic concerts, going on national and international tours in performances with jazz instrumentalists. Fitzgerald made recordings with Louis Armstrong and Louis Jordan (*see box on p. 46*). "Stone Cold Dead in the Market" (1946) with Jordan reached No. 1 on the rhythm-and-blues (R&B) chart

Career takes off
In 1953 Granz became Fitzgerald's manager and her musical career began to soar. Under his direction she embarked on a series of "songbook" recordings on the Verve label. From 1956 to 1964 Fitzgerald sang the songs of some of the United States's best-known composers and lyricists, including Duke Ellington, Cole Porter, Irving Berlin, Johnny Mercer, Jerome Kern, and George and Ira Gershwin. The recordings exposed Fitzgerald to a wider audience who admired her enormous musical talent and as a result she became a frequent guest on television variety shows including the *Bing Crosby Show*, the *Ed Sullivan Show*, the *Tonight Show*, and the *Nat King Cole Show*.

Fitzgerald also appeared in a number of films, including *Ride 'Em Cowboy* (1940), *Pete Kelly's Blues*

▼ **Ella Fitzgerald in 1970, the year she gave a concert in Budapest, Hungary, and then released the live album.**

As a child Ella Fitzgerald listened to the records of Mamie Smith and the Mills Brothers. She always credited Connee Boswell (1907–1976), a popular white solo artist and leader of the Boswell Sisters trio, as her idol and chief early musical influence. It was Fitzgerald's singing of the song "The Object of My Affection," popularized by Boswell, that brought her success at the Apollo Theater's Amateur Night contest.

Another early and important influence on Fitzgerald was Louis Jordan (1908–1975). Born in Brinkley, Arkansas, Jordan learned saxophone and clarinet from his father and joined his first band in his teens. He made his professional debut in 1929 and moved to Philadelphia in 1932. In 1936 Jordan joined Chick Webb's Orchestra and sang with Fitzgerald. He left in 1938 to form his own group, the Tympany Five.

From 1942 to 1951 Jordan had 57 R&B hits. His first million-seller hit was "G.I. Jive" in 1944, which won him the title "King of the Jukeboxes." In addition Jordan appeared in a number of films. In 1951 Jordan formed a 15-piece band, which was not successful. He continued to work through the 1950s and 1960s, recording for different labels, and in the 1970s he re-formed the Tympany Five.

Jordan's music acted as the bridge between the old band style and early R&B and the new rock-'n'-roll. His showmanship and music were immensely popular with black and white audiences and influenced scores of musicians—both contemporaries and future generations.

(1955); *St. Louis Blues* (1958), and *Let No Man Write My Epitaph* (1960).

Fitzgerald continued to perform and tour all over the world. In 1974 she spent a celebrated two weeks performing in New York with Count Basie and Frank Sinatra. In the same year the University of Maryland named its 1,200-seat theater and concert hall the Ella Fitzgerald Center for the Performing Arts.

In Fitzgerald's later years she suffered with health problems that limited her performances. In 1993, in honor of her 75th birthday, her "songbook" recordings and her recordings with Chick Webb were reissued on compact disk. Fitzgerald died in 1996 in California.

Awards and influence

During her lifetime Fitzgerald received hundreds of awards and honors, including 13 Grammy awards, the Kennedy Center for Performing Arts' Medal of Honor Award, the National Medal of Art, the Peabody Award for Outstanding Contributions in Music, and the NAACP Award for lifetime achievement. In addition, she was awarded honorary degrees from Dartmouth, Talladega, Howard, and Yale universities.

Fitzgerald was one of the first singers to use her voice as a horn in the bebop jazz style and was instrumental in the transition of the jazz singer from the styles of swing to bop. Her use of the harmonic and rhythmic vocabulary of the bebop sound developed by musicians such as saxophonist Charlie Parker and trumpeter Dizzy Gillespie led to her mastery of the vocal technique of scat. She performed with numerous famous names including Count Basie, Louis Armstrong, Dizzy Gillespie, Oscar Peterson, Benny Goodman, Roy Eldridge, Louis Jordan, Clark Terry, and Joe Pass, recording over 2,000 songs. More than 40 million of her records have been sold and her albums continue to be reissued.

KEY DATES

1918	Born in Newport News, Virginia, on April 25.
1934	Makes first stage appearance.
1936	Records first song, "Love and Kisses" on Decca Records.
1938	Records first hit song "A-Tisket, A-Tasket."
1987	Receives the National Medal of Arts.
1996	Dies in Beverly Hills, California, on June 15.
2005	Posthumously given the Ford Freedom Award for improving the African American community and the world in general.

See also: Armstrong, Louis; Basie, Count; Cole, Nat King; Eldridge, Roy; Ellington, Duke; Gillespie, Dizzy; Parker, Charlie; Smith, Mamie

Further reading: Nicholson, Stuart. *Ella Fitzgerald: A Biography of the First Lady of Jazz.* New York, NY: Da Capo Press, 1995.
www.ellafitzgerald.com (Official site).

FLETCHER, Arthur
Activist

Arthur A. Fletcher devoted his life to achieving equality for African Americans. He advocated affirmative action policies that gave preferential treatment to ethnic minorities in education and employment. He is often called the "father of affirmative action."

Fletcher was born in Phoenix, Arizona, in 1924. He attended Junction City High School, Kansas, where he organized his first civil rights protest on learning that black students' photographs were to be included only at the back of the school's 1943 yearbook.

Fletcher joined the Army on leaving high school and served under General George Patton during World War II (1939–1945), earning a Purple Heart. After the war he went to Washburn University, Topeka, Kansas, and graduated with a degree in political science and sociology in 1950. While at Washburn Fletcher excelled in football, joining the Los Angeles' Rams as a professional player after graduation and becoming the Baltimore Colts' first black team member.

Working for social change

Fletcher's career in public service began in 1954, when he worked on Fred Hall's campaign to win the Kansas governorship before he accepted a post with the Kansas

▼ **Arthur Fletcher helped open up employment and education opportunities to many black Americans.**

Highway Commission. Concerned about the lack of opportunities that the U.S. economy offered African Americans, Fletcher began encouraging black businesses to bid for government contracts.

On moving to Washington, D.C., in the 1960s, Fletcher worked in several government posts. In 1969 President Richard Nixon made Fletcher assistant secretary of wage and labor standards in the Labor Department. In that position Fletcher developed the "Philadelphia Plan," which enforced equal opportunities for black and other minority businesses pursuing government-funded contracts. Although affirmative action flourished under Nixon, the requirement that federal contractors set goals and targets for minority employment was soon challenged in the courts. On leaving the federal government in 1972, Fletcher became executive director of the United Negro College Fund and helped coin its slogan, "A mind is a terrible thing to waste." In later years Fletcher was appointed to the U.S. Commission on Civil Rights, which he chaired from 1990 to 1993. He also entered the 1996 presidential race on a proaffirmative action platform.

Learning systems

The recipient of many honors and a respected writer on equal opportunity rights, Fletcher was president and CEO of Fletcher's Learning Systems, which provided education and training materials to help companies comply with government equal opportunity guidelines. He died in 2005.

KEY DATES	
1924	Born in Phoenix, Arizona, on December 22.
1954	Begins career in public service.
1969	Appointed by President Nixon to work at the Labor Department.
1990	Becomes chair of and later a commissioner on the U.S. Commission on Civil Rights (until 1995).
2005	Dies in Washington, D.C., on July 12.

See also: Affirmative Action

Further reading: Anderson, Terry H. *The Pursuit of Fairness: A History of Affirmative Action*. New York, NY: Oxford University Press, 2004.

FLIPPER, Henry Ossian
Soldier, Engineer

Henry Ossian Flipper, the fifth black cadet to attend the U.S. Military Academy at West Point, was the first African American to graduate from the academy. He did so in the face of a sustained campaign of prejudice directed toward him by white officers and cadets.

Flipper was born on March 21, 1856, in Thomasville, Georgia, into an enslaved family. He managed to obtain an education through the American Missionary Association and entered Atlanta University in 1873. In the same year he won a place at West Point.

Military service

On June 14, 1877, Flipper graduated from West Point, ranked 50 out of 76 graduates. He was commissioned as a second lieutenant and the following year joined the Tenth United States Cavalry. For three years Flipper was posted to Texas and the Indian Territory, where he commanded several military engineering projects, including road and telegraph-line construction, and also fought in battles around Eagle Springs, Texas, in 1880. He was promoted to quartermaster positions at Fort Davis, Jeff Davis County.

In 1881 the new commander of Fort Davis, Colonel William Rufus Shafter, arrived, and Flipper found himself the object of persecution. In 1882 embezzlement charges were brought against him after some post funds disappeared. Although a court martial found Flipper not guilty, he was dismissed from the army for "conduct unbecoming to an officer and a gentleman" in 1882.

A second career

Flipper's great personal success after his dismissal is testimony to his character. He held a series of engineering positions with commercial companies and then assisted

▲ *Henry Ossian Flipper was the first black graduate of West Point and the Army's first black officer.*

the government in land rights disputes. The early 1900s saw Flipper take on legal and engineering responsibilities with mining companies working in Mexico and Spain. In 1919 he became assistant to the secretary of the Interior in Washington, D.C. In addition, Flipper was a prolific author, publishing technical, historical, and personal works. He retired in 1931 and died of a heart attack in 1940. In 1976 a bust of Flipper was unveiled at West Point, and an annual honor in his name is now given to high-performing cadets.

See also: Military and African Americans

Further reading: Flipper, Henry Ossian. *Black Frontiersman: The Memoirs of Henry O. Flipper: First Black Graduate of West Point*. Fort Worth, TX: Texas Christian University Press, 1997.
http://www.tsha.utexas.edu/handbook/online/articles/FF/ffl13.html (Detailed biography and bibliography).

KEY DATES	
1856	Born in Thomasville, Georgia, on March 21.
1877	Graduates from West Point.
1882	Dismissed from the Army on trumped-up charges of embezzlement on June 30.
1919	Becomes assistant to the Secretary of the Interior in Washington, D.C.
1940	Dies in Atlanta, Georgia, on May 3.

FLOOD, Curt
Baseball Player

Despite being a three-time All-Star and seven-time Gold Glove winner, Curt Flood is a baseball player better remembered for his experiences off the field than on.

Akin to slavery

In the landmark 1970 legal case *Flood v. Kuhn*, Flood challenged the "reserve clause," which bound a player one year at a time in perpetuity to the club owning his contract. Flood likened the inability of baseball players to control the terms of their labor to a kind of slavery, protesting in particular to players being treated "as pieces of property." Flood also placed his legal challenge in the spirited context of 1960s social movements, such as the fight for civil rights and Vietnam. He argued, "I could not ignore that what was going on outside the walls of Busch Stadium was truly hypocrisy and now I found that all of those rights that these great Americans were dying for, I didn't have in my own profession." While Flood ultimately lost his suit against professional baseball, his case paved the way for pitchers Andy Messersmith and Dave McNally to challenge the reserve clause successfully and begin free agency.

▼ ***Baseball player Curt Flood was also a civil rights activist and painter, seen here completing a portrait of Martin Luther King, Jr.***

KEY DATES	
1938	Born in Houston, Texas, on January 18.
1957	Traded to the St. Louis Cardinals.
1964	Wins World Series with the Cardinals.
1967	Wins second World Series.
1969	Traded to the Philadelphia Phillies in October.
1970	Brings case *Flood v. Kuhn*.
1997	Dies in Los Angeles, California, on January 20.

Background

Flood was born on January 18, 1938, in Houston, Texas, although his family moved to California when he was two years old. Graduating from high school in 1956, he signed a contract with the Cincinnati Reds and moved to the Deep South, playing Class B and Class A ball in the Carolina and South Atlantic leagues. Traded to the St. Louis Cardinals on December 5, 1957, after only 15 games of Triple A ball, Flood became a key member of the Cardinals' squad. He embarked on a highly successful career as a major league centerfielder. During his 12 years in St. Louis, Flood won seven Gold Gloves and batted over .300 six times—he helped the team win three National League pennants and two World Series.

On October 7, 1969, as part of a seven-player trade, Flood was traded to the Philadelphia Phillies. He was opposed to the move, in part because he considered Philadelphia to be a racist city. In 1970 he filed an antitrust suit against major league baseball, sitting out the season while he waited for the verdict. Flood lost the trial and his appeals, including a Supreme Court decision in 1972. He never returned to the majors and died of throat cancer in 1997. A year later Congress passed the Curt Flood Act, which gave major league baseball players the same antitrust protection that other athletes had. Despite the major effect his actions had on baseball, Flood has not been elected to the Baseball Hall of Fame.

Further reading: Flood, Curt. *The Way It Is.* New York, NY: Trident Press, 1971.
http://espn.go.com/classic/biography/s/Flood_Curt.html (Biography).

FLOWERS, Vonetta
Athlete

The first African American to win a winter Olympic gold medal, Vonetta Flowers and her story inspired admiration in athletes and sports fans around the world when she was part of the winning women's two-man bobsled team less than two years after taking up the sport.

Early success
Flowers was born Vonetta Jeffrey in Birmingham, Alabama, on October 29, 1973. She was raised in the nearby town of Helena. She trained in track events from age nine, showing great promise as a runner, and went on to earn honors as an all-state basketball player while attending Jackson-Olin High School in Birmingham. Flowers's talents led to her being awarded a sports scholarship to the University of Alabama (UAB), where she became a track and field star, winning titles in the 100 meters, 200 meters, long jump, and triple jump.

Following graduation in 1997, she worked as an assistant track coach, where she met and married fellow UAB track athlete Johnny Flowers. Although Vonetta Flowers competed in the 1996 and 2000 Olympics trials for the summer games, she failed to make the U.S. team on either occasion.

Changing track
Hampered by old injuries and disappointed after failing to qualify in the long jump at the 2000 Olympic trials, Flowers resigned herself to returning to her old coaching job. Her husband refused to let her give up, however. After reading a U.S. Bobsled Federation flier wanting to recruit track and field athletes for winter sports, Johnny persuaded Flowers to try out for the bobsled team.

After scoring well in the sprinting and jumping tests, Flowers was invited to a trial at a bobsled track in Germany. She learned how to act as a "brakeman,"

▲ **U.S. teammates Vonetta Flowers (left) and Jean Racine attend the 2005 Women's World Cup of 2-Man Bobsled in Lake Placid, New York.**

pushing the sled at the start of the run and applying the brakes at the end. A month later Flowers teamed up with leading bobsled driver Bonny Warner; the duo finished second at the national team trials in Park City, Utah. They went on to do well during the 2000–2001 season, finishing third in the World Cup and eighth in the 2001 World Championships.

A winning partnership
On parting company with Warner, Flowers was recruited by another bobsled driver, Jill Bakken. The women worked well together and came in second in the 2002 Olympic trials. They went on to win the Olympic gold in the two-woman bobsledding event at Salt Lake City, Utah, in February 2002. Flowers was the first black athlete from any nation to win a gold medal in the Winter Olympics.

A devout Christian, the mother of twin boys, and the author of the autobiography *Running on Ice*, Flowers joined a new partner, Jean Racine, to prepare for the 2006 Winter Games in Turin, Italy.

Further reading: Flowers, Vonetta, with W. Terry Whalin. *Running on Ice: The Overcoming Faith of Vonetta Flowers.* Birmingham, AL: New Hope Publishers, 2005.
http://www.vonettaflowers.com (Flowers's site).

KEY DATES	
1973	Born in Birmingham, Alabama, on October 29.
1997	Graduates with a BA from the University of Alabama, Birmingham.
2000	Takes up bobsledding.
2002	Becomes first black athlete to win gold medal in any winter Olympic sport.

FORD, Arnold
Musician, Religious Leader

Arnold Josiah Ford (also known as Rabbi Ford) was a black nationalist and follower of Judaism who became the musical director for the New York chapter of the United Negro Improvement Association (UNIA), founded by Marcus Garvey in 1917.

Garvey intended the UNIA to unite all the people of the world with African ancestry to establish their own country and government. In addition to his work within the UNIA, Ford is known for his musical accomplishments and his influence in spreading Judaism among African Americans.

Music

Ford was born in Barbados in 1877 to Edward Thomas and Elizabeth Augustine Ford. As a child growing up in Bridgetown, Ford received musical instruction on several instruments, including the bass, violin, and harp. He later studied music theory and joined the musical corps of the British Royal Navy in 1899.

Moving to Harlem, New York, in 1910, Ford joined the Clef Club Orchestra, directed by James Reese Europe. In 1912 Ford performed with the orchestra in a landmark concert at Carnegie Hall in which all the music performed was by African American composers. The concert is seen as the first jazz performance at Carnegie Hall.

In addition to being musical director of the UNIA, Ford was responsible for planning the formal procedures of the organization. A song that he cowrote with fellow UNIA officer Benjamin E. Burrell, "Ethiopia," was sung at every UNIA gathering. In 1920 Ford published the *Universal Ethiopian Hymnal*, which contained 20 hymns that he had either written or collected from other sources.

Black Jews

Ford's involvement with Judaism reflected a historical link between the Jewish faith and Africans. In the West Indies some blacks had converted to Judaism under the influence of Jewish plantation owners. In the late 19th century some of these black Jews immigrated to the United States and started all-black synagogues.

Meanwhile a centuries-old legend told of black Jews, descendants of the biblical queen of Sheba who had once lived in the African kingdom of Ethiopia. In 1769 Scottish explorer James Bruce rediscovered Ethiopia's black Jews, the Falashas. In 1867 Joseph Halevy, a Jewish scholar, visited the Falashas and became an advocate for the

KEY DATES	
1877	Born in Bridgetown, Barbados, on April 23.
1912	Performs with Clef Club Orchestra at Carnegie Hall.
1920	Publishes the *Universal Ethiopian Hymnal*.
1924	Establishes the Beth B'nai Abraham congregation.
1935	Dies in Ethiopia on September 16.

community. For many black Americans, meanwhile, Ethiopia's victory over their Italian invaders in 1896 and its continued independence represented a beacon of freedom. Ethiopia's example fueled Garvey's dream of returning African Americans to Africa.

In 1908 rabbis from 44 countries declared that the Falashas were authentic Jews. In 1919 Ford met an Ethiopian goodwill mission to the United States, who invited him to visit Ethiopia. Inspired by the meeting, Ford tried to turn the religious direction of the UNIA toward Judaism, but Garvey remained firmly Christian. In 1923 he expelled Ford from the UNIA.

In 1924 Ford established the Beth B'nai Abraham congregation in Harlem. By 1928 he had created a business component, the B'nai Abraham Progressive Corporation, which owned buildings, leased apartments, and operated a religious and vocational school. The corporation went bankrupt in 1930.

Move to Ethiopia

In 1930 Ford moved to Ethiopia. He and his small group of musicians performed at the November coronation ceremony of Emperor Haile Selassie (1892–1975) and played at local hotels in the capital city of Addis Ababa. Ford remained in Ethiopia until his death in September 1935.

See also: Europe, James Reese; Garvey, Marcus; Religion and African Americans

Further reading: Landing, James E. *Black Judaism: Story of an American Movement.* Durham, NC: Carolina Academic Press, 2002.
www.unia-acl.org (Official UNIA site).

FORD, Barney
Entrepreneur, Activist

An escaped slave, Barney Lancelot Ford, who took his name from the steam locomotive *Lancelot Ford*, became a successful businessman and one of the most respected black activists of his time.

Road to freedom

Born in about 1822 in Virginia, Ford grew up a slave on a plantation in South Carolina. He worked in the fields until age 18, when his owner hired him out as a waiter on a Mississippi steamboat. Ford managed to escape with the help of the Underground Railroad and fled north to Chicago. The Railroad was a secret network of safe houses and transportation run by abolitionists that helped slaves escape from the South. While in Chicago Ford helped other slaves and taught himself to read and write. He also met escaped slaves Julia Lyoni (his future wife) and her brother Henry Wagoner.

In 1851 Ford and his wife left to make their fortunes in the gold fields of California. On the way, however, they decided to stay on in one of the ship's ports of call, Greytown, Nicaragua, where they opened a small hotel and restaurant. Nine years later and $5,000 richer, the couple left Central America with their three children after a U.S. ship shelled and destroyed their hotel during a dispute between the United States and Britain. After returning

▼ *By the time of his death in 1902 Barney Ford was one of Denver's most respected citizens.*

briefly to Chicago, the Ford family headed west to Colorado in search of gold. They boarded with Aunt Clara Brown, the first black pioneer.

Ford's first staked claim near Denver was taken by white men. He and some other black prospectors then staked a claim on a hill southeast of Breckinridge, Colorado; but because African Americans were denied land rights, they asked a white lawyer to file the claim. Believing that Ford had struck it rich, the lawyer filed the claim in his own name and ran Ford and his friends off the land. The lawyer was unable to find gold, however.

Ford returned to Denver, securing a loan to start a barbershop and a restaurant. He built a series of luxurious hotels in Denver, followed by hotels in Cheyenne, Wyoming, and San Francisco, California. By the 1870s Ford's fortune was close to a quarter of a million dollars.

Known as the "Black Baron of Colorado," Ford devoted himself increasingly to improving African American rights. He promoted black suffrage as a member of the Republican Election Commission and started adult literacy programs for freed slaves. He was also the first black American to serve on a Colorado grand jury. Ford died in 1902.

See also: Brown, Clara

Further reading: Talmadge, Marian, and Iris Gilmore. *Barney Ford: Black Baron.* New York, NY: Dodd Mead, 1973.
http://www.undergroundrailroad.net/tnt/2002/stories/page3.html (Fictional diary of Barney Ford with notes on his life).

KEY DATES

1822	Born in Virginia at about this time.
1851	Opens the United States Hotel and Restaurant in Greytown, Nicaragua.
1860	Travels to Colorado; boards with Aunt Clara Brown.
1865	Fights for black suffrage.
1902	Dies in Denver, Colorado, on December 22.

FOREMAN, George
Boxer

George "Big George" Foreman is a true sporting legend, known as much for his character as for his demonstrated talent in the boxing ring.

▲ George Foreman (right) lands a right hook on the chin of Russia's Iones Chepulis to win the gold medal at the 1968 Olympics in Mexico City.

Early life

Foreman was born on January 10, 1949, in Marshall, Texas, the fifth of seven children in a poor family. By the time he was a teenager, Foreman was in trouble with the law. Foreman dropped out of high school in the 10th grade and in 1965 found work with the Job Corps, a program developed by the Department of Labor for disadvantaged youth as part of President Lyndon B. Johnson's War on Poverty. Foreman also began training as a boxer; his coach, "Doc" Broadus, told him that if he stopped being an alley fighter he could be an Olympic champion.

Foreman excelled at his new sport, and won 16 of his 18 amateur matches. In 1968 he won the National Amateur Athletic Union (NAAU) championship title, and earned a place on the U.S. Olympic team destined for Mexico City later in the year. There Foreman took an Olympic gold in

KEY DATES	
1949	Born in Marshall, Texas, on January 10.
1965	Joins the Job Corps.
1968	Wins the NAAU boxing championship and a gold medal at the Olympics in Mexico City
1973	Wins the world heavyweight title from Joe Frazier.
1974	Loses title to Muhammad Ali and retires from boxing three years later.
1987	Returns to boxing ring, and reclaims the heavyweight title in 1994.
2003	Inducted into the International Boxing Hall of Fame.

FOREMAN, George

INFLUENCES AND INSPIRATION

George Foreman first heard Muhammad Ali on the radio in 1962 before his fight with Sonny Liston. In a 2003 interview for *Counterpunch*, Foreman recalled running around with friends desperately looking for a radio just to hear Ali talk. "We all liked him because he said he was pretty. None of us thought we were pretty. And here is this man saying 'I'm pretty. I'm pretty.' And we thought we're goodlooking too."

When the two men faced each other in Kinshasa in 1974, Foreman was hurt by his childhood hero's taunts both outside and inside the ring. As a result Foreman lost his temper and judgment. The two men were very different—one, Ali, all quicksilver wit and lip, the other, Foreman, speaking very little and therefore disliked by the press and the crowds for being standoffish.

In later years, when asked about the famous "rumble in the jungle," Foreman said that he lost because Ali drew such strength from the love and support of the audience: "They loved him, and I love him too. He's the greatest man I have ever known." Today the two men are good friends.

the heavyweight class. Years later Foreman said that the victory "was the highlight of my whole athletic career." In 1969 he turned professional.

Title fighter

Foreman made an explosive entrance into professional boxing, inflicting a shock defeat on Joe Frazier for the world heavyweight championship in Kingston, Jamaica, on January 22, 1973. Foreman twice defended the title successfully, but on October 30, 1974, he lost the crown to his childhood hero Muhammad Ali (*see box*) in one of the most famous fights in history. Held in Kinshasa, Zaire (now the Democratic Republic of Congo), it became known as the "rumble in the jungle." Ali let Foreman punch himself out before knocking him out in the eighth round. Foreman had to take a year off to recover.

In 1976 Foreman boxed Ron Lyle in a brutal fight in Las Vegas, Nevada. In the fourth round Lyle knocked Foreman down, only for Foreman to get up and knock him down in turn. Lyle knocked Foreman down again in that round before Foreman knocked him out in the fifth round. He won three more fights before the end of the year.

In 1977 Foreman lost a 12-round decision to Jimmy Young. Foreman became very sick after the fight and converted to Christianity. He retired from boxing and became an ordained minister with a church in Texas.

Return to the ring

In 1987, at age 38, Foreman returned to the ring in a move that stunned the boxing world. He said that he had come back partly to prove that older people could still excel at sports, and partly to make money for the youth center he and his brother-in-law had opened in Texas for disadvantaged children.

Between 1987 and 1991 Foreman won 24 fights. In April 1991 he fought Evander Holyfield for the world title but lost in a 12-round points decision. In 1994 Foreman beat International Boxing Federation (IBF) and World Boxing Association (WBA) champion Michael Moorer at age 45, becoming the oldest heavyweight champion ever and setting a record for the longest time between losing one world championship and winning the next.

Foreman won three more fights, but in March 1995 he was stripped of his WBA title for refusing to fight their contender; in June he resigned his IBF title in June rather than fight a rematch with Axel Schultz. Foreman retired again in 1997. In 2003 he was elected to the International Boxing Hall of Fame and named boxing's ninth greatest puncher of all time by *Ring Magazine*.

Retirement

Foreman became a popular boxing commentator. His autobiography, *By George,* was published in 1995. Also in 1995 he launched the George Foreman Lean Mean Grilling Machine, promoting it himself on television. By 1999 he had sold over 10 million grills around the world, making more money from them than he did in his entire boxing career. Foreman has had four wives and 10 children; his five sons are all named George.

See also: Ali, Muhammad; Frazier, Joe

Further reading: Foreman, George, and Joel Engel. *By George: The Autobiography of George Foreman.* New York, N.: Simon & Schuster, 2000.
http://www.biggeorge.com/ (Foreman's official site).
http://www.eastsideboxing.com/news.php?p=2100&more=1 (Foreman–Ali fight).

FORMAN, James
Civil Rights Activist

James Forman was one of the most influential figures in the Student Nonviolent Coordinating Committee (SNCC). In 1969 he became one of the first major black leaders to demand slavery reparations.

Born James Rufus (his stepfather's surname) in 1928 in Chicago, Forman spent the first six years of his life with his grandparents on a farm in Marshall County, Mississippi. When he was brought back to Chicago, he discovered his real father, a cab driver, and reverted to his family name.

Forman graduated from Englewood High School in 1947 and joined the Air Force, fighting in the Korean War (1950–1953). In 1952 he enrolled at the University of Southern California. At the beginning of his second semester, Los Angeles policemen falsely arrested him for robbery and beat him in jail before releasing him without charge. As a result of the experience Forman needed treatment in a psychiatric hospital. Resuming his studies,

▼ *James Forman leaves the Episcopal Church's headquarters in 1969 after demanding reparations for injustices suffered by African Americans.*

Forman transferred to Roosevelt University in Chicago, where he became a leader in student politics and in 1956, his final year, chairman of the university's delegation to the National Student Association conference.

On graduating, Forman took a job on a Chicago newspaper, where his editor assigned him to report on northern civil rights workers in Tennessee. Although he went South as an observer, he soon became involved in political activism in support of dispossessed black tenants.

Forman became a member of the SNCC. In the summer of 1961 he was sent to jail for boarding a segregated bus in North Carolina. When his sentence was suspended, he immediately joined the SNCC committee. A week later he became its executive secretary, and in that post he took a leading role in the 1963 civil rights march on Washington, D.C., as well as in the campaign to register voters and start "freedom schools" in Mississippi. In 1966 Forman was ousted from the SNCC for not being sufficiently radical.

Forman visited Africa the following year, served briefly as the radical Black Panther Party's foreign minister, and in 1969 helped organize the Black Economic Development conference in Detroit, Michigan. His "Black Manifesto" sought $500 million from white churches for their role in slavery and the later subjugation of blacks. Forman continued to actively promote the cause of African Americans throughout his life. He died of cancer in 2005.

KEY DATES	
1928	Born in Chicago, Illinois, on October 5.
1956	Graduates from Roosevelt University.
1961	Becomes executive secretary of the SNCC.
1966	Is replaced by Stokely Carmichael in the SNCC.
2005	Dies in Washington, D.C., on January 10.

See also: Carmichael, Stokely; Civil Rights; National Organizations

Further reading: Forman, James. *The Making of Black Revolutionaries.* Seattle, WA: University of Washington Press, 1997.
http://www.washingtonpost.com/wp-dyn/articles/ A1621-2005Jan11.html (*Washington Post* obituary).

FORTEN, Charlotte
Educator, Author

A gifted teacher, Charlotte Forten believed passionately that education could be used to achieve freedom and equality for African Americans and heal the wounds inflicted by slavery.

Forten was born in Philadelphia, Pennsylvania, in 1837 to a wealthy family of fervent abolitionists. Her grandfather was the successful businessman and antislavery campaigner, James Forten, Sr.; her father, Robert Bridges Forten, was a key member of the Philadelphia Vigilant Committee, a slavery assistance network; and her mother, Mary Woods Forten, belonged to the Philadelphia Female Anti-Slavery Society.

Following the death of her mother in 1840, Forten's father moved to Massachusetts to immerse himself in the abolitionist movement. Forten remained with her relatives

in Pennsylvania, where she was educated at home by private tutors. Eventually she moved to Salem, Massachusetts, to be near her father.

Begins keeping a diary

In 1854 Forten began living with the leading African American abolitionist, Charles Lenox Redmond, and his family (*see box*), and enrolled at the Higginson Grammar School, where she was the only African American student in a school of 200. It was at this time that she began to keep the diaries for which she is best known.

After her graduation from Higginson in 1855, Forten enrolled in the Salem Normal School for "young ladies who wish to prepare themselves for teaching." However, Forten's father, now living in Canada, did not approve of her ambitions. He instructed her to return to Philadelphia, and then reluctantly allowed her to continue her studies at the Normal School but refused to supply the money she needed to pay for her education. When Forten enrolled again she wrote in her diary that she found the teaching "so thorough and earnest that it increases the love of knowledge and the desire to acquire it." The day she received her diploma was "among the happiest in my life."

Becomes a teacher

Forten began teaching third and fourth grades at Salem's Epes Grammar School in June 1856, becoming Salem's first African American school teacher. She graduated from the Normal School in July. However, in 1858 Forten was forced to resign and move back to Philadelphia after suffering from tuberculosis. She had recovered by September 1859,

▼ *Charlotte Forten in the 1870s, when she was working for the Treasury in Washington, D.C.*

INFLUENCES AND INSPIRATION

The foremost influence on Forten was the abolitionist movement. Born to a family of prominent abolitionists and belonging to an intellectual circle that included the essayist and poet Ralph Waldo Emerson, the abolitionist William Lloyd Garrison, and the activist Maria Weston Chapman, Forten developed a social conscience from an early age.

Forten's mission to eliminate slavery and empower her fellow African Americans evolved with the encouragement of her teachers at the Higginson Grammar School and later at the Salem Normal School. Forten was especially inspired by the example of her principal at Higginson, Mary L. Shepard. In addition to acting as a mentor to Forten, Shepard offered to pay for her education at the Normal School when her father refused to continue doing so and later provided Forten with a teaching post at Higginson.

Forten was also influenced by her friend Sarah Redmond, sister of Charles Redmond, who advocated using education specifically as an instrument to advance African American people.

Forten was hungry for knowledge and was a regular visitor to the Essex Institute, which exhibited historical and scientific artifacts. She was profoundly influenced by her reading of literature, particularly Chaucer, Shakespeare, Milton, Wordsworth, Byron, Elizabeth Barrett Browning, Phillis Wheatley, and Emerson. Forten also enthusiastically attended lectures, particularly finding inspiration in those delivered by people who had traveled to Britain, where slavery had been abolished in 1833.

and took up a teaching post at Higginson. She enrolled in the Advanced Program at the Normal School, her financial difficulties alleviated by an anonymous grant from Boston lawyer and philanthropist Nathaniel Ingersoll Bowditch. Forten was also discovering a talent for poetry; several of her poems were published in abolitionist magazines, such as the *Liberator*.

While on a visit to Boston, Massachusetts, in 1862, Forten applied for a teaching job at the Boston Port Royal Commission, which had been established to provide support for newly freed slaves settling on the Sea Islands of South Carolina. When the Boston Commission did not reply, Forten applied to and was accepted by the Philadelphia Commission. She was the first African American to be hired for the Port Royal Experiment.

Sea Islands teacher

Forten arrived on St. Helena Island in October 1862. Initially she found that there was a vast gulf between her and the islanders. She had been fortunate to have had a privileged upbringing, while the islanders had suffered the harsh realities of slavery. Many of her students had no experience of school practices and spoke Gullah, an African dialect. Forten recorded in her diary her shock at their "barbaric" form of worship.

However, over time Forten learned about African spirituality and culture as she taught the islanders reading, writing, and math, and gradually she was accepted by the community. Forten's mission required great courage. The Civil War (1861–1865) exposed the islands to the constant threat of Confederate attack, yellow fever was prevalent, and the Union soldiers, as Forten wrote in her diary, "talked flippantly and sneeringly of the Negroes." Eventually, the combination of physical and emotional anxiety caused Forten to become ill, and she left St. Helena in May 1864.

After the islands

On her return to New York City, Forten published "Life on the Sea Islands" in the *Atlantic Monthly*, documenting her work as part of the Port Royal Experiment. She continued to teach and in the late 1860s played an important part in recruiting new teachers. In 1873 she was appointed as a clerk at the Treasury. In 1878 Forten married Francis J. Grimke, a Presbyterian minister. Her only child, a daughter, died in 1880. Supporting her husband in his work as the pastor of the Fifteenth Street Presbyterian Church in Washington, D.C., Forten established a woman's missionary group. After a long period of ill health, Forten died in 1914.

See also: Slavery

Further reading: Graves, Kerry, and Christy Steele (eds.). *A Free Black Girl Before the Civil War: The Diary of Charlotte Forten, 1854*. Mankato, MN: Blue Earth Books, 1999.
http://www.salemstate.edu/150/150-charlotte_forten.php (Biography on Salem State College Anniversary site).

FORTEN, James
Sailmaker, Abolitionist

In the early 19th century James Forten ran a successful sailmaking business employing about 40 people, a remarkable achievement for an African American at that time. He was also an active campaigner for civil rights for African Americans, including the right to vote.

Forten was born in Philadelphia, Pennsylvania, on September 2, 1766. His parents, Thomas and Sarah Forten, were free, so Forten was able to go to a local Quaker school. From age eight Forten also worked with his father at Robert Bridges's sail loft, making sails. In 1775, when his father died in an accident, Forten was forced to take on a number of other jobs to help support the family.

Seafaring and sailmaking

At age 14 Forten began working as a powder boy aboard the navy vessel *Royal Louis*. It was a powder boy's job to carry bags of gunpowder from the magazine below to the gun deck when the guns were being fired. Forten was at sea during the American Revolution (1775–1783) and was captured by the British. He refused the offer of a home in Britain, saying, "I am here a prisoner for the liberties of my country. I never, never shall prove a traitor to her interests!" After seven months of captivity he was released and returned home.

Back in Philadelphia Forten became an apprentice sailmaker in Robert Bridges's sail loft. Such was his ability that in 1786 he was made foreman of the company. In 1798 Bridges retired from the sailmaking business, but he loaned Forten the money to purchase his company.

Forten took the sail loft to new heights. He experimented with different types of sails and invented one that improved ship speed and maneuverability, which became very profitable. He came to employ about 40 people, both blacks and whites, and eventually built up his personal fortune to $100,000.

Abolitionist

Despite his successful lifestyle, Forten never forgot the injustices visited on other less fortunate African Americans. He was a vigorous campaigner for equal rights for all African Americans and votes for women, and he put his money to work supporting abolitionist William Garrison's antislavery newspaper *The Libertarian*. In 1800 Forten presented a petition to Congress calling for the emancipation of all slaves. He also wrote and published

KEY DATES	
1766	Born in Philadelphia, Pennsylvania, on September 2.
1780	Begins to work as a powder boy on the *Royal Louis*.
1786	Becomes foreman at Robert Bridges's sail loft.
1798	Buys the sail loft when Robert Bridges retires.
1800	Petitions Congress for black emancipation.
1833	Helps found the American Anti-Slavery Society.
1842	Dies in Philadelphia on February 24.

a pamphlet attacking the Pennsylvania legislature for prohibiting the immigration of freed black slaves from other states.

In 1816 Paul Cuffe, a wealthy black shipping merchant, took 38 black colonists to settle in Sierra Leone, Africa. Cuffe and Forten were friends, and Forten agreed to recruit colonists from Philadelphia. In 1817 Forten and other black leaders called a meeting that was attended by 3,000 people. However, none was in favor of emigrating to Africa. Taken aback by the strength of feeling expressed at the meeting, the leaders agreed to put aside their private opinions and join their fellow African Americans in opposing colonization. Together with activist Richard Allen, Forten helped form the Convention of Color to support the settlement of escaped slaves in Canada, opposing plans for repatriation to Africa.

Forten was founder and president of the American Moral Reform Society, which was dedicated to "the promotion of education, temperance, economy, and universal liberty." He also helped set up the American Anti-Slavery Society in 1833. Individual acts of kindness included using his money to free black slaves and open a school for black children. When Forten died in 1842, about 5,000 black and white Philadelphians attended his funeral.

See also: Allen, Richard; Cuffe, Paul

Further reading: Davis, Burke. *Black Heroes of the American Revolution.* New York, NY: Harcourt Brace & Co., 1976.
http://www.blackinventor.com/pages/jamesforten.html
(Biography and portrait).

FORTUNE, T. Thomas
Publisher, Journalist, Activist

The leading African American journalist of the late 19th century, T Thomas Fortune used the newspapers he edited, notably the *New York Age*, to protest racism and to instill pride in his black readers. Many of his concerns, including the plight of African American women and the economic exploitation of black labor, foreshadowed those of the 1960s civil rights movement.

From slave to militant journalist
Timothy Thomas Fortune was born into slavery in 1856 in Marianna, Florida. Seven years later the Emancipation Proclamation brought slavery to an end in the United States. Fortune's father Emanuel was elected to the Florida House of Representatives in 1868; he was,

▼ **T. Thomas Fortune ghostwrote A Negro for A New Century (1899) for Booker T. Washington.**

however, forced out of office and town in 1871, as were many other African American officials at the end of Reconstruction. The Fortune family resettled in Jacksonville, Florida, where Thomas received a basic education in the Freedman Bureau's schools and learned to love books.

Fortune learned his trade as a printer's devil, or apprentice; he also worked for the post office briefly until appointed a special inspector of customs.

Fortune enrolled at Howard University. Washington, D.C., in 1874 to study law. After graduating, he taught for a short time before leaving for New York City, where he worked for a white religious paper called the *White Witness*. In 1884 he founded the *New York Freeman*, which later became the *New York Age*.

The *Age* employed some of the most outstanding black journalists of the era but was best known for Fortune's editorials. Fortune was sensitive to the way in which language could be used as a tool of oppression: He coined the term "Afro-American" as a way of asserting both black racial pride and national identity.

In 1890 Fortune founded the Afro-American League, one of the nation's first equal-rights organizations. He resigned from the *Age* in 1907 but continued to edit and write. Before his death in 1928, Fortune became editor of Marcus Garvey's *Negro World*.

See also: Civil Rights; Emancipation and Reconstruction; Garvey, Marcus; Washington, Booker T.

Further reading: Thornbrough, Emma Lou. *T. Thomas Fortune: Militant Journalist.* Chicago, IL: University of Chicago Press, 1972.
www.pbs.org/blackpress/news_bios/newbios/nwsppr/Biogrphs/fortune/fortune.html (Biography).

FOSTER, Andrew J.
Educator

Andrew Foster was declared "Father of Deaf African Education" in 2004, an apt description of his lifetime of service for disadvantaged children in Africa. Driven by his religious commitment to bring hope to the hearing impaired, within a span of 30 years Foster had established at least 31 schools for the deaf in 13 African countries.

Early life

Andrew Jackson Foster was born in Ensley, near Birmingham, Alabama, in 1925, the son of a coal miner. He became totally deaf at age 11 from spinal meningitis, an infection and inflammation of the membrane and fluid surrounding the brain and spinal cord.

Foster attended the Alabama School for the Negro Deaf in Talladega until he moved to Michigan at age 17. Foster then took correspondence courses and evening studies until he obtained his high school diploma.

In 1951 Foster received a congressional scholarship to go to Gallaudet College (later University), in Washington, D.C. Gaullaudet had been founded on April 8, 1864, when President Abraham Lincoln signed a charter establishing it as the world's first university for the deaf and hard of hearing. In 1954 Foster became the first African American to graduate from Gallaudet. He later obtained his master's degree in special education from the East Michigan College and another degree in missions from the Seattle Pacific Christian College in Washington.

African mission

On a visit to Africa Foster was moved by the oppressive conditions for deaf people that he found there. He discovered that in many places the deaf were largely hidden away and excluded from everyday life. Foster determined to help bring about change. In 1956 he founded the Christian Mission for the Deaf (CMD), a nonprofit organization to promote gospel and education work in Africa with its headquarters in Detroit, Michigan.

In 1957 Foster opened his first school, the Accra Mission School for the Deaf, in Ghana. Foster went on to establish schools in Nigeria, Chad, Togo, Ivory Coast, Cameroon, Chad, Senegal, Benin, Central African Republic, Democratic Republic of Congo, Burkino Faso, Burundi, and Gabon. About the same number of Sunday schools and religious centers were established in the same countries, as well as in Kenya, Sierra Leone, Congo, and Guinea. One of the key aims of CMD was to train local African Christian workers and leaders. Foster also taught sign language to many Africans so they could fulfill his favorite Bible verse, Isaiah 29:10: "In that day, the deaf will hear the words of the book."

Tragic death

In 1970 Foster received an honorary doctorate in humane letters from Gallaudet College for his dedication to deaf education. On December 3, 1987, he died, along with 11 other passengers when their small plane crashed into a mountain in Rwanda, East Africa.

Legacy

In October 2004 Gallaudet University dedicated a new auditorium to Foster's memory. The National Black Deaf Advocates (NBDA) raised the money to commission a bust of Foster from New York sculptor Virginia Cox, the first time a deaf African American had been so honored. The bust was presented to Gallaudet in May 2004. It was placed in the glass-enclosed auditorium lobby, where it is lit 24 hours a day and is visible at all times.

The university also supports the Andrew Foster Endowment Fund, which provides scholarships for deaf African American students to study at Gallaudet.

Further reading: Carroll, Cathryn, and Susan M. Mather. *Movers and Shakers: Deaf People Who Changed the World.* San Diego, CA: Dawn Sign Press, 1997.
http://president.gallaudet.edu/andrewfoster/ (Biographical sketch on Gallaudet College site).
http://www.cmdeaf.org/ (CMD site).

KEY DATES	
1925	Born in Ensley, Alabama.
1954	Graduates with a BA from Gallaudet College, Washington, D.C.
1956	Founds the Christian Mission for the Deaf.
1957	Opens first school in Africa.
1970	Receives honorary doctorate from Gallaudet.
1987	Dies in an airplane crash in Rwanda on December 3.

FOSTER, Andrew "Rube"
Baseball Player, Manager

Player, manager, and owner Andrew "Rube" Foster left an indelible imprint on the game of baseball in the early decades of the 20th century. Foster first achieved success on the diamond as a pitcher. Considered the best black pitcher of his time, Foster earned his nickname "Rube" by defeating white pitching superstar Rube Wadell in an exhibition game in 1902—that same year Foster was credited with 51 victories. However, it was in his capacity as a manager and founder of the Negro National League that Foster is best remembered.

Early life

Foster was born in Calvert, Texas, on September 17, 1879, to Andrew and Sarah Foster. His father was an elder of the African Methodist Episcopal Church. Foster was an asthmatic who dropped out of school after eighth grade.

Foster first demonstrated his pitching talent with the Waco Yellow Jackets at age 17. He was a huge man for the time, standing 6 foot 3 inches (1.9m) tall and weighing 220 pounds (100kg).

Foster began his professional career in 1902, when he signed with the Chicago Union Giants. In 1903, playing with the Cuban X-Giants, he was responsible for four of the team's five wins in the seven-game Colored Championship of the World, which pitted the X-Giants against the Philadelphia Giants. In 1904 Foster moved to the Philadelphia Giants and won both their victories in a three-game series against the Cuban X Giants, striking out 18 batters in one game and pitching a 2-hitter in the other.

While playing for Chicago's Leland Giants in 1907, Foster assumed the role of team manager, a position he would occupy for the next several years. As a player and manager, he led his team to 110 wins and 10 losses in 1907 and 123 wins and 6 losses in 1910, establishing the Giants as the best team in black baseball. His trademark

▲ *Rube Foster is known as the father of baseball for his influence on the game.*

play was the bunt and run, in which a baserunner had the potential to go from first to third on a ball dropped in front of the plate.

Chicago American Giants

In conjunction with white saloon owner John Schorling, Foster founded the Chicago American Giants in 1911. Foster billed the team as "the greatest aggregation of colored baseball players in the world." They played their home games in old South Side Park, which Schorling had purchased and renovated to seat 9,000 fans.

Once again Foster provided the team with a formula for success—the American Giants won all but one of the recorded championships between 1910 and 1922; in 1916 the Indianapolis ABCs temporarily broke the Giants' winning streak. The Giants barnstormed across the nation

KEY DATES	
1879	Born in Calvert, Texas, on September 17.
1911	Founds Chicago American Giants.
1920	Founds Negro National League in February.
1930	Dies in Illinois on December 9.
1981	Inducted into Baseball Hall of Fame.

INFLUENCES AND INSPIRATION

William (Willie or Bill) Hendrik Foster (1904–1978) was Rube's younger half-brother. He played briefly with the Memphis Red Sox before Rube persuaded him to join the Chicago American Giants in 1923. For three years Rube taught Willie the art of pitching. In 1926 Willie won 26 consecutive games, leading the Giants to the playoffs against the Kansas City Monarchs. He won the last two games 1–0 and 5–0 to win the league championship. For over 10 years Foster was the Giants' star pitcher. His tenure included pennants in 1926, 1927, 1932, and 1933, and near misses in 1928 and 1934. In 1927 Foster posted a Negro League record of 18–3. Available box scores show Foster winning 11 of 21 confrontations with the legendary Satchel Paige. He also won six of seven games against white major leaguers. Willie's last year in baseball was spent with a white semipro team in Elgin, Illinois, and a black team called the Washington Browns in Yakima, Washington. In 1960 he returned to his alma mater, Alcorn College, Mississippi, as baseball coach and dean of men. Foster was elected to the Baseball Hall of Fame in 1996.

playing exhibition and regular games against any willing opponents. Their innovative baseball with its base-stealing, hit-and-running, and bunting was popular with the fans. After Foster's retirement the Giants won pennants in 1926 and 1927, as well as winning the world series in those years. From 1923 to 1930 Foster's young half-brother Willie, an outstanding left-hand pitcher, played on the team (*see box*). Despite many changes in ownership the Giants remained the longest continuous franchise in the history of black baseball before closing in 1950.

Negro League

On February 13, 1920, Foster convinced seven other owners to join him in forming the Negro National League, which provided a showcase for talented black players and flourished until Foster's death 10 years later. According to Foster, the objective behind the league was "to create a profession that would equal the earning capacity of other professions, and keep colored baseball from the control of whites." At Foster's insistence, all clubs, with the exception of the Kansas City Monarchs, whom he reluctantly accepted, were controlled by African Americans. Foster hoped that if the Negro National League was successful, eventually black teams would be allowed into the major leagues. Eight teams formed the league—the Kansas City Monarchs, Indianapolis ABC's, Dayton Marcos, Chicago Giants, Chicago American Giants, Detroit Stars, St. Louis Giants, and the Cuban Giants. By 1923 the league was such a success that 400,000 fans came out to see their favorite black players perform on the field.

Foster, as president, took 5 percent of the gate and laid down strict rules for managers and players. He was determined that no wrongdoing would jeopardized any chance they might have of integrating with the majors.

When white businessmen saw the profits being made by black baseball they formed the Eastern Colored League, which included the Philadelphia Hilldales, Cuban Stars, Brooklyn Royal Giants, Atlantic City Bacharach Giants, Baltimore Black Sox, and New York Lincoln Giants.

The Negro leagues played short seasons, compared with those of white major league teams. Some black players competed in Caribbean winter leagues during the off-season. The short season allowed teams time to barnstorm—play exhibition games on tour.

In 1924 the two leagues played their first World Series. The Kansas City Monarchs of the National League beat the Philadelphia Hilldales of the Eastern League in 10 games. In 1925 the Hilldales beat the Monarchs. The ECL collapsed in the spring of 1928 but the member teams reemerged in 1929 as the American Negro League.

The years of the Great Depression were tough for black baseball. The Negro National League folded in 1931. In 1937 teams in the South and the Midwest formed the Negro American League, which operated as the last black major league division through 1960.

Legacy

Foster quit baseball in 1926 because of mental illness. He died in an Illinois asylum four years later. At his funeral, attended by about 3,000 people, Foster was eulogized as the "father of Negro baseball." In 1981, decades after his death, later generations honored Foster's legacy by inducting him into the Baseball Hall of Fame.

Further reading: Peterson, Robert W. *Only the Ball Was White.* New York, NY: Gamercy, 1999.
www.negroleaguestore.com/Rube_Foster.htm (Biography).
http://www.blackbaseball.com/ (Negro League site).

FOXX, Jamie
Actor

Award-winning actor Jamie Foxx has a reputation for playing extremely diverse roles and adopting very different looks in his movies. He has starred with some of the leading names in Hollywood. In 2005 Foxx became the first African American and the second person ever to be nominated for two Academy Awards for two different roles.

Early life
Foxx was born Eric Morlon Bishop in Terrell, Texas, on December 13, 1967. His parents separated when he was young, and he spent most of childhood with his grandmother. Foxx was interested in music from a young

▼ *In 2005 actor Jamie Foxx won an Oscar for best performance by an actor in a leading role at the 77th Annual Academy Awards Ceremony. Foxx played the legendary singer Ray Charles in the movie* **Ray.**

age; he played the piano and sang in the local church choir, of which he later became the director. Foxx attended the local school, where he excelled in sports and music. He went to study at the prestigious Juilliard School, studying classical piano. He supplemented his income performing as a standup comedian; in 1990 he changed his name to Jamie Foxx, adding the extra "x" as a tribute to the actor Redd Foxx.

Television
In 1991 Foxx was given a spot on the TV show *In Living Color*, on which Jim Carrey and the Wayans brothers also appeared. Five years later WB Network gave Foxx his own program, *The Jamie Foxx Show*. Foxx eventually executive produced the series. He began to appear in movies, such as the comedy *The Truth about Cats and Dogs* (1996) and Oliver Stone's *Any Given Sunday* (1999). He also appeared in Michael Mann's *Ali,* starring Will Smith as boxing legend Muhammad Ali.

Stardom
Foxx's career really started to take off in 2004. He achieved wide recognition when he played a cab driver opposite Tom Cruise's assassin in Michael Mann's blockbuster movie *Collateral* (2004). Foxx's role won him a nomination for best supporting actor at the 2005 Academy Awards. He also landed the prime role of legendary musician Ray Charles in the biographical movie *Ray* (2004). Foxx won a Golden Globe, Screen Actors Guild Award, and an Oscar for Best Actor for his brilliant performance.

KEY DATES	
1967	Born in Terrell, Texas, on December 13.
1991	Appears on *In Living Color*.
1996	Given his own program, *The Jamie Foxx Show*.
2005	Becomes first African American and second person ever to be nominated for two different Oscars; wins the Oscar for Best Actor for his performance in *Ray*.

See also: Charles, Ray; Foxx, Redd; Smith, Will

Further reading: http://www.imdb.com/name/nm0004937 (International Movie Database entry).

FOXX, Redd
Comedian, Entertainer

The comedian Redd Foxx enjoyed success as a stage entertainer before breaking into movies and starring in the popular Emmy-winning sitcom *Sanford and Son* (1972–1977), in which he played a junkman. Born John Elroy Sanford, he took his stage name, Redd, from his nickname "Chicago Red" and his last name as a tribute to baseball star Jimmie Foxx (1907–1967).

Road to success

Born on December 9, 1922, in St. Louis, Missouri, Foxx was raised by his mother, Mary, after his father left home; his mother worked as a domestic in Chicago.

Foxx quit high school early to play in a washtub band with two friends. In 1939 the three young men moved to New York, where they earned money playing mostly on the streets and in the subway, although they occasionally performed at the Apollo Theater. After being rejected by the Army during World War II (1939–1945), Foxx started to play in a tramp band. He adopted his stage name at about this time.

Foxx perfected his stand-up routine working in nightclubs in New York. His first regular spot was at a club in Baltimore; he played there for a couple of years before moving back to New York with a much more polished routine in 1945. He began to play with another comedian, Slappy White (1921–1995), and the pair was given a spot opening for Dinah Washington in Los Angeles in 1952. Although Foxx and White split, Foxx remained in Los Angeles and came to the notice of Dootsie Williams, who owned Dooto Records. Williams suggested that Foxx record an album completely made up of stand-up comedy. In 1956 Foxx released the first of more than 50 of these "party albums"; they sold more than 10 million copies.

▲ *Comedian Redd Foxx stars in the television series* **Sanford and Son** *(1972–1977).*

The albums helped make Foxx popular with white audiences. His career was further helped by the TV host Hugh Downs, who booked Foxx for the *Today* show. Foxx was such a hit that other talk shows such as *The Tonight Show* also booked him. In 1968 he stepped in after Aretha Franklin failed to appear at a performance; members of the Hilton Hotel group were in the audience and offered Foxx a $960,000 contract. In 1970 Foxx broke into movies with *Cotton Comes to Harlem*, but his best-known role was playing junkman Fred Sanford in *Sanford and Son*. He never quite repeated this success. Foxx died of a heart attack while filming *The Royal Family* in October 1991.

See also: Franklin, Aretha; Washington, Dinah

Further reading: Bogle, Donald. *Blacks in American Films and Television.* New York, NY: Garland, 1988.
http://www.tvparty.com/foxx.html (Redd Foxx Comedy Hour with clips).

KEY DATES	
1922	Born in St. Louis, Missouri, on December 9.
1956	Records first of his popular "party albums."
1970	First film role in *Cotton Comes to Harlem*.
1972	Stars as the lead in the hit sitcom *Sanford and Son*.
1991	*The Royal Family* premieres in September; dies in Hollywood, California, on October 11.

FRANKLIN, Aretha
Singer

Known as the "queen of soul," or simply "Lady Soul," Aretha Franklin has been regarded as the premiere voice of soul and rhythm-and-blues (R&B) music since her phenomenal emergence onto the music scene in the 1960s. Her artistry became known throughout the world with such hits as "Respect," "I Never Loved a Man the Way I Love You," "Chain of Fools," "(You Make Me Feel Like a) Natural Woman," "I Say a Little Prayer," and many others. She has received more than 15 Grammy Awards, including a Lifetime Achievement Award in 1994.

Early life
Born in Memphis, Tennessee, on March 25, 1942, Franklin grew up immersed in the gospel tradition through the church in Detroit, Michigan, where her father, Reverend C. L. Franklin, was preacher. C. L. Franklin, himself a good singer, knew many of the greats of gospel music, including Mahalia Jackson, Sam Cooke, Clara Ward, and the Reverend James Cleveland (*see box on p. 66*). With her sisters Carolyn and Erma, Aretha sang regularly at her father's church. Her parents separated when she was six, and Franklin remained with her father in Detroit. Her mother died when Franklin was 10. She first became a featured soloist with the choir at age 12. Two years later she made her first recording, *The Gospel Sound of Aretha Franklin*, after accompanying her father on a preaching tour across the United States.

Early career
Franklin left school at age 15 and moved to New York City three years later to pursue her singing career. She was heard by the talent scout and Columbia Records producer John Hammond, who declared the 18-year-old Franklin "an untutored genius, the best natural singer since Billie Holiday." She signed with that label in 1961, producing 10 albums over six years. These records, containing mostly jazz and pop songs, were often impressive, yet they do not reveal the true breadth of the talent that would emerge later. Many critics have felt that Columbia made the mistake of steering Franklin away from the intensity of her gospel roots and R&B temperament.

When her contract with Columbia expired, Franklin signed in 1967 with Atlantic Records, where producer Jerry Wexler was determined to let her voice gravitate to its natural territory: R&B and soul. Their first album together,

I Never Loved a Man the Way I Love You, was an enormous commercial and critical success, producing several Top 10 hits, including her signature song "Respect." The album was her first million-seller and has become one of the classics of the genre.

Career success
After *I Never Loved a Man*, Franklin's career skyrocketed. Her albums with Atlantic throughout the remainder of the 1960s and early 1970s continued to spin off Top 10 hits at a remarkable rate. In a year and a half—from early 1967 through late 1968, she had 10 Top 10 hits. Later Franklin recalled that "when I went to Atlantic, they just sat me down at the piano and the hits started coming."

When the Grammy Awards added a separate category for "Best Rhythm and Blues Vocal Performance, Female" in

▼ *Aretha Franklin in 1967, the year she signed with Atlantic Records.*

INFLUENCES AND INSPIRATION

Aretha Franklin told an interviewer in the mid-1990s that although her father, C. L. Franklin, did not sing a lot, he "could have sung with the best of them." Indeed, her father, and the gospel tradition he introduced her to, represented one of the most important influences on Franklin's musical career. Guests at the Franklin house included such figures as Sam Cooke, Art Tatum, and the greatest gospel singer of all, Mahalia Jackson.

Cooke's pioneer career move from gospel to pop was crucial in encouraging the young Franklin to pursue a music career in the secular repertoire of R&B. Yet she never left her gospel roots behind. Drawing frequently on that deep influence and combining it with R&B, Franklin's classic 1967 recordings "I Never Loved a Man the Way I Love You," "Respect" and "Do Right Woman-Do Right Man," are considered to be the high point of soul music.

Franklin's voice was so overwhelming in its force and artistry that she is often underestimated as a piano player. Franklin credits the gospel singer Clara Ward (1924–1973) as perhaps her most important role model, sparking Franklin's desire to play the piano and sing. Ward accompanied the Ward Trio, a family group that included her mother and sister. From 1948 the Ward Trio began a 15-year career with W. Herbert Brewster, producing a string of hits that made them one of the most popular female gospel groups of the time. Ward was known for her ability to convey drama in slow gospel songs and her distinctive technique of inserting shrieks and growls that foreshadowed what became known as "hard" gospel.

1967, Franklin won the award for eight consecutive years. She would go on to win three more awards in that category in the 1980s.

Civil rights activist

Achieving international prominence in the late 1960s, at the height of the civil rights movement, Franklin became a symbol of black accomplishment and black pride. Her song "Respect" became a kind of rallying cry for social progress and empowerment in both black activist and feminist circles. Franklin's searing rendition of that song won her two Grammy Awards in 1967 and a special civil rights award from Martin Luther King, Jr.

From the mid-1970s onward

Franklin's remarkable early period with Atlantic was followed by a solid run of critically acclaimed hit songs into the mid-1970s. They included "Spanish Harlem" and her cover of Paul Simon's "Bridge Over Troubled Water." By the end of the decade, however, her record sales were dwindling.

In 1980 Franklin joined Arista Records and once again enjoyed several hit songs, including "Jump to It" and "Freeway of Love." Also in 1980 Franklin appeared in *The Blues Brothers* movie, giving a strong performance of her 1968 song "Think" and exposing her music to a new generation of listeners.

Franklin returned to her gospel roots in such albums as *Amazing Grace* in 1972 and *One Lord, One Faith, One Baptism* in 1987. Also in 1987, Franklin became the first woman to be inducted into the Rock and Roll Hall of Fame. In 2005 Franklin was awarded the Lena Horne Award For Outstanding Career Achievements at the Tenth Annual Soul Train Lady of Soul Awards.

KEY DATES

1942	Born in Memphis, Tennessee, on March 25.
1961	Signs contract with Columbia Records.
1967	Moves to Atlantic Records; records the landmark album *I Never Loved a Man the Way I Love You*.
1987	Inducted into the Rock and Roll Hall of Fame—the first woman to be inducted.
1994	Receives Lifetime Achievement Grammy.

See also: Civil Rights; Cooke, Sam; Franklin, C. L.; Holiday, Billie; Jackson, Mahalia; King, Martin Luther, Jr.; Tatum, Art

Further reading: Bego, Mark. *Aretha Franklin: The Queen of Soul.* New York, NY: Da Capo Press, 2001.
Werner, Craig. *Higher Ground: Stevie Wonder, Aretha Franklin, Curtis Mayfield, and the Rise and Fall of American Soul.* New York, NY: Crown, 2004.
http://www.legacyrecordings.com/arethafranklin/ (Official Sony Music site).

FRANKLIN, C. L.
Preacher, Civil Rights Activist

Widely known as the "man with the golden voice," C. L. Franklin was among the best-known and most influential preachers of the 20th century. His impassioned sermons, which blended rapturous religious faith with indignant political fervor, played an important role in the civil rights movement of the 1960s. They served to highlight the crucial contribution made by religion to the rising black activism of the period.

Early life
Clarence LaVaughn Franklin was born on January 22, 1915, in Sunflower County, Mississippi, where his mother, father, and, later, stepfather were poor farmers, or sharecroppers. In 1925 the family moved to the nearby city of Cleveland, where the young Franklin became deeply involved in St. Peter's Rock Baptist Church. At age 16 he was ordained as a pastor; through the 1930s he worked as a "circuit rider," touring and preaching in different churches on successive Sundays.

In 1936 Franklin married pianist and gospel singer Barbara Siggers; the couple separated in 1948. Among their five children was Aretha, later an outstanding singer and recording artist, who began her gospel singing career accompanying her father on his tours.

Golden voice
Franklin rapidly won fame for his fiery, inspirational sermons, as well as for his distinctive chantlike, whooping delivery. He served as pastor at New Salem Baptist Church in Memphis and Friendship Baptist Church in Buffalo, New York. In 1946 he became pastor at the New Bethel Baptist Church in Detroit, Michigan, where he served for the next 33 years and where he soon established himself as a national figure. Franklin started a food ministry at Bethel for those who could not afford food for themselves or their families, offered financial and legal help for the homeless, and conducted a prison ministry.

Franklin also embarked on preaching tours and broadcast his sermons live over the radio. Some 75 of them were recorded by Chess Records and became best sellers across the United States, selling millions of copies. His soul-stirring sermons set a style and standard for preaching that still influences preachers today. In a 2005 interview with the *Detroit Free Press*, Reverend E. L. Branch remembered going to New Bethel Church to hear Franklin preach. "A group of us young ministers would go to New Bethel to listen and learn from the master. That's how we defined preaching. C. L. Franklin." Branch said of Franklin's preaching style, "He had music in his voice. He had rhythm and the ability to close a sermon in a musical style that was so unique and so powerful it stirred the emotions of people almost to a frenzy."

Singing for freedom
In his sermons Franklin called on African Americans not only to proclaim their faith but also to assert their dignity and political rights. In one of his most famous sermons, "Without a Song," he compared African Americans to the Israelites during their captivity in Babylon. However, Franklin believed that unlike the Israelites, who in the Bible refused to sing for their captors, African Americans should stand up and "sing out" their desire for freedom.

Franklin's rousing sermons brought him into the center of the civil rights movement. He was close to Martin Luther King, Jr., and helped organize the famous "Walk Toward Freedom" march of 1963. Franklin was also actively involved in the Urban League and the National Association for the Advancement of Colored People (NAACP).

In 1979 Franklin was shot during an armed robbery at his home in Detroit; he remained in a coma until his death in 1984. Over 10,000 people came to his funeral service at the New Bethel Baptist Church.

KEY DATES	
1915	Born in Sunflower County, Mississippi, on January 22.
1946	Becomes pastor of the New Bethel Baptist Church in Detroit, Michigan.
1963	Helps organize and takes part in the "Walk Toward Freedom" march.
1984	Dies in Detroit, Michigan, on July 27.

See also: Civil Rights; Franklin, Aretha; King, Martin Luther, Jr.

Further reading: Salvatore, Nick. *Singing in a Strange Land: C. L. Franklin, the Black Church, and the Transformation of America.* New York, NY: Little Brown, 2005. www.nicksalvatore.com (Includes audio excerpts from Franklin's sermons).

FRANKLIN, Carl
Actor, Film Director

Film director Carl Franklin received critical acclaim with the 1992 award-winning movie *One False Move*. Franklin was already an established actor.

Early life

Born in Richmond, California, on April 11, 1949, Franklin was raised by his mother and stepfather—Franklin's father died before he was born. A good student, Franklin won a scholarship to attend the University of California, Berkeley, where he studied history. He took up acting as a pastime, but it soon became his grand passion; he moved to New York after his graduation to see if he could make a career of it.

From actor to director

Franklin's professional acting career began with performances at the New York Shakespeare Festival. He appeared in other stage roles, then in 1973 starred in the film comedy *Five on the Black Hand Side*. Between 1973 and 1986 Franklin became a successful television star. The shows he appeared in were some of the most popular of the 1970s and 1980s, including *The Streets of San Francisco*, *The Incredible Hulk*, *The Rockford Files*, *MacGyver*, and *The A-Team*.

While the work paid the bills, Franklin found acting increasingly less fulfilling. In 1986 he enrolled in an MA course in directing at the American Film Institute (AFI). His thesis film was so impressive that he was hired by veteran filmmaker Roger Corman's company Concorde Productions. While working for Corman, Franklin refined his writing, producing, and directing skills on fairly low-budget video films.

In 1991 he decided to make his own film. He wrote and directed *One False Move*, starring Billy Bob Thornton and Bill Paxton. Although the film initially had limited commercial success, the critics loved it. Franklin won several awards, including the MTV Movie Award for Best New Filmmaker and a New Generation Award from the Los Angeles Film Critics Association. Such awards turned Franklin into a much sought-after director.

In 1995 Franklin directed the film adaption of crime writer Walter Mosley's book *Devil in a Deep Blue Dress*, starring Denzel Washington. Although the film was critically well received, it did not do well at the box office. Likewise the 1998 movie *One True Thing* won actor Meryl

▲ *Carl Franklin's directorial career has received more critical acclaim than box-office success.*

Streep both an Oscar and a Golden Globe nomination but was not a financial success.

Franklin also directed Ashley Judd and Morgan Freeman in the naval thriller *High Crimes* in 2002. He worked with Denzel Washington again on the 2003 movie *Out of Time*.

KEY DATES	
1949	Born in Richmond, California, on April 11.
1973	Makes his film debut in *Five on the Black Hand Side*.
1983	Lands his most popular TV role in *The A-Team*.
1986	Enrolls at the American Film Institute (AFI).
1992	Releases his first major feature film, *One False Move*.

See also: Freeman, Morgan; Mosely, Walter; Washington, Denzel

Further reading: Bogle, Donald. *Primetime Blues: African Americans on Network Television.* New York, NY: Farrar Straus Giroux, 2001.
http://www.imdb.com/name/nm0002083/ (IMDB page on Franklin).

FRANKLIN, John Hope
Historian, Civil Rights Activist

One of the most revered and celebrated academics in America, John Hope Franklin is the nation's leading expert on the history of African Americans and their struggle for freedom and citizenship. During his long career Franklin has used his expertise and influence to promote black civil rights and interracial understanding.

The African American historian

Born in Rentiesville, Oklahoma, in 1915, Franklin was named for John Hope, the first African American president of Atlanta University. His family was middle class: his father, Buck Colbert Franklin, was a lawyer and his mother, Mollie Parker, an elementary school teacher. In 1921 Franklin's father moved to Tulsa, Oklahoma, and set up a law practice. The family was about to join him in Tulsa, until his office was burned down during the notorious Tulsa race riot—75 blacks were killed, and thousands lost their homes. They finally moved in 1925.

▼ *John Hope Franklin's interests go beyond academia: He is an expert on orchid cultivation.*

Franklin was a gifted student; he was valedictorian of his high school class. Franklin decided to study at Fisk University in Tennessee, from which he graduated in 1935. He continued his studies at Harvard, from which he gained his MA (1936) and PhD (1941). He embarked on a distinguished career as a university teacher and lecturer, holding positions at historically black colleges such as Howard University, and at Brooklyn College and the University of Chicago. In 1985 Franklin was named James B. Duke Professor of History Emeritus at Duke University, North Carolina.

Making a name for himself

Franklin has written more than 20 books, but he made his name with *From Slavery to Freedom: A History of Negro Americans* (1947). This groundbreaking book reshaped the way in which black Americans perceived their own history and helped foster a shared sense of identity and commitment to the ongoing struggle for civil rights. Franklin's interest in equality also led Supreme Court justice Thurgood Marshall to invite him to document the historical part of the brief on the 1954 landmark *Brown v. Board of Education*, which ended segregation in schools.

Franklin has received many honors, including the NAACP Spingarn Medal and the Presidential Medal of Freedom (both 1995). In 2001 Duke University opened the John Hope Franklin Research Center.

KEY DATES	
1915	Born in Rentiesville, Oklahoma, on January 2.
1941	Awarded PhD from Harvard University.
1947	Publication of *From Slavery to Freedom: A History of Negro Americans;* it was the first of many editions.
1995	Awarded the Presidential Medal of Freedom.

See also: Historically Black Colleges and Universities; Marshall, Thurgood

Further reading: Franklin, John Hope, and Alfred A. Moss. *From Slavery to Freedom: A History of Negro Americans.* New York, NY: Knopf, 2000.
www.acls.org/op4.htm (1988 lecture given by Franklin about his life and commitment to learning).

FRAZIER, E. Franklin
Sociologist, Educator

Edward Franklin Frazier was a sociologist whose books and essays set out to show that many of the problems within the African American family came from racist attitudes and how African Americans were treated outside the home.

Frazier was born on September 24, 1894, in Baltimore, Maryland. His father, a bank messenger, stressed the importance of education for self-improvement, and Frazier worked hard through his school career. In 1912 he graduated from Baltimore Colored High School, winning a scholarship to Howard University, Washington, D.C.

After graduating from Howard, Frazier taught before studying for his master's degree at Clark University, Worcester, Massachusetts, where he majored in sociology and graduated in 1920. Two years' research followed, including a year at the University of Copenhagen, where he studied Denmark's rural high schools.

Returning to the United States in 1922, Frazier married Marie Brown. Based in Atlanta, Georgia, he worked as director of the Atlanta University School of Social Work and taught sociology at Morehouse College. He also

▼ **E. Franklin Frazier dedicated his life to changing perceptions of race and the politics of race relations.**

started to publish articles on African American life. His views on racial discrimination were controversial and he was forced to leave Atlanta after receiving death threats.

A career in sociology

While studying for his PhD from the University of Chicago, Frazier began teaching at Fisk University, Nashville, Tennessee, before moving to Howard. In 1934 he was appointed professor and head of the department of sociology, where he remained until his retirement as professor emeritus in 1959. While there, Frazier published his most influential works. In 1932 his PhD dissertation was published as *The Negro Family in Chicago*. It was followed in 1939 by *The Negro Family in the United States*, which won the Anisfield Award for the most important book on race relations.

Frazier's most controversial book, and the one that made his popular reputation, was *Black Bourgeoisie* (1957) in which he argued that the African American middle classes, interested in status and consumerism, were more like the white upper class than middle class. In 1948 he was elected president of the American Sociological Society, the first African American to become chief officer of a national professional organization. Frazier died in 1962.

Further reading: Frazier, E. Franklin *The Negro Family in the United States*. Notre Dame, IN: University of Notre Dame Press, 2001.
http://www.asanet.org/page.ww?name=E.+Franklin+Frazier&section=Presidents (Biography).

FRAZIER, Joe
Boxer

Joe Frazier is a boxing legend, and one of the few fighters to beat the great Muhammad Ali in the ring. He won the world heavyweight title in 1970 and successfully defended it a year later in an epic match with Ali.

Early life

Frazier was born in 1944, in Beaufort, South Carolina, the 11th child of a poor farmer, or sharecropper. In his late teens Frazier moved to Philadelphia, Pennsylvania, and began attending a gym in an attempt to get into shape. There he discovered a talent for boxing, and was soon fighting on the amateur circuit.

Heavyweight champion

Frazier distinguished himself as an amateur heavyweight, losing only to Buster Mathis in the trials for the 1964 Tokyo Olympics. However, Mathis subsequently suffered a hand injury, and Frazier stepped up to fight in Tokyo. He won the gold medal, and in 1965 he turned professional. As a pro, "Smokin' Joe"—the title by which he became known—seemed unstoppable, taking his first 19 fights with no defeats. On March 4, 1968, he met Buster Mathis in a fight in New York, and defeated his former opponent in the 11th round. In 1970 Frazier became the world heavyweight champion after defeating Jimmy Ellis.

Beating the best

In 1967 Muhammad Ali refused to serve in Vietnam when he was drafted into the Army. His titles were stripped from him and he was not allowed to box again until 1970, when a judge ruled in his favor. Ali immediately aimed to reclaim the heavyweight title from Frazier. A match was scheduled for March 8, 1971, at Madison Square Garden in New York City. Newspapers billed it "the fight of the century." The two men traded insults and tempers rose. After an epic battle, Frazier's trademark left hook put Ali on the canvas in the 15th round. Ali got back up, but the judges declared Frazier the winner.

Defeat and retirement

In 1973 Frazier lost his title to George Foreman in Jamaica after being knocked down six times in the first two rounds. In January 1974 Frazier was defeated by Ali in a 12-round unanimous decision. In October Ali took Foreman's title. In 1975 Frazier and Ali met again in the Philippines. The

▲ Joe Frazier poses for the cameras in April 1968, not long after defeating Buster Mathis. Two years later Frazier was the world heavyweight champion.

match became known by boxing fans as the "Thrilla in Manila." After 14 rounds of heavy slugging on both sides, Frazier's trainer would not let him come out for the final round, and Ali won. The following year Frazier lost to Foreman. After some brief comeback attempts, Frazier retired in 1981. Following his retirement Frazier worked as a boxing trainer. He also performed as a singer in his own band, the Knockouts.

KEY DATES	
1944	Born in Beaufort, South Carolina, on January 12.
1964	Wins a gold medal in the Tokyo Olympics.
1970	Takes the world heavyweight title.
1971	Retains title in a challenge from Muhammad Ali.
1973	Loses heavyweight title to George Foreman.
1975	Is defeated by Muhammad Ali in Manila.
1981	Retires from boxing.

See also: Ali, Muhammad; Foreman, George

Further reading: Frazier, Joe, and Phil Berger. *Smokin' Joe: The Autobiography*. New York, NY: Macmillan, 1996.
http://espn.go.com/classic/biography/s/Frazier_Joe.html
(Extensive biography of Frazier).

FRAZIER, Walt
Basketball Player

Walt Frazier—usually known by the nickname "Clyde" on the basketball court—was one of the New York Knicks' greatest basketball players for a decade between 1967 and 1977.

Walter Frazier, Jr., was born in 1945 in Atlanta, Georgia, the first of nine children in the Frazier family. As a teenager at the David Howard High School, he excelled in sports, particularly football, baseball, and basketball. Colleges were more interested in his skills as a football quarterback than in his basketball talent, but Frazier chose to go to Southern Illinois University on a basketball scholarship.

Playing for the Knicks

At Southern Illinois Frazier began to show the powerful defensive tactics for which he was to become famous. He was central to the team's victory in the 1966 National Invitation Tournament and as a senior was given All-American team honors. The path was being laid for a pro career, and in 1967 he was drafted into the National Basketball Association (NBA) by the New York Knicks.

Frazier would play for the Knicks for almost his entire professional career, from 1967 to 1977. His first season did not see him at his best—he averaged only nine points per game. However, his scoring soon began to pick up, and he steadily became feared by his opponents for a lightning-fast ability to steal balls, turn around, and put the ball through the hoop. In 1969 Frazier was selected to the NBA All-Defensive First Team (the first of six such titles), and in 1970 he was chosen for the NBA All-Star First Team. By then Frazier was helping the Knicks to ever greater achievements, with an average of 20.9 points per game. In the 1970 NBA finals against the Los Angeles Lakers, Frazier scored 36 points, and the Knicks won 113–99.

▲ *Walt Frazier's nickname "Clyde" is taken from the the robber in the story of* **Bonnie and Clyde** *and referred to his ability to steal balls from opponents.*

Retirement

Frazier continued to be central to the Knicks' success throughout the 1970s, being part of another championship defeat of the Lakers in 1973. In 1975 Frazier was named All-Star Most Valuable Player. However, Frazier's points average began to decline, and in 1977 he was traded to the Cleveland Cavaliers. While with the Knicks Frazier had scored 14,617 points over 759 games. However, the player was not happy with the move to Cleveland, and he never regained his previous form.

Frazier retired from basketball in 1981, working as a sports agent, then as a charter-boat captain, and finally as a sports commentator. In 1996 he was elected to the NBA 50th Anniversary All-Time Team.

Further reading: Frazier, Walt. *Rockin' Steady: A Guide to Basketball and Cool.* Englewood Cliffs, NJ: Prentice-Hall, 1974. Frazier, Walt. *Walt Frazier: One Magic Season and a Basketball Life.* New York, NY: Harper Collins, 1989.
http://www.nba.com/history/players/frazier_summary.html (Biography and NBA statistics).

KEY DATES	
1945	Born in Atlanta, Georgia, on March 29.
1967	Drafted to play for the New York Knicks.
1969	Selected to the NBA All-Defensive First Team.
1970	Chosen for the NBA All-Star First Team.
1977	Traded to the Cleveland Cavaliers.
1981	Retires from professional basketball.

FREELON, Allan
Artist, Art Educator

Allan Freelon was the first African American to become a supervisor of art education in his local school district. He was also a successful artist, known for his landscapes and harbor scenes executed in free brushstrokes and vivid colors.

Early life

Allan Randall Freelon was born in 1895 in Philadelphia, Pennsylvania, into a middle-class family that valued art and education. Freelon was the first African American to be awarded a four-year scholarship to study at the Pennsylvania Museum School of Industrial Art (now the University of the Arts). He went on to earn a BA from the University of Pennsylvania and a master of fine arts from Temple's Tyler School of Art. Freelon served in the Army as a second lieutenant during World War I (1914–1918), an experience that caused him to suffer a nervous breakdown.

In 1919 Freelon was employed as an art teacher in Philadelphia public schools. In 1921 he was appointed supervisor of art education in the district, becoming the first African American in the nation to hold such a position.

Artistic career

From the 1920s Freelon also pursued his career as an artist. In 1921 an exhibition of his paintings was held at the Harlem branch of the New York Public Library. From 1927 to 1929 Freelon studied at the Barnes Foundation,

just outside Philadelphia, which had opened in 1922 to promote education and the fine arts. The foundation had a collection of modernist European and American paintings that inspired Freelon to continue his exploration of light and color effects. During summer breaks he spent time at an artists' colony in Gloucester, Massachusetts, where he was influenced by the impressionist style of Hugh Breckenridge (1870–1937).

Both black and white critics have criticized Freelon for producing artworks that developed European traditions of painting rather than exploring the African and black American cultural themes advocated by the New Negro Movement of the Harlem Renaissance in the 1920s and 1930s. Freelon disagreed with Harlem Renaissance writer Alain Locke, who believed that black artists should look solely to Africa for inspiration. Freelon believed that he should be free to pursue his own artistic interests and directions. Nonetheless, he spoke out against racism, and painted *Barbecue American Style* (1935), which attacked lynching, for an exhibition sponsored by the National Association for the Advancement of Colored People (NAACP).

Printmaker and social role

As well as being an educator and painter, Freelon was a talented printmaker and an active member of black cultural life in Philadelphia. In 1921 he became the first African American member of the Philadelphia Print Club. He was also a member of the Tra Club, a group of Philadelphia artists and their supporters, and exhibited in its annual shows in the 1930s. In 1937 a group of African Americans set up the Pyramid Club because they were excluded from membership in white clubs. It became a venue for prominent members of the black community to socialize and network. In 1940 the club sponsored the first of its annual invitational art exhibitions when Freelon was invited to speak about the role of the black artist. He died in his home city in 1960.

See also: Freelon, Philip; Harlem Renaissance; Locke, Alain

Further reading: http://www.ncat.edu/~museum/freelon.htm (Information about Allan Freelon on the occasion of an exhibition of his work by North Carolina A&T State University).

KEY DATES

1895 Born in Philadelphia, Pennsylvania, on September 2.

1913 Begins studies at the Pennsylvania Museum School of Industrial Art.

1919 Begins teaching art in Philadelphia's public schools.

1921 Exhibition of his paintings is held at the Harlem branch of the New York Public Library.

1927 Begins studying at the Barnes Foundation.

1929 Work included in a traveling exhibition organized by the Harmon Foundation.

1935 Participates in NAACP-sponsored exhibition against lynching.

1960 Dies in Philadelphia.

FREELON, Nnenna
Singer

Nnenna Freelon is a jazz vocalist who has received increasing acclaim since the late 1990s. She is a singer in the tradition of Ella Fitzgerald and Sarah Vaughan who has brought freshness and originality to the standard repertoire.

Late developer
Born in 1954 in Massachusetts, Chinyere Nnenna Pierce sang gospel music at an early age but did not pursue a career as a singer until later, putting her family first. She graduated from Simmons College in Boston with a degree in health-care administration. In 1979 she married acclaimed architect Philip Freelon. Although working in

▼ *Nnenna Freelon has sung with many of the greatest African American musicians.*

health care in Durham, North Carolina, and a mother of three children, Freelon did not discard her music interests. In the 1980s she studied with Yusef Lateef and performed locally with a band that included Bill Anschell (piano), John Brown (bass), and Woody Williams (drums).

At the 1990 Federal Jazz Forum in Atlanta, Georgia, Freelon was heard by jazz pianist Ellis Marsalis (the father of trumpeter Wynton Marsalis). Marsalis has championed Freelon's singing career ever since.

Freelon's first recording contract was with Columbia, and her first record was released in 1992. She became a supporting artist on tour with musicians such as Ray Charles, Al Jarreau, and Ellis Marsalis. Her first record, *Nnenna Freelon*, received unfavorable criticism as an impersonation of Sarah Vaughan, but after her second album, *Heritage* (1993), critics became more positive.

Singing success
In 1996 Freelon started recording with the Concord Jazz Label and has since had five Grammy nominations. She considers her fifth album, *Maiden Voyage* (1998), the true beginning of her voyage as a singer. It contains Freelon's versions of Herbie Hancock and Stevie Wonder songs. She also sang "Fly Me to the Moon" in *The Visit* (2000) and made her first appearance in film as a nightclub singer in *What Women Want* (2000).

Freelon is a winner of the Billie Holiday Award from the French Academie du Jazz and the Eubie Blake Award. Her eighth album, *Live*, was recorded at the Kennedy Center in Washington, D.C., in February 2003.

See also: Blake, Eubie; Charles, Ray; Fitzgerald, Ella; Freelon, Philip; Hancock, Herbie; Marsalis, Wynton; Vaughan, Sarah; Wonder, Stevie

Further reading: http://www.nnenna.com/home.html (Official site).

FREELON, Philip
Architect

Philip Freelon is the principal architect and president of the Freelon Group. In 2001 the firm was awarded the North Carolina Chapter of the American Institute of Architect's Firm Award. In addition to his professional achievements Freelon has shown a deep commitment to public service.

Early life

Freelon was born in Philadelphia in 1953 and educated at public high schools, including Central High. He came from an artistic family, being the grandson of the talented Harlem Renaissance painter Allan Freelon. Freelon's father marketed medical equipment and supplies and his mother was an elementary school teacher.

In 1975 Freelon graduated from the College of Design at North Carolina State University with a BA in environmental design and top design honors. He continued his architectural education with a master's degree in architecture from the Massachusetts Institute of Technology (MIT). In 1979 Freelon married Chinyere Nnenna Pierce, who became an international jazz star.

Architectural career

Returning to North Carolina in 1982, Freelon worked for the large architectural practice of O'Brien/Atkins Associates, holding positions there as senior designer, project manager, and vice president of architecture. In 1989 Freelon spent a year at the Harvard Graduate School of Design on a Loeb Fellowship.

In 1990 Freelon resigned from O'Brien/Atkins to start his own firm, the Freelon Group, which has grown to an 18-architect firm with over 50 employees. The firm's commissions include educational buildings—several buildings for the campus of the North Carolina State University—airport buildings, including the award-winning parking deck at Raleigh-Durham International Airport, and museums.

The Freelon Group designed several prestigious African American cultural projects that opened in 2005, while others were still being constructed. They included the Museum of the African Diaspora in San Francisco, the Museum of Maryland African American History and Culture in Baltimore (with the firm RTKL), the International Civil Rights Center and Museum in Greensboro, North Carolina, and the Amistad Research Center at Tulane University in

New Orleans. The firm also acted as adviser on the planning of new facilities for the National Museum of African American History and Culture in Washington, D.C. Freelon argues that "It's important to be of the culture if you're talking about a culture-specific museum."

Honors and awards

The work of the Freelon Group has received seven awards from the American Institute of Architects (AIA) and the Outstanding Firm Award from the North Carolina section of the AIA in 2001.

Freelon is also involved in architectural education. He has lectured at several universities, including Harvard, Howard, North Carolina, and Hampton, and his firm offers apprenticeships to local high school students. Each semester one student in a drafting class is selected for an internship with the firm, where he or she is paid to learn more about architecture and contribute to the firm's work.

In 2002 the North Carolina State University College of Design selected Freelon as its Distinguished Alumnus of the year. In 2003 Freelon was elected to the College of Fellows of American Institute of Architects (FAIA) for his contribution to architectural education.

In addition to teaching, Freelon has served as a member of the Design Guild Board, including a term as president. He is also a member of the NC State Board of Visitors, the African-American Community Advisory Committee, and the Chancellor's Circle.

See also: Freelon, Allan; Freelon, Nnenna

Further reading: http://www.freelon.com (Freelon Group's official site).
http://www.ncsu.edu/news/press_releases/02_10/283.htm (North Carolina State University page on 2002 award).

KEY DATES

1953   Born in Philadelphia, Pennsylvania.

1975   Graduates from North Carolina State University with BA in environmental design.

1990   Founds the Freelon Group.

2003   Elected to FAIA for his contribution to architecture.

FREEMAN, Elizabeth
Slave

Elizabeth Freeman, nicknamed "Mumbet," was the first African American woman to be freed from slavery by bringing and winning a legal case for freedom under the Massachusetts Constitution.

Slavery

Freeman was born to slave parents in Claverack, New York, in 1742 or 1748. Along with her sister Lizzy, Freeman was sold to the Dutchman Pietre Hoogeboom when she was about six months old.

In 1758, when Freeman was in her early teens, she was given to Colonel John Ashley, a well-known judge and patriot, and his wife, Hannah, who was Pietre's daughter. Freeman worked as a slave on the Ashley homestead in Sheffield, Massachusetts, for almost three decades. By then she was known as "Mum Bett," or "Mumbet" and had a young daughter known as "Little Bett." Her husband had been killed while fighting in the American Revolution (1775–1783).

Freeman served meals at the political meetings held in the Ashley household and often overheard conversations among Colonel Ashley, lawyers Theodore Sedgewick and Tapping Reeve, and others, about the proposed constitution. In 1773 these men had been influential in putting together the Sheffield Resolves, a petition against British tyranny and a manifesto for individual rights.

In 1780 Massachusetts adopted its own constitution. It is the oldest still-governing written constitution in the world and was the model for the U.S. Constitution, which was drafted seven years later. The first article states "All men are born free and equal, and have certain natural, essential, and unalienable rights; among which may be reckoned the right of enjoying and defending their lives and liberties; that of acquiring, possessing, and protecting property; in fine, that of seeking and obtaining their safety and happiness."

Court case

In 1781 Freeman took a blow from her mistress with a heated kitchen shovel that had been meant for her sister Lizzy. The next day Freeman went to the law offices of Theodore Sedgewick and asked "Every man has a right to freedom. … I am not a dumb critter; won't the law give me any freedom?" Sedgewick agreed to take her case and that of another of Ashley's slaves, Brom, to court.

KEY DATES

1742	Born in Claverack, New York, at about this time.
1758	Is given to Colonel John Ashley.
1781	Files a legal suit for freedom after being hit with a kitchen shovel; may have gained her freedom this year.
1829	Dies in Massachusetts on December 28.

On August 21, 1781, *Brom & Bett v. Ashley* appeared in front of a county court. Sedgewick argued two points in his case. First, that no law in Massachussetts had established slavery; second, that even if it had, that law would be annulled by the new constitution. A jury granted Freeman and Brom their freedom and ordered Ashley to pay them 30 shillings and costs. The case set a precedent and led to the 1783 abolition of slavery in Massachusetts.

After the case

After winning her freedom, Mumbet changed her name to Freeman. She refused an offer of work for wages from Ashley. Instead she accepted a paid job in the Sedgewick household, where she worked for many years. When she left to live in her own house, she continued to work as a nurse and midwife until just before her death in 1829. Nearly 40 years later one of her great-grandchildren was born in Great Barrington, Massachusetts. His name was W. E. B. DuBois and he later became one of the most influential black leaders of the early 20th century.

Freeman was buried in the Stockbridge Cemetery. Her gravestone reads: "She was born a slave and remained a slave for nearly thirty years. She could neither read nor write yet in her own sphere she had no superior or equal. She neither wasted time nor property. She never violated a trust nor failed to perform a duty. In every situation of domestic trial, she was the most efficient helper, and the tenderest friend. Good mother, farewell."

See also: DuBois, W. E. B.; Slavery

Further reading: Wilds, Mary. *Mumbet: The Life and Times of Elizabeth Freeman.* Greensboro, NC: Avisson Press, 1999.
http://www.juntosociety.com/founders/mumbett.html (Junto Society page on Freeman).

FREEMAN, John
Businessman

John Freeman escaped slavery in the South to become one of the most successful African American businessmen of the mid-19th century, only to face the injustice of losing most of his wealth when he was accused of being an escaped slave.

Early life

Freeman was born free in Virginia in 1807 and lived there until age 24, when he moved to Monroe, Georgia. He registered at the courthouse and received a document certifying his free status from John B. Lucas. In about 1936 Freeman accompanied Lucas, who was an Army colonel, to Florida during the Second Seminole War (1835–1842) between the U.S. government and the Seminoles.

In 1844 Freeman moved to Indianapolis, Indiana. He became a sexton in the church of Congregationalist preacher Henry Ward Beecher, a leader of the antislavery movement and the brother of Harriet Beecher Stowe (1811–1896), author of *Uncle Tom's Cabin* (1852).

Wealth

Freeman began to buy land in 1844 and continued to add to his holdings until 1852. By 1850 the census recorded that Freeman had become the richest African American in Marion County, Indiana. He had earned much of his wealth from a restaurant in Indianapolis and the surrounding 4 acres (1.6ha) of land on which he grew crops for sale and for use in his own kitchens.

Court case

In 1853 Missouri farmer Pleasant Ellington lodged a legal claim that Freeman had been his slave Sam until 1836. According to the charge, Freeman had taken

KEY DATES	
1807	Born in Prince Edward County, Virginia.
1844	Moves to Indianapolis, Indiana.
1853	Fights court proceedings to have him returned to slavery in Missouri.
1863	Moves to Canada at about this time.
1870	Returns to the United States.
1902	Dies on October 2.

advantage of his owner's temporary absence in Kentucky to escape across the state line via Illinois into Indiana. Although Freeman had documents identifying him as a free person, he was arrested and jailed.

Under the second Fugitive Slave Act, passed by Congress in 1850, it was up to Freeman to prove his innocence; if he failed to do so, he would be shipped back to Ellington.

A supporter of Freeman's offered to pay his bail, but the court refused. Ellington was offered money to buy Freeman but refused to accept any amount.

Freeman fought the case vigorously, but at great personal cost. He had to sign over his properties in trust to William Hubbard, clerk of the state bank, to help pay costs for his defense. He also had to pay for witnesses to come from Georgia, Alabama, and Kentucky to testify on his behalf. He paid for two attorneys to go to Canada to search for the real Sam, whom they succeeded in finding.

Innocent, but at a price

As a result of overwhelming evidence that Sam and Freeman were not the same man and testimony that proved Freeman was a free black, the case was dismissed. Freeman, however, had nearly bankrupted himself in the process. He was saved from ruin by friends and members of his local community, who joined together to help him pay off his debts and hang on to some of his property, including his restaurant.

In an attempt to regain some of his property, Freeman sued Ellington in the fall of 1853. Freeman was awarded $2,000 in damages and costs but was never able to collect the money. In 1854 a local paper described Freeman as destitute, and records show that between 1855 and 1860 he worked at semiskilled jobs such as house painting.

In 1863 or 1864 Freeman moved with his family—his wife, Letitia Draper, and their children Henry, John, Jr., Elijah, Martha, and Harriet—to Canada. They remained north of the 49th parallel until 1870, when they returned to the United States to live in Topeka, Kansas. Freeman died in 1902.

See also: Slavery

Further reading: http://www.IN.gov/judiciary/ (Indiana court records and timeline on Freeman).

FREEMAN, Morgan
Actor

Morgan Freeman is a highly respected film, stage, and television actor. While many other African American actors were being overlooked by major film studios, Freeman consistently received roles that were not specifically written for black actors. He has played a variety of parts, from God to the director of the CIA. Freeman also has many other interests, including owning a restaurant and blues club in the Mississippi Delta (*see box*).

Making an impact
Born in Memphis, Tennessee, on June 1, 1937, Freeman was brought up by his grandparents in Mississippi. He spent his summers in Chicago with his parents, who had moved there to find work. From an early age he was conscious of the difference in the way that black and white people were treated. He said, "When I was growing up I learned American history from the movies. But only

▼ *Morgan Freeman is often cast in thrillers such as* **Seven** *and* **Kiss the Girls.**

white people were history. You know, you'd see a movie set in the future, after the world has been bombed out of existence, and only a few people are left and you realize those few people are white. I thought, wait a minute, where's everybody else?"

Freeman attended Los Angeles Community College before joining the Air Force in 1955. He had dreamed of being a fighter pilot as a child, but he worked as a mechanic and found Air Force life disappointing. After resigning in 1959, Freeman turned his attention to acting, making his theater debut in a production of *The Niggerlovers*. He got his first movie break in Leo Penn's drama *A Man Called Adam* (1966), which starred Louis Armstrong and Sammy Davis, Jr. A year later he made his Broadway debut in an all-black production of *Hello Dolly!*

In the 1970s Freeman continued to work on stage. He also appeared in the PBS children's television show *The Electric Company* as the character Easy Reader. Freeman's performance in the film *Brubaker* (1980) and on the soap

INFLUENCES AND INSPIRATION

Morgan Freeman believes strongly in the preservation of Mississippi Delta culture, particularly its food and music, and has invested both time and money in doing this.

In 2000, along with attorney and friend Bill Luckett, Freeman opened Madidi, a restaurant specializing in southern-inspired food. Situated in Clarksdale, Mississippi—"ground zero" to blues aficionados around the world—the venture was so successful that in 2001 Freeman and Luckett opened the Ground Zero Blues Club, also in Clarksdale. Freeman said that he was prompted to set up his own club when he realized that there was nowhere to go to see live blues in the area. Located in an old warehouse, Ground Zero Blues has been designed in the style of an old blues club. It serves soul food alongside live music and has showcased many black musicians and singers. Ground Zero draws audiences from all over the world, as well as Freeman's celebrity friends like actor Ashley Judd and her family, the acclaimed country band the Judds.

Freeman said that Clarksdale is "not just 'the Crossroads' for the blues. It's ... ground zero for our nation's musical heritage. Everything from jazz to rock is rooted in blues born in the Delta."

opera *Another World* (1982–1984), along with his theater work in the early 1980s, led to more challenging film roles, but the road to success was a long one. When Freeman was finally nominated for an Academy Award for best supporting actor for his performance as a dangerous hustler in *Street Smart* (1987), he was 50 years old. Two years later he received a second Oscar nomination for best actor for his performance as Hoke in *Driving Miss Daisy* (1989), a role he had originally played Off Broadway two years earlier. He won a Golden Globe award instead.

Freeman received critical acclaim for stage performances that ranged from Shakespearean leads to drunks. On screen he starred in several roles written specifically for black actors, such as a disciplinarian principal in *Lean on Me* (1989) and a Civil War soldier in the drama *Glory* (1989). He also directed the anti-apartheid film *Bopha!* (1993).

Unforgiven and beyond

After playing aging gunslinger Ned Logan in Clint Eastwood's critically acclaimed western *Unforgiven* (1992), Freeman received even more lucrative film offers. His performance as Red, the prison inmate who befriends actor Tim Robbins in the film *The Shawshank Redemption* (1994), won him another Oscar nomination.

Part of Freeman's success lies in the fact that he is just as convincing as a man in prison for murder as he is as a policeman. He played a weary detective and mentor to Brad Pitt in the thriller *Seven* (1995), and he starred as criminal psychologist Alex Cross in the popular crime movie *Kiss the Girls* (1997), alongside Ashley Judd, with whom he has since appeared in many films. Freeman was president of the United States in the disaster movie *Deep*

KEY DATES	
1937	Born in Memphis, Tennessee, on June 1.
1987	Receives first Oscar nomination for *Street Smart*.
1990	Wins a Golden Globe award for *Driving Miss Daisy*.
1992	Stars in *Unforgiven*; nominated for an Oscar.
1995	Stars in *Seven*.
2000	Opens Madidi; a year later opens blues club.
2005	Wins Oscar for Best Supporting Actor in *Million Dollar Baby*.

Impact (1998), a military officer in *Dreamcatcher* (2003), and God in the comedy *Bruce Almighty* (2003). Continuing his successful collaboration with Eastwood, Freeman starred in *Million Dollar Baby* (2004) as ex-prize fighter Eddie "Scrap Iron" Dupris. His performance earned him an Oscar for Best Supporting Actor.

Freeman still calls Mississippi home and believes that it is less racist than other parts of the United States. He observed: "I grew up in a segregated society, and that was purposely, obviously, openly segregated and I wasn't given any business about it or anything else. And then I went up to the north and you see it…. It's painful and it's insidious, because you want to think something else is going on and it's not. You want to think you're free there. You're not."

See also: Armstrong, Louis; Davis, Sammy, Jr.

Further reading: http://www.pbs.org/wnet/aaworld/reference/articles/morgan_freeman.html (Biography).

FUDGE, Ann
Corporate Executive

Ann Fudge was the first African American woman to head a major corporate division and the first African American to head a major advertising agency.

Ann Marie Fudge was born in Washington, D.C., in 1951. Her father was an administrator for the U.S. Postal Service and her mother was a manager at the National Security Agency. After graduating from Simmons College, Boston, Massachusetts, in 1973, Fudge worked as a human resources specialist for General Electric until 1975.

Rising to the top
In 1977, straight after graduating from Harvard Business School, Fudge started a marketing assistant position at General Mills, the sixth-largest food manufacturing company in the United States. She quickly rose through the ranks to assistant product manager, project manager, and, in 1983, marketing director in charge of four brands. Fudge led the team that developed and introduced Honey Nut Cheerios and established it as one of the United States's most popular breakfast cereals.

▼ *In 1998* **Fortune** *listed Ann Fudge as one of the 50 most powerful women in American business.*

In 1994 Fudge became the first African American woman to head a major corporate division when she was named president of Kraft General Foods' Maxwell House Coffee Company. In 1995 Fudge was appointed executive vice president of Kraft Foods, Incorporated.

In 1997 Fudge was made president of Kraft's Maxwell House and Post coffee and cereal division. She oversaw the manufacture, promotion, and sales of renowned brand products such as Minute Rice, and was responsible for radically improving the appeal of Kool-Aid. Fudge soon developed a reputation as an outstanding manager with a track record of improving the fortunes of failing brands. However, after a year at the head of Kraft, Fudge shocked the business world by walking out of her job to spend time with family and friends.

In 2003 Fudge returned to the world of business when she was appointed chairman and chief executive officer (CEO) of Young & Rubicam, one of the most powerful advertising firms in the world. She had once again made history in corporate America by becoming the first African American to head a major advertising agency.

Among Fudge's honors are leadership awards from the Minneapolis and New York City YWCAs, Advertising Woman of the Year (1995), the Alumni Achievement Award from Harvard Business School (1998), the 2000 Achievement Award from the Executive Leadership Council, and University of Arizona 2005 Executive of the Year.

KEY DATES

1951 Born in Washington, D.C., on April 23.

1977 Graduates from Harvard Business School

1994 Becomes the first African American woman to head a major corporate division when named president of Kraft General Foods' Maxwell House Coffee Company.

2003 Appointed chairman and CEO of Young & Rubicam advertising firm.

Further reading: Barkley Brown, Elsa, Darlene Clark Hine, and Rosalyn Terborg-Penn (eds.). *Black Women in America: An Historical Encyclopaedia*. Bloomington, IN: Indiana University Press, 1994.
http://www.cnn.com/SPECIALS/2002/black.history/stories/04.fudge/ (CNN page on Fudge).

FULANI, Lenora
Psychotherapist, Activist

Lenora Fulani made history by becoming the first woman and the first African American to appear on the ballot in all 50 states when she ran for president in 1988 as an independent.

Leonora Branch was born into a working-class family in Chester, Pennsylvania, in 1950. She later took the name "Fulani." The Fulani people of West Africa are the largest nomadic group in the world.

Fulani became a youth leader in the local Baptist Church, where she regularly played the piano for the choir. As a senior at the predominantly African American Chester High School, Fulani threatened to organize a walkout if her class was forced to integrate its all-black class cabinet, the first in the school's history. Eventually the school administration was forced to back down.

In 1968 Fulani won a scholarship to Hofstra University, Long Island. After graduating with a major in psychology, she went on to study at Columbia University's Teachers College and then the City University of New York, where she earned a PhD in developmental psychology.

Fred Newman and social therapy

In 1973, while completing her doctorate and working at the Rockefeller Institute in New York City, Fulani attended a therapy group run by Fred Newman, a controversial psychotherapist who had developed what he called "social therapy." Social therapy uses a supportive group setting to help people work through emotional problems and stress. Fulani undertook postgraduate training at Newman's New York Institute for Social Therapy clinic and later become the best-known supporter of his work. She chose to remain with the New York Institute for Social Therapy and began her therapy practice working with people in Harlem.

▲ *Lenora Fulani (right) with Danny Forbes and Mary Tyler Moore at a 2001 benefit for the All Stars.*

In 1979 Fulani cofounded the National Alliance Party (NAP) with Newman. Its aim was to bring about political change without resorting to the policies of the Republican or Democratic parties. As a NAP candidate Fulani ran for lieutenant governor of New York in 1982, mayor of New York City in 1985, governor of New York in 1986 and 1990, and president of the United States in 1988 and 1992. Fulani's brand of independent politics has involved many tactics: She has led drives for voter registration, instigated lawsuits to open up ballot access to independent parties, and fought to be included in debates with major candidates at state and national levels.

Fulani has also worked on a number of community outreach projects. In 1983 she and Newman founded the All Stars Talent Show Network, a program for young people from the poorest neighborhoods of New York City, Newark, San Francisco, Los Angeles, Boston, and Atlanta. In 1984 she helped found the Castillo Cultural Center in New York, which produces plays dedicated to multiculturalism.

KEY DATES

1950   Born in Chester, Pennsylvania, on April 25.

1983   Founds the All Stars Talent Show Network for deprived urban youth.

1988   Runs for president and is the first woman and the first African American to appear on the ballot in all 50 states.

1992   Publishes her autobiography, *Making of a Fringe Candidate*.

Further reading: Fulani, Lenora. *Making of a Fringe Candidate*. New York, NY: Castillo International, 1992.
http://leonora-fulani.biography.ms/ (Biography).

FULLER, Charles
Writer

Charles Fuller is a playwright, screenwriter, and television scriptwriter who, since the 1960s, has been influential in developing drama that explores themes of black life. He is best known for *A Soldier's Play* (1981), for which he became the second African American to win the Pulitzer Prize for Drama in 1982.

Early life

Charles H. Fuller, Jr., was born in Philadelphia, Pennsylvania, in 1939, the son of Charles H. Fuller, a printer, and his wife, Lillian. Fuller was educated at Villanova University (1956–1958) and La Salle College (1965–1967). He served in the Army from 1959 to 1962.

Playwright and theater founder

In 1967, while working as a safety inspector for houses, Fuller cofounded the Afro-American Arts Theater in Philadelphia to encourage black theater professionals and to explore and improve the understanding of issues relating to the lives of African Americans. Fuller was codirector until 1971. He commented in an interview in 1999, "My struggle all these years has been to do nothing more than to change how people see us [black Americans], and in so doing perhaps change how we see ourselves."

Having opened a theater, Fuller began writing plays, and first came to critical attention with his two-act drama *The Perfect Party* (1969), in which he explored tensions within interracial marriages.

Fuller examined the realities of African American life in domestic dramas such as *In Many Names and Days* (1972), *In the Deepest Part of Sleep* (1974), and the hard-hitting *Zooman and the Sign* (1980), which centers on a black father's search for the teenage killer (Zooman) of his daughter. The New York *Village Voice* awarded Fuller an Obie Award for screenwriting for the play.

Fuller has also explored relationships and tensions among African Americans and between black and white Americans in two military dramas: *The Brownsville Raid* (1975) is based on the true story of the wrongful dishonorable discharge of an entire black regiment in 1906. The Pulitzer-prize-winning *A Soldier's Play* (1981) deals with a black captain's investigation into the death of a black soldier just outside a segregated Army camp in Louisiana during World War II (1939–1945). During discussions about opening on Broadway, Fuller was asked

KEY DATES	
1939	Born in Philadelphia, Pennsylvania, on March 5.
1967	Cofounds the Afro-American Arts Theater in Philadelphia, which he codirects until 1971.
1981	Receives Obie Award for Screenwriting for *Zooman and the Sign.*
1982	Awarded the Pulitzer Prize for Drama for *A Soldier's Play.*
1984	*A Soldier's Story* is released by Columbia Pictures.

to delete the controversial line that ends the play: "You'll have to get used to Black people being in charge." When he refused, the play did not appear on Broadway. In addition to the Pulitzer the play also won him the New York Drama Critics' Circle Award for Best American Play and the Edgar Allen Poe Award for Best Mystery.

Fuller adapted his play into the feature movie *A Soldier's Story* (1984), starring the then unknown Denzel Washington, and received a Golden Globe nomination for the best adapted screenplay as well as two Academy Award nominations for best screenplay and best movie.

A change of direction

From the 1990s Fuller increasingly concentrated on writing for film and television. He said, "I always wanted to reach the most people with my work. Not enough people go to the theater."

In 1985 Fuller's adaptation of *The Sky is Gray*, based on an Ernest Gaines story, was shown on PBS. Since then other major networks such as Showtime and CBS have produced several of his screenplays.

Fuller is a member of the Writers Guild of America, and the recipient of the Rockefeller Foundation Fellowship, a Guggenheim Fellowship, and the National Endowment of the Arts Fellowship in Playwriting.

See also: Gaines, Ernest; Washington, Denzel

Further reading: Fuller, Charles. *Zooman and the Sign.* New York, NY: Samuel French Plays, 2003.
http://www.bridgesweb.com/blacktheatre/fuller.html (Biography on site promoting black theater, including plot outlines of major plays and critical reactions).

FULLER, Meta Warrick
Sculptor

Meta Warrick Fuller was one of the first black women artists to achieve success in the United States. She addressed African and African American themes in her work, and her best-known sculpture, *Ethiopia Awakening* (about 1914–1921), is widely regarded as a precursor to the New Negro Movement's celebration of African and black American culture in 1920s Harlem, New York.

Early years
Born into a middle-class family in Philadelphia in 1877, Meta Vaux Warrick soon showed artistic talent. She received a scholarship to the Pennsylvania Museum School of Industrial Art before moving to Paris, France, in 1899. There she studied sculpture at the Académie Colarossi and drawing at the École des Beaux-Arts. She met and was encouraged by the French sculptor Auguste Rodin and socialized with the African American painter Henry Ossawa Tanner, who had settled in Paris, and the activist W. E. B. DuBois. Like Rodin, Fuller was interested in exploring the expressive qualities of sculpture and the psychological aspects of human experience; she also became increasingly motivated by racial consciousness.

Return to the United States
On her return to the United States, Fuller found it difficult to sell her sculpture in an art world that was prejudiced against both women artists and black artists. In 1907, however, her series of tableaux on the theme of the "Negro's progress" at the Jamestown Tercentennial Exposition brought her recognition. In 1909 she married Solomon Carter Fuller.

In 1913 Fuller sculpted the *Spirit of Emancipation* for DuBois to mark the 50th anniversary of emancipation. Shortly afterward she produced *Ethiopia Awakening*. Fuller wrote that the sculpture symbolized the black American "awakening, gradually unwinding the bandages of his past and looking out on life again, expectant, but unafraid." *Ethiopia Awakening* embodied the shared heritage of Africans and African Americans, and has become a symbol of liberation from racism.

Although being a wife and mother took up much of Fuller's time, she continued to sculpt, producing many works that addressed black life, among them *A Silent Protest Against Mob Violence* (1919), *The Talking Skull* (1937), and *The Crucifixion* (1964). She died in 1968.

▲ *In 1910 a fire in a Philadelphia warehouse destroyed 16 years of Meta Warrick Fuller's work.*

KEY DATES

1877 Born in Philadelphia, Pennsylvania, on June 9.

1894 Attends the Pennsylvania Museum School of Industrial Art.

1899 Studies art in Paris, where she meets Auguste Rodin, Henry Ossawa Tanner, and W. E. B. DuBois.

1907 Is awarded a gold medal for her tableaux at the Jamestown Tercentennial Exposition.

1914 Produces *The Awakening of Ethiopia* at about this time.

1968 Dies in Framingham, Massachusetts, on March 18.

See also: DuBois, W. E. B.; Fuller, Solomon; Tanner, Henry O.

Further reading: Farrington, Lisa E. *Creating Their Own Image: The History of African-American Women Artists*. New York, NY: Oxford University Press, 2005.
http://www.indiana.edu/~jah/teaching/2003_03/index.shtml
(Detailed resources on Fuller's 1907 Jamestown tableaux).

FULLER, Solomon Carter
Psychiatrist

Solomon Carter Fuller is the first recorded black psychiatrist. Before the advances in civil rights in the 1960s he was one of just a handful of African American psychiatrists. Fuller was not known just because of his color; he achieved recognition in the medical profession for his work both as a practitioner and researcher. In particular, he is remembered for his studies of degenerative brain diseases such as Alzheimer's.

Born in Africa
Fuller was born into a family of coffee planters and government officials in 1872 in Liberia in West Africa. He went to the United States in 1889 to attend Livingstone College in Salisbury, North Carolina. He completed his BA in 1893. He then started his medical training at the Long Island College Hospital in Brooklyn, New York, and completed it at Boston University Medical School, finally receiving his medical degree in 1897.

Fuller undertook his internship at Westborough State Hospital in Westborough, Massachusetts. After two years of service he became the resident pathologist at the hospital. (He would later become the head pathologist and was a member of the medical team at Westborough State until 1944.) In 1899 Fuller also started teaching at Boston University Medical School. He held various professorships in psychiatry, pathology, and neurology until 1933.

Research career
Fuller pursued postgraduate studies throughout his medical career. At first he studied at the Carnegie Laboratory in New York. Between 1904 and 1905 Fuller moved to the University of Munich, Germany. There he studied under Emil Kraepelin (1856–1926) and Alois Alzheimer (1864–1915) at the Royal Psychiatric Hospital. Kraepelin was the world leader in the study of schizophrenia and bipolar disorder at the time. Alzheimer was an expert in dementia. In 1906 he described the changes produced inside the brain brought about by a particular form of dementia. This disease is now known as Alzheimer's disease.

Challenging findings
Returning to the United States in 1906, Fuller continued to concentrate his research on the degenerative diseases of the brain. In 1912 he challenged the widely held assumption that the main cause of Alzheimer's disease was arteriosclerosis. Research findings finally proved Fuller right in 1953, the year that he died.

Richly awarded
Fuller was a member of several professional bodies, including the American Psychiatric Association (APA) of which he became a fellow in 1942. From 1923 he helped the National Medical Association recruit doctors to staff the newly created Tuskegee Veterans Hospital, a medical facility for African American war veterans in Alabama.

Fuller received several honors after his death. In 1974 the APA created the Solomon Carter Fuller Award to honor a black citizen "who has pioneered in an area which has significantly benefited the quality of life for black people." The Solomon Carter Fuller Mental Health Center in Boston was also named in his honor. In 1972, Framingham, Massachusetts, the town in which Fuller lived his final years, dedicated a public park to him and his wife, Meta. A biography by Mary Kaplan, *Solomon Carter Fuller: Where My Caravan Has Rested*, was published in 2005.

KEY DATES	
1872	Born in Monrovia, Liberia, on August 11.
1889	Moves to the United States.
1897	Qualifies as a medical doctor.
1899	Begins to teach at Boston University Medical School.
1905	Studies in Germany under Alois Alzheimer.
1939	Awarded honorary doctor of science by Livingston College.
1953	Dies in Framingham, Massachusetts, on January 16.
1974	American Psychiatric Association creates the Solomon Carter Fuller Award to honor African Americans.

See also: Fuller, Meta Warrick

Further reading: Kaplan, Mary. "Solomon Carter Fuller: A Pioneer in Alzheimer's Disease Research." *Journal of the History of the Neurosciences, 9*. London: Talyor & Francis, 2000. http://pn.psychiatryonline.org/cgi/content/full/37/17/19 (*Psychiatric News*, American Psychiatric Association).

FULLER, Thomas
Mathematician

During the 18th century a slave named Thomas Fuller amazed audiences with his feats of mental arithmetic. In 1788, for example, he was asked to calculate the number of seconds lived by a man 70 years, 17 days, and 12 hours old, and came back with the correct answer— 2,210,500,800—in only a minute and a half. What was more, his computation even took account of the number of leap years—and thus the extra days—that the man's lifetime would have encompassed.

Such mathematical skill earned Fuller the nickname the "African Calculator" and was used by abolitionists to argue against the then-prevailing viewpoint among whites that Africans were a mentally inferior race. White supremacists suggested that Fuller was not a genius but an idiot savant, an otherwise mentally subnormal individual who displayed an extraordinary ability in a limited field. (Today savants are diagnosed as autistic.) Very little is known about Fuller beyond a small number of contemporary newspaper accounts describing his mathematical feats. However, the few personal accounts attest to Fuller's high intelligence in all fields, so it is unlikely that he was a savant. It is more probable that he had learned techniques to help him perform calculations quickly.

"African Calculator"

Fuller was born and raised in West Africa in 1710. It is not known where he was born, but it was probably along the Gulf of Guinea between what is now Liberia and Benin. At age 14 he was kidnapped, endured the brutal Middle Passage across the Atlantic, and was sold as a slave to a Virginia plantation owner. In Virginia the boy was given the name Thomas Fuller. Fuller was the name of his owner.

It is likely that Fuller was already in possession of his remarkable mathematical gifts before he came to America. Many of the peoples of West Africa had efficient counting systems that they used not only for trade and account keeping but also in number games and astronomical calculations. European and Asian math systems used a base 10 system (with units, tens, hundreds, etc.) to make calculations. However, African mathematicians performed calculations by juggling very large numbers in their heads using a range of sophisticated algorithms. Most evidence for this comes from the accounts of European slavers who describe the great mental arithmetic skills of African slave traders they did business with.

Proof of equality

However and wherever he gained his skills, Fuller is likely to have put them to practical use on the plantation where he worked. His reputation as a mathematical "wizard" spread, and he seems to have attracted a stream of visitors—both admirers and unbelievers—who came to test his ability. Many witnesses dismissed Fuller and his skills, suggesting that his feats were just tricks of memory. For others, however, Fuller was living proof of the real equality that existed between black and white people.

Fuller specialized in calculating things such as the number of months, days, or weeks a person had lived. Similarly he would figure out how many feet and inches were in any large distance. He was also skilled at squaring and cubing figures, even multiplying numbers to considerably greater powers. Fuller was unable to read and write because he was never taught. However, part of his demonstrations involved challenging others to race him to do a calculation using pencil and paper. Invariably, Fuller would complete the calculation first.

Black math

In 2005 just 0.25 percent of professional mathematicians in the United States are African American—the legacy of years of underachievement because of lack of adequate education. In their efforts to combat this poor record, teachers often cite Fuller as an early example of black achievement in math. In this way they hope to encourage young black students to enjoy manipulating numbers and perhaps even take up math as a career.

Further reading: Fauvel, John, and Paulus Gerdes. "African Slave and Calculating Prodigy: Bicentenary of the Death of Thomas Fuller." *Historia Mathematica 17*, 1990. www.math.buffalo.edu/mad/ special/fuller_thomas_1710-1790.html (Mathematicians of the African Diaspora).

GABRIEL
Slave, Rebel

Also known as Gabriel Prosser, so named for his owner Thomas Prosser, Gabriel was a slave who planned a rebellion that aimed to kidnap the governor of Virginia in order to force the end of slavery in that state and create greater equality for all its citizens.

Born into slavery

Born in 1776 on Prosser's tobacco plantation in Henrico County, Virginia, Gabriel was unusual among slaves in that he was taught to read and write, and also trained as a blacksmith from the age of 10. By the time he was 20, he had become a tall, enormously strong, and intelligent individual whom other slaves looked to as a leader.

When Prosser died in 1798, his son Thomas Henry became the new plantation master. In common with many other owners of the time, he hired out his skilled slaves, a practice that allowed them to earn a small wage while paying a share to their masters. Although still exploitative, the system allowed slaves to travel and socialize with other slaves, free blacks, and white laborers. Gabriel became known throughout the area and, perhaps inspired by the slave uprising of 1791 in Haiti, began to plot for freedom.

In 1799 Gabriel was caught stealing a pig, and he assaulted a white man while resisting arrest. He escaped execution but his left hand was branded with a hot iron and he spent a month in jail. The incident appears to have pushed Gabriel toward open defiance of the slavery laws.

Betrayal and bad weather

In 1800 Gabriel and a group of mainly slaves, some free blacks, and white abolitionists began to collect weapons and recruit forces to take Richmond, Virginia's, state capital. The uprising was planned for August 30 and involved a three-pronged assault on the city, killing plantation owners and other whites who resisted. However,

▲ *More than 60 years before the Civil War ended slavery, Gabriel and a band of followers attempted to use force to have slavery abolished in Virginia.*

groups that supported abolition, such as Methodists and Quakers, were to be spared. The rebels would then kidnap Governor James Monroe (1758–1831), who later became president, and force him to agree to their demands.

The plot failed before it started. A rainstorm washed away a key bridge and made roads impassable. As the rebels rescheduled, two slaves betrayed the plot, and the state militia was sent in to quash the attack. With a reward on his head Gabriel was captured on September 24. He was hanged in Richmond shortly after, the last of some 30 slaves who were similarly executed.

See also: Slavery

Further reading: Bontemps, Arna. *Black Thunder: Gabriel's Revolt, Virginia, 1880.* Boston, MA: Beacon Press, 1992.
http://www.pbs.org/wgbh/aia/part3/3p1576.html (History of Gabriel's conspiracy).

GAINES, Clarence
Basketball Coach

Clarence "Big House" Gaines was an exceptional figure in the history of collegiate basketball. He was a man known as much for his humane and encouraging character as for the victories of his players on the court.

Early life

Gaines was born on May 21, 1923, and was raised in Paducah, Kentucky. He attended Lincoln High School, where he discovered that he was good at basketball and football. In those games he was helped by his size—at age 18 he was 6 feet 4 inches (1.93m) tall and weighed 250 pounds (113kg)—and impressive speed.

In 1941 Gaines graduated from high school. He had scholarship offers from three predominantly black colleges and decided on Morgan State University, Baltimore, Maryland, where he threw himself into both his sports and his academic studies. As well as being a star player on the university's football team and showing his capabilities in basketball, Gaines graduated from the university in 1945 with a BS in chemistry. He also gained his nickname at Morgan State. Gaines recalled that a student "saw me and just said 'You're as big as a house.' And I guess the name Big House stayed with me all these years."

Turning coach

Gaines wanted to go to dental school but could not afford the money for tuition and living expenses. Intending to earn enough money to finance his studies, he became assistant football and basketball coach at Winston-Salem State University in North Carolina. After four years he gave up football to concentrate on his first love, basketball.

The sports facilities at Winston-Salem were chronically underfunded, but by 1947—by which time he was the athletic director—Gaines had turned the team into one of the most successful in collegiate basketball.

Track record

Gaines coached the Rams at Winston-Salem for 47 years. During that time the team won 828 games, a record only surpassed by National Collegiate Athletic Association (NCAA) coach Adolph Rupp. Under Gaines's tutelage, Winston-Salem became a fast-paced, athletic force in collegiate basketball, winning the Central Intercollegiate Athletic Association (CIAA) championships 12 times. His teams won 20 or more straight games on 18 occasions.

KEY DATES	
1923	Born in Paducah, Kentucky, on May 21.
1941	Attends Morgan State University, Baltimore, where he excels at sports.
1945	Becomes a sports coach at Winston-Salem State University, North Carolina.
1967	Receives the NCAA College Division Basketball Coach of the Year Award.
1993	Retires from coaching.
2005	Dies in Winston-Salem, North Carolina, on April 18.

In 1950 Gaines earned an MA in physical education from Columbia University, New York, and married Clara Berry. They had two children.

In 1967, Gaines's finest season, the Rams' 31–1 win made Winston-Salem the first predominantly black school to win an NCAA basketball title. Gaines was awarded the NCAA College Division Basketball Coach of the Year Award, the first African American to receive that honor. Gaines also was named the CIAA Basketball Coach of the Year five times (1961, 1963, 1970, 1975, 1980). Other awards included CIAA Outstanding Tournament Coach (1957, 1960, 1961, 1963, 1966, 1970, 1972, 1979), and the Indiana Sports Lifetime Achievement Award (1990).

Gaines's official positions included CIAA president (1970–1974) and serving as a member of the U.S. Olympic Committee (1973–1976). Gaines retired in 1993, having been enshrined in eight halls of fame for his service to collegiate sport. He died in 2005 of complications from a stroke.

On his death North Carolina senator Richard Burr said of Gaines, he "was more than a coach. He was a community leader, an educator, a mentor and a father figure. His most important achievement was the near 80 percent graduation rate of his student athletes—a legacy that all college coaches should look to emulate."

Further reading: Gaines, Clarence, and Clint Johnson. *They Call Me Big House*. Winston-Salem, NC: John F. Blair Publisher, 2004.

http://www.hoophall.com/halloffamers/Gaines.htm (Biography and statistics).

GAINES, Ernest J.
Writer

Ernest Gaines's novels evoke the rural community of southern Louisiana where he was raised. While his work is not autobiographical, it contains elements and characters from his own country upbringing.

Early life

Gaines was born in 1933 in the old slave quarters of the Riverlake Plantation near Oscar, Louisiana. The eldest of nine children, he was largely raised by his disabled great aunt after his parents separated. His schooling began in a one-room church and was followed by three years at St. Augustine, a Catholic school for African Americans.

Unable to complete his education in rural Louisiana because he was an African American, Gaines joined his mother in Vallejo, California, when he was 15. Homesick for Louisiana, he spent many hours in the local library and began writing. On graduation from high school he joined the Army before enrolling at San Francisco State College, where he majored in English.

On his graduation in 1957 he won a creative writing fellowship to Stanford University. While there he decided to pursue a career as a writer. His first novel, *Catherine Carmier*, was published in 1964.

The Autobiography of Miss Jane Pittman, one of Gaines's most successful novels, was published in 1971 while he was writer in residence at Denison University in Granville, Ohio. It tells the story of a 110-year-old woman whose life spans the Civil War to the civil rights movement. The novel made Gaines's reputation and was turned into a television movie in 1974.

▲ *Ernest Gaines at his birthplace on the Riverlake Plantation near the False River, Louisiana.*

Recognition

Gaines received a Guggenheim Fellowship between 1973 and 1974, and in 1981 he joined Southwestern Louisiana State University at Lafayette as a visiting professor of creative writing. In 1983 he was made writer-in-residence at the university, a position he holds today.

During the 1980s Gaines received numerous awards in recognition of his literary achievements. Another novel, *A Gathering of Old Men* (1983), was made into a movie. Gaines gained an even wider audience in 1997 when Oprah Winfrey chose *A Lesson before Dying* (1993) for her book club. The novel had already won the National Book Critics Circle Award in 1994 for best book.

Gaines's work explores the rural world of ordinary African Americans in the South. In so doing, it creates a microcosm that reflects the experiences of a much wider community that reaches far beyond Louisiana.

See also: Winfrey, Oprah

Further reading: Carmean, Karen. *Ernest J. Gaines: A Critical Companion*. Westport, CT: Greenwood Press, 1998.
http://aalbc.com/authors/ernest.htm (African American Literature Book Club page on Gaines).

KEY DATES	
1933	Born near Oscar, Louisiana, on January 16.
1948	Moves to Vallejo, California.
1957	Graduates from San Francisco State College.
1959	Graduates from the creative writing program at Stanford University.
1964	Publishes first novel, *Catherine Carmier*.
1983	Becomes writer in residence at Southwestern Louisiana State University.
1997	*A Lesson before Dying* (1993) is picked for Oprah Winfrey's book club.

GAITHER, Jake
Football Coach

Jake Gaither was one of the most successful coaches in the history of college football. Gaither is most remembered for introducing the split-line T-formation in 1963, which was immediately imitated by almost every other football coach.

Early life

Alonzo Smith Gaither was born in 1903 in Dayton, Tennessee. The son of a preacher, in his youth Jake, as he became known, thought that he would become a minister like his father. However, he later decided to become a lawyer. His mother suggested the career because her son was "always running at the mouth."

While attending Knoxville College, Gaither played football. However, just as he was completing his master's degree at Ohio State University, his father died. Gaither opted to abandon any further academic studies and took a job in order to support his mother.

When the United States entered World War II (1939–1945) in 1941, Gaither joined the Army. In 1942 he was diagnosed with brain cancer and was lucky to survive.

▼ *Jake Gaither (right) and Paul "Bear" Bryant (left) are awarded Kodak Coach of the Year awards by Gerald Zarow, vice president of Kodak, in 1961.*

KEY DATES

1903	Born in Dayton, Tennessee, on April 11.
1927	Graduates from Knoxville College.
1937	Completes MA at Ohio State University.
1945	Appointed head football coach at Florida A&M College.
1962	Voted Small College Coach of the Year.
1994	Dies in Tallahassee, Florida, on February 18.

Football career

In 1945 Gaither was appointed head football coach at Florida Agricultural and Mechanical College in Tallahassee (now FAMU). The job was by no means sought after—there were no other applicants—but Gaither soon showed what could be done.

He quickly turned the college team, the Rattlers, into a major force in the black college league. Over the next 25 seasons under his leadership Florida A&M won six national black college titles and 20 Southern Intercollegiate Athletic Conference championships. In his final season Gaither masterminded his team's historic 34–28 victory over the University of Tampa in the South's first interracial college game.

By the time Gaither retired from coaching at the end of his 25th season in 1969 his career record was 203 wins, 36 losses, and four ties, the highest winning percentage (.844) of anyone who has coached more than 13 seasons of college football.

Gaither was a charismatic and inspirational coach. On at least one occasion he hid an onion up his sleeve to fool his players into believing that their performance had reduced him to tears. On the rare occasions when the Rattlers lost, their coach did not require onions to show his emotions. His stated selection criteria were simple— "I like my boys to be agile, mobile, and hostile"—but that was no more than a soundbite. He was in fact a deep thinker and a great football innovator.

Further reading: Curry, George E. *Jake Gaither: America's Most Famous Black Coach*. New York, NY: Dodd Mead, 1977.
http://www.theledger.com/static/top50/pages/gaither.html
(Top 50 Floridians of the 20th century).

GAMBLE, Kenny
Producer, Songwriter

Grammy-winning producer and songwriter Kenny Gamble is probably most famous for his partnership with Leon Huff. Together the two men created one of the most distinctive musical styles of the 1970s, the Philly Soul Sound.

Making an impression

Born in Philadelphia, Pennsylvania, on August 11, 1943, Gamble was interested in music from an early age. He began singing in groups and worked on several songs, including Danny & the Juniors' hit "At the Hop." In 1962 he met Leon Huff while working as a background singer and lyricist at Philadelphia's Schubert Theater. The two men played with the group the Romeos. They worked well together and in 1964 produced their first Gamble/Huff song, "The 81," recorded by Candy and the Kisses. Three years later Gamble and Huff had their first Top Five hit with the Soul Survivors' "Expressway to Your Heart."

After working with several independent labels, including Atlantic Records, Gamble decided to set up his own company, Gamble Records, in 1967. Two years later he cofounded Neptune Records with Huff. The highly successful independent label Chess Records, owned by Phil and Leo Chess, distributed Neptune's records. The company had a string of hits, including Jerry Butler's "Only the Strong Survive." In 1970 the company changed its name to Philadelphia International Records (PIR), backed by Columbia. Within the first nine months of business PIR sold around 10 million records; its hits included Billy Paul's "Me and Mrs. Jones."

▲ *Kenny Gamble (left) and Leon Huff helped establish the careers of the O'Jays, among others.*

Gamble and Huff's sound included sweeping strings, moody horns, and insistent drum rhythms, and became the definitive soul sound of the early 1970s. The style later influenced disco in the second half of the 1970s. Most of the PIR tracks were recorded at the Sigma Sound Studios in Philadelphia with the help of a group of session musicians, including Huff himself on keyboards and Don Renaldo on strings and horns. In 1975 the label was involved in the payola scandal, when it was accused of offering bribes in exchange for radio airplay: Gamble was fined, but Huff was acquitted.

Gamble also founded Universal Companies, a nonprofit organization that developed programs to help the local community, including adult education, job training, and housing for low- and moderate-income families in Philadelphia. Gamble has received many awards: In 1999 he and Huff received a Grammy for Lifetime Achievement.

KEY DATES

1943   Born in Philadelphia, Pennsylvania, on August 11.

1962   Begins working with Leon Huff while a member of the Romeos.

1970   Launches Philadelphia International Records with Huff.

1979   Has major hit with "Ain't No Stoppin' Us Now."

1989   Wins Grammy for best R&B song, "If You Don't Know Me by Now," a No. 1 for the British band Simply Red.

1999   Receives (with Huff) a Grammy for Lifetime Achievement.

See also: Huff, Leon

Further reading: http://www.bsnpubs.com/columbia/gamble.html (Looks at Gamble-Huff discography in detail).

GARNER, Erroll
Musician

Erroll Louis Garner's individual style of play earned him a special place among jazz pianists. His technique involved producing continuous rhythmical chords with the left hand and then superimposing free melodic interpretations with the right. This stood outside the traditions of jazz piano at the time, and his virtuosity has enabled him to remain unique. He was one of the few jazz pianists to be acclaimed by a mainstream audience. He was also the first jazz musician to be signed by the classical impresario Sol Hurok (1888–1974).

Musical roots
Garner was born into a musical family in 1921. Both his parents were accomplished singers, and his brother Linton (1915–2003) was also to become a notable jazz pianist.

▼ *Erroll Garner taught himself the piano. His distinctive swing style grew from listening to his mother's ragtime records.*

Garner, however, was a prodigy. From age two he played on the piano the songs he heard on his mother's Victrola record player. He received formal piano lessons from age six but never learned to read music. At age 10 Garner played on Radio KQV Pittsburgh as a member of the Kan-D-Kids.

Professional career
Garner moved to New York in 1944, where he consolidated his career with his own trio performing in nightclubs. By the 1950s he was established on the jazz scene. Two recitals in 1950, at the Cleveland Music Hall and the New York Town Hall, established him as a solo player. The various recordings, television appearances, and national and overseas engagements that followed eventually consumed his career as a nightclub performer.

Garner did not compose in a methodical manner, but his scores for film and Broadway shows were written down by arrangers. Garner's piano solos, *Erroll Garner Piano Solo*, were published by M. Feldman; *The Erroll Garner Songbook*, compiled by Sy Johnson (1977), and *The Erroll Garner Anthology* are still available. His most famous song, "Misty" (1955), has been published as a separate score for solo piano (1964, 1984) and for orchestra (1959). It was used in Clint Eastwood's film *Play Misty for Me* in 1971. Garner rerecorded the song for the film, which won Eastwood an Oscar for best director. A number of new compilations have been issued regularly since Garner's death in 1977. Linton Garner also composed *I Never Said Goodbye*, an eight-movement tribute to his brother. A documentary, *Linton Garner: I Never Said Goodbye*, was screened in 2002.

KEY DATES	
1921	Born in Pittsburgh, Pennsylvania, on June 15.
1944	Moves to New York.
1950	Plays solo concert at Cleveland Music Hall.
1977	Dies in Los Angeles, California, on January 2.

Further reading: Doran, James M. *Erroll Garner: The Most Happy Piano*. Mettuchen, NJ: Scarecrow Press, 1985.
http://www.erroll-garner-archives.com (Erroll Garner Archives).

GARNER, Margaret
Slave

Margaret Garner was a slave mother who tried to kill her children, and succeeding in killing one, rather than see them returned to slavery when their attempted escape failed.

A slave's life

Margaret was born on the Maplewood plantation of John Pollard Gaines in Kentucky in 1833. In her early years she led a relatively stable life as a domestic servant. In 1949 ownership of Maplewood passed to Gaines's younger brother, Archibald Kinkead Gaines. The new owner is believed to have brought abuse and hardship to Margaret's life. That same year Margaret married Robert Garner, a fellow slave from a neighboring estate. Their first child Thomas was born in 1850, although the family was rarely able to be together. By 1856 Garner had four children and was pregnant with a fifth.

The escape

On the night of January 27, 1856, the Garner family, together with Robert's parents, escaped across the frozen Ohio River to the free state of Ohio. When they were discovered by pursuers, Margaret killed her two-year old daughter and attempted to kill her other children and herself but was overpowered.

The trial

Garner's trial lasted for two weeks and involved a legal debate on whether she should be tried for "murder," as argued by abolitionists, or "destruction of property," as argued by slave masters. The latter view eventually prevailed and the family was returned to slavery. Some reports say that Margaret drowned in a shipwreck on her way back to slavery; others report that she died of typhoid two years after reentering slavery.

Repercussions

Margaret Garner's story fueled the debate about slavery. For abolitionists the terrible act had been brought about by the horrors of slavery; for slave masters, however, it was proof that black slaves were subhuman. In the years that followed, the story appeared in numerous poems, essays, and novels. In 1867 Thomas Satterwhite Noble painted Margaret as the *Modern Medea*, drawing parallels with an ancient Greek myth about a mother who killed her children. Garner was then forgotten until her story was revived by Toni Morrison in her novel *Beloved* (1987). The opera *Margaret Garner* by composer Richard Danielpour, with a libretto by Morrison, premiered in Detroit in 2005.

▼ *This engraving based on Thomas Satterwhite Noble's 1867 painting* **Modern Medea** *shows Margaret Garner facing her pursuers over the dead and unconscious bodies of her children.*

KEY DATES	
1833	Born in Boone County, Kentucky, on June 4.
1849	Changes ownership together with the estate.
1856	Attempts to escape; stands trial for "destruction of property" for the murder of her daughter.
1858	Dies at about this time.

See also: Morrison, Toni; Slavery

Further reading: Weisenburger, Steven. *Modern Medea: A Family Story of Slavery and Child-Murder from the Old South.* New York, NY: Hill and Wang, 1998.
http://www.rootsweb.com/~kypendle/slavemargaretgarner.htm (Margaret Garner resources with links).

GARNET, Henry Highland
Abolitionist, Minister

Henry Highland Garnet was a significant abolitionist in the United States. He was born into slavery in 1815 in New Market, Maryland, to George and Henrietta "Henny" Trusty. George Trusty was the son of a West African prince who had been captured in combat. In 1824 the Trustys were allowed to attend a family funeral: They never returned. After briefly staying in New Hope, Pennsylvania, the family moved to New York in 1825, where George Trusty gave his family new first names and the Trustys became the Garnets.

KEY DATES	
1815	Born in New Market, Maryland, on December 23.
1824	Escapes with his family from slavery.
1840	Has leg amputated; is a founding member of American and Foreign Anti-Slavery Society;
1881	Becomes minister to Liberia.
1882	Dies in Monrovia, Liberia, on February 12.

Radical tendencies

While attending the African Free School Garnet developed an interest in abolitionist politics. Garnet's schoolmates were a talented group: they included Alexander Crummell and Samuel R. Ward who went on to become prominent abolitionists; James McCune Smith (1813–1865), the first African American doctor; actor Ira Aldridge; and Charles Reason, the first black college professor.

In 1828 Garnet went to sea for a year. On his return from a voyage he discovered that his family had gone into hiding from slave hunters. Garnet went to work on a farm on Long Island, New York, where he seriously injured his

▼ *Henry Highland Garnet, photographed in about 1881, just before he went to Liberia.*

leg in an accident two years later. In 1835 Garnet and two school friends, including Crummell, traveled to the Noyes Academy in Canaan, New Hampshire, a college recently opened to African Americans. Shortly afterward a group of local people opposed to the education of blacks destroyed the school building. They then set upon the house where the 14 black students were staying. According to Crummell, Garnet saved the boys' lives by firing a warning shot over the mob's heads. The boys fled Canaan and enrolled in Oneida Institute in New York.

By 1840 when he graduated, Garnet had built up a formidable reputation as an abolitionist speaker. In that same year Garnet had to have his crippled leg amputated, but this did not stop him from becoming a founding member of the American and Foreign Anti-Slavery Society. Three years later Garnet was ordained a minister and became pastor of the Liberty Street Presbyterian Church in Troy, New York, a position that he held for five years. A powerful orator, Garnet advocated active resistance to slavery and argued for blacks to form their own colonies abroad. In 1865 he was the first black person to deliver a speech before the House of Representatives. In the 1870s he continued campaigning for equal rights and went to work at the Shiloh Presbyterian Church, New York. In 1881 Garnet was given a diplomatic post in Liberia, which he took up on December 28. He died on February 12, 1882.

See also: Aldridge, Ira; Crummell, Alexander; Reason, Charles; Slavery; Ward, Samuel R.

Further reading: Pasternak, Martin B. *Rise Now and Fly to Arms: The Life of Henry Highland Garnet.* New York, NY: Garland Publishing, 1995.
http://www.pbs.org/wgbh/aia/part4/4p1537.html (Biography).

GARVEY, Amy Ashwood
Activist

Amy Ashwood Garvey was an activist who became the first wife of Marcus Garvey, founder of the Universal Negro Improvement Association (UNIA). Although her association with Garvey quickly ended, she continued to be a strong voice for pan-Africanism—the promotion of unity among people of African descent—all her life.

Amy Ashwood was born in 1897 in Jamaica but lived in Panama during her childhood. She returned to Jamaica to study at Westwood High School in Trelawny. At age 17 Ashwood met Garvey at a debate. When he set up the UNIA in 1914–1915, she became intensely involved, organizing its regular activities and setting up a Ladies Auxiliary Wing. She also planned to start an industrial school. The UNIA had its early offices in a house rented by the Ashwoods.

Ashwood and Garvey were secretly engaged in 1916, and despite resistance from her parents, Ashwood followed Garvey to the United States in 1918. There she became general secretary of the UNIA and a director of the UNIA's

▼ *Amy Ashwood Garvey was an enthusiastic advocate of pan-Africanism all her life.*

Black Star Line shipping company. Ashwood also helped establish the *Negro World*, UNIA's newsletter. She married Garvey in 1919 but their relationship soon dissolved. They were officially divorced in 1922.

Ashwood Garvey continued an active political life both in Jamaica and abroad. In 1924 she helped found the Nigerian Progress Union, which later became the West African Student's Union, an organization to further the interests of Africans abroad. Between 1935 and 1938 Ashwood Garvey owned a restaurant in London, England, which served as a meeting place for pan-Africanists. She also made friends with British suffragists such as Sylvia Pankhurst and fought for equal employment opportunities for Jamaican women in the United States and Britain.

In 1937 Ashwood Garvey was a founding member of the International African Service Bureau, a network that coordinated correspondence between African and Caribbean nationalists, trade unionists, editors, and intellectuals. In 1944 she became president of the Jag-Smith Party in Jamaica and their candidate to the Jamaican House of Representatives. She organized the Fifth pan-African Congress of 1945, which was seen as a high-water mark for Pan-Africanism. Ashwood Garvey died in 1969.

KEY DATES	
1897	Born in Port Antonio, Jamaica, on October 28.
1918	Moves to the United States; becomes general secretary of the UNIA.
1919	Marries Marcus Garvey.
1922	Divorces Garvey.
1937	Cofounds International African Service Bureau.
1945	Organizes Fifth Pan-African Congress.
1969	Dies.

See also: Garvey, Amy Jacques; Garvey, Marcus

Further reading: Martin, Tony. *Amy Ashwood Garvey: Pan-Africanist, Feminist and Wife No. 1*. Dover, MA: Majority Press, 1998
www.aaregistry.com/african_american/1954/
Amy_Garvey_businesswoman_and_frontline_activist
(Biography).

GARVEY, Amy Jacques
Feminist, Journalist

Amy Jacques Garvey, the second wife of Marcus Garvey, founder of the Universal Negro Improvement Association (UNIA), gained recognition in her own right as a journalist, feminist, and leading figure of the pan-African movement to unite people of African descent.

Amy Euphemia Jacques was born in Kingston, Jamaica, on December 31, 1896, to Samuel and Charlotte Jacques. Her parents were middle-class, educated, and propertied. Jacques graduated from the Wolmers' Girl's High School and moved to the United States in 1917 to study to become a teacher.

Jacques's roommate was Amy Ashwood Garvey, who introduced Jacques to the UNIA and to her husband, Marcus. Jacques soon became involved in the UNIA and it was not long before she became Garvey's personal secretary. When Garvey and Ashwood divorced in 1922, Jacques became Garvey's traveling companion and later his wife. The Garveys had two sons.

▼ *Amy Jacques Garvey's father brought her up to be self-confident and high-achieving.*

In 1923 Marcus Garvey was imprisoned on charges of fraud in connection with his shipping line. This thrust Jacques into the forefront of the UNIA movement and his defense. Between 1923 and 1925, to raise funds, she edited and published two volumes of her husband's speeches and writing as the *Philosophy and Opinions of Marcus Garvey*. In 1924 she became associate editor of the *Negro World*, UNIA's newsletter. Jacques held strong feminist ideas and wrote a column titled "Our Women and What They Think."

When Garvey was released from prison and deported to Jamaica in 1927, Jacques went with him. She continued to work for the UNIA as contributing editor of *Negro World*.

Garvey died in 1940, but his death did not end Jacques's link with the pan-African movement. She contributed to the *African*, a Harlem-based journal, in the 1940s and founded the African Study Circle in Jamaica. In 1944 Jacques wrote "A Memorandum Correlative of Africa, West Indies and the Americas," a submission to the representatives of the United Nations for the consideration of an African Freedom Charter. She also published *Garvey and Garveyism* (1963), *Black Power in America,* and *The Impact of Garvey in Africa and Jamaica* (1968). Jacques was awarded the Musgrave Medal by the Institute of Jamaica in 1971. She died on July 25, 1973.

KEY DATES	
1896	Born in Kingston, Jamaica, on December 31.
1917	Moves to the United States.
1922	Marries Marcus Garvey.
1944	Publishes "A Memorandum Correlative."
1963	Publishes *Garvey and Garveyism*.
1971	Awarded the Musgrave Medal.
1973	Dies in Jamaica on July 25.

See also: Garvey, Amy Ashwood; Garvey Marcus

Further reading: Taylor, Ula Yvette. *The Veiled Garvey; The Life and Times of Amy Jacques Garvey*. Chapel Hill, NC: University of North Carolina Press, 2002.
http://www.marcusgarvey.com/wmview.php?ArtID=535 (Biography).

GARVEY, Marcus
Political Leader

Black Nationalist leader, publisher, and entrepreneur Marcus Garvey is best known for his Back to Africa movement. One of the most eloquent orators in African American history, he motivated blacks to return to Africa. He also argued that black people should establish an independent economy within the United States, practice black capitalism, live in a separate black society, and be free from racial oppression.

His Universal Negro Improvement Association (UNIA) was the first African American movement to appeal to impoverished blacks. Garvey promoted the idea that black people were capable of anything they put their minds to. His rallying cry was "Up you mighty race. You can accomplish what you will."

Early life
Mosiah Garvey, Jr., was born in 1887 to Marcus Mosiah Garvey, a mason, and Sarah Jane Richards, a domestic worker, in St. Ann's Bay, Jamaica, West Indies. While still in school Garvey began working as an apprentice at his godfather's printing business in St. Ann's Bay. At age 14 he quit school. By age 16 he had published his first newspaper, called *Garvey's Watchman*. Only three issues were published.

Between 1910 and 1912 Garvey traveled around Central America, writing and editing in Port Limon, Costa Rica, and in Colon, Panama. He then returned to Jamaica before moving to London, England, to pursue higher education at Birkbeck College from 1912 to 1914. In the meantime he traveled extensively in Europe and published several articles on the future of Africans living in the Americas. Garvey also wrote Booker T. Washington, founder of Tuskegee Institute, asking for support. Washington invited Garvey to visit him in Tuskegee. However, Washington died shortly before Garvey arrived.

Political career
In 1914 Garvey returned to Jamaica and met Amy Ashwood, who would become a playwright, feminist, and lecturer. Together, Garvey and Ashwood founded the Universal Negro Improvement and Conservation Association and African Communities League.

In 1916 Garvey moved to New York and began working as a printer. He developed a following by speaking on street corners. In May Garvey held a public meeting in a

▲ *Rastafarians believe that Marcus Garvey was the reincarnation of John the Baptist because he predicted the 1930 coronation of Haile Sellassie in Ethiopia.*

church that ended badly when he fell off the stage. Undeterred, Garvey set off a few weeks later on a grueling speaking tour of 38 states.

In 1917 Garvey opened the New York branch of his organization, now called the Universal Negro Improvement Association (UNIA). In 1918 Ashwood joined Garvey in New York, against the wishes of her parents. The UNIA published the first issue of its official newspaper the *Negro World*. The publication soon fell afoul of the colonial powers in Central America and the West Indies.

By 1919 the UNIA had two million members. That same year Garvey established a shipping company, the Black Star Line, whose goal was to transport African Americans to Africa and to establish mutually beneficial trade links between Africans and African Americans. He also set up the

INFLUENCES AND INSPIRATION

During the Great Depression a young man of 22 met Marcus Garvey in Detroit, Michigan. Before that he had already traveled to Chicago to hear one of Garvey's lectures about the redemption of Africa and the importance of racial identity and pride. The man, Elijah Poole, had recently lost his job at the Cherokee Brick Company in Macon, Georgia, and yearned to hear something that would give more meaning to his life. Poole was influenced by Garvey's hopeful and encouraging speech, as were other African Americans like historian and activist John Henrik Clarke. Soon after his encounter with Garvey, Elijah Poole made a decision to improve the plight of his people. He later renamed himself the Honorable Elijah Muhammad and took control of the Nation of Islam, which influenced Malcolm X, Muhammad Ali, and many others.

KEY DATES

1887	Born in St. Ann's Bay, Jamaica, on August 17.
1914	Founds UNIA.
1919	Opens Black Star Line shipping company.
1920	Announces Liberian colonization plan.
1927	Is deported from the United States.
1940	Dies in London on June 10.

Negro Factories Corporation and a chain of restaurants, grocery stores, laundries, a hotel, and a printing press. In about 1917 Garvey attracted the attention of the Justice Department and its head, J. Edgar Hoover (1895–1972), later to become director of the FBI. Referring to Garvey as a "notorious negro agitator," Hoover suggested that his irregular business dealings might provide a means by which to deport him.

Garvey and Ashwood married on Christmas Day 1919. By 1920 Garvey had established branches of the UNIA throughout northern U.S. cities, as well as in South and Central America, Africa, Europe, and Australia.

Back to Africa

In 1920 Garvey announced the Liberian Colonization Plan. The UNIA had negotiated with the government of Liberia for land to settle 20,000 families from the United States, the Caribbean, and South and Central America. The new arrivals would pay off all of Liberia's debt, which was in excess of $2 million, and the UNIA's headquarters would move to the capital, Monrovia. The Liberian government agreed, but then the U.S. government convinced the Monrovian authorities to change their mind before the settlers arrived. Nevertheless, the UNIA sent its first delegation to Liberia in 1921. The Black Star Line delivered just two boatloads of African Americans to Liberia before poor business management and criminal investigations by the U.S. authorities forced it to shut down operations in 1922. About 5 percent of Liberia's modern population is descended from the African Americans and West Indians who arrived in those years.

Decline

As Garvey's other businesses failed, so did his marriage to Ashwood. Amy Jacques, Garvey's secretary who had been the maid of honor at his first wedding, became Garvey's second wife in 1922. Jacques was herself a prolific writer and published articles in the *Negro World* and the *African*. The couple had two children, Marcus Mosiah Garvey III (1931–) and Julius Winston Garvey (1933–). Both were born in Jamaica but later became U.S. residents.

In 1922 James Eason formed the rival Universal Negro Alliance. At the beginning of 1923 Eason was shot, dying a few days later. Two of Garvey's associates were arrested for the murder. A matter of weeks later the UNIA closed after failing to pay rent. In May Garvey was tried for mail fraud in the illegal sale of Black Star Line stock. He was sentenced to five years in jail but instead he was deported to Jamaica in 1927. In 1934 a bankrupt Garvey moved to London, England. He died of brain hemorrhage in 1940.

See also: Ali, Muhammad; Clarke, John Henrik; Garvey, Amy Ashwood; Garvey, Amy Jacques; Malcolm X; Muhammad, Elijah; Political Movements; Washington, Booker T.

Further reading: Caravantes, Peggy. *Marcus Garvey: Black Nationalist*. Greensboro, NC: Morgan Reynolds Pub., 2004. Jimson, Linda, S. (ed.). *Marcus Garvey, Man of Vision and Action: His Life, Ideology, and Work*. Indianapolis, IN: LifeStar Enterprises, 1995.
http://www.pbs.org/wgbh/amex/garvey/timeline/index.html (Timeline of Garvey's life).

GASTON, A. G.
Businessman

Arthur George "A. G." Gaston was a millionaire businessman who used much of his wealth in philanthropy and supporting the civil rights movement.

The grandson of slaves, A. G. Gaston was born in 1892 in Alabama. An only child, he left school after the 10th grade and served in the Army in World War I (1914–1918). At the end of the hostilities Gaston returned to Alabama and took a series of odd jobs. In 1923 he used his savings of $5,000 to found the Booker T. Washington Insurance Company in Birmingham, Alabama. The firm began by selling insurance policies to steelworkers but soon branched out to provide other forms of coverage.

▼ *A. G. Gaston inspects the damage caused after his home in Birmingham, Alabama, was set on fire by white supremacists in 1963.*

Making opportunities

One successful business venture led to another. Gaston became a partner in the Smith and Gaston Funeral Home. He then founded the Booker T. Washington Business College, a vocational training institution for African Americans. This established a pattern that was repeated throughout Gaston's long life. First, he would either create or acquire various companies, including at different times the Citizen's Federal Savings Bank, a motel, a construction firm, two cemeteries, and two radio stations. He would then redirect some of the profits into philanthropic endeavors that would benefit the needy, especially socially disadvantaged African Americans. Among Gaston's achievements in this area were a seniors' home and the A. G. Gaston Boys Club (which now also includes girls) in Birmingham, Alabama. He was also a leading member of the African Methodist Episcopal Church.

In the 1960s Gaston became active in the civil rights movement. Most of his work was done behind the scenes, but in 1963 he famously posted a $5,000 bail bond for Martin Luther King, Jr., after the campaigner had been jailed for marching to protest segregation.

In 1987 Gaston sold his nine corporations to his 350 employees for $3.4 million, about one-tenth of their true value. He then took a job in what had been his own bank and kept working until six months before his death, at age 104

KEY DATES	
1892	Born in Demopolis, Alabama, on July 4.
1923	Founds Booker T. Washington Insurance Company.
1963	Posts bail for Martin Luther King, Jr.
1987	Sells all his businesses to his staff.
1996	Dies in Demopolis, Alabama, on January 19.

See also: King, Martin Luther, Jr.; Washington, Booker T.

Further reading: Jenkins, Carol, and Elizabeth Gardner Hines. *Black Titan: A. G. Gaston and the Making of a Black American Millionaire.* New York, NY: One World, 2004.
http://www.anb.org/articles/10/10-02211.html (Biography).

GATES, Henry Louis, Jr.
Academic, Writer

Henry Louis "Skip" Gates, Jr., is one of the most prominent academics and cultural critics in the country. In 1991 he became the W. E. B. DuBois Professor of Humanities in the department of African American studies at Harvard University. His authoritative research has revitalized the field of African American history and literature, and brought it into the mainstream.

Gates was born in 1950 in Keyser, West Virginia. His father was a factory worker and janitor, and his mother a cleaner. He graduated from Yale University in 1973 and began to study at Clare College, Cambridge, England. At Cambridge Gates met the Nobel-prize-winning Nigerian playwright Wole Soyinka (1934–), who influenced his interest in African culture. In 1979 Gates became the first

▼ *Henry Louis Gates, Jr., has been voted one of the 25 most influential Americans by* **Time** *magazine.*

KEY DATES	
1950	Born in Keyser, West Virginia, on September 16.
1973	Graduates from Yale University.
1979	Earns PhD from Clare College, Cambridge.
1991	Becomes W. E. B. DuBois Professor at Harvard.
1997	Wins *Time* magazine's Influential American Award.
2004	Publishes *America behind the Color Line*.

African American to obtain a PhD from Cambridge. Since then Gates has held teaching positions at Yale, Cornell, Duke, and Harvard universities.

Gates is also a prolific writer and editor. In 1983 his rediscovery and republication of Harriet E. Wilson's *Our Nig* (1859), the first novel by an African American, which had previously been credited to a white man, brought him great acclaim. His interest in women writers of that time led him to edit the 30-volume *Oxford-Schomburg Library of Nineteenth Century Black Women Writers* (1988). In 2001 he published another rediscovered work, the *Bondwoman's Narrative* (1850) by Hannah Crafts, a fugitive slave.

In addition to major projects such as *Encarta Africana* (with K. Anthony Appiah, 1999), *The African American Century: How Black Americans Have Shaped Our Century* (with Cornel West, 2000), and the 1999 PBS documentary *Wonders of the African World*, which he wrote and presented, Gates has developed a critical approach to black literary works that is both influential and controversial. In his work *The Signifying Monkey: Towards a Theory of Afro-American Literary Criticism*, which won the 1989 American Book Award, Gates argued that black writing should not be judged by Western culture and standards. Gates has received numerous awards and honorary degrees for his work on African American culture.

See also: Appiah, Anthony; DuBois, W. E. B.; West, Cornel; Wilson, Harriet E. Adams

Further reading: Gates, Henry Louis, Jr. *Colored People: A Memoir.* New York, NY: Vintage, 1995.
http://www.galegroup.com/free_resources/bhm/bio/gates_h.htm (Biography).

GAYE, Marvin
Singer

One of the most famous soul singers of the 20th century, Marvin Gaye influenced many musicians through such songs as "I Heard It through the Grapevine," "What's Going On?" and "Sexual Healing."

Early life

Marvin Pentz Gay, Jr., was born in 1939 in Washington, D.C. Like most black singers before him, Gaye (as he would later call himself) got his singing start in the church. His family followed the strict religious doctrine of a small branch of the Pentecostal Church, which observed the Sabbath on Saturday. The family lived by many rules, including no television. This made Marvin (the eldest son) and his siblings odd in the eyes of the children in the neighborhood, and Marvin grew into a shy but rebellious youngster. Marvin, Sr., monitored the Gaye children closely and whipped them to keep them in line. Marvin sought escape through listening to the music on the radio and inside his own head, often telling his younger brother Frankie that he heard music.

Marvin sang with his friends in a group called the D. C. Tones while attending Cardoza High School. After graduating from high school, Gaye enrolled in the Air Force for a brief period. He then joined a singing group called the Marquees. Through the connections of Elias McDaniel, better known as bluesman Bo Diddley, the Marquees recorded a couple of unremarkable songs at OKeh Records in September 1957. Their debut failed to make an impression, and Gaye was forced take nonsinging work. Gaye then met Harvey Fuqua, a record promoter who was looking to re-form his "doo-wop" swing group the Moonglows. The Marquees auditioned for Fuqua in Chicago and shortly thereafter became known as Harvey and the Moonglows.

Joining Motown

The Moonglows toured around small venues, many in the segregated South. They experienced much discrimination, often forced to sleep and eat in their cars because whites would not provide them with accommodations. In 1959 the Moonglows encountered the Gordy family in Detroit—the Motor City. Berry Gordy, Jr., was a songwriter who also ran a rhythm-and-blues (R&B) record label. He was so impressed with Gaye that he bought 50 percent of his contract from Fuqua. At the end of that same year Gordy set up the legendary Motown Records. Gaye was signed as one of the label's first artists, along with the likes of Smokey Robinson and Jackie Wilson (1934–1984).

In the beginning Gordy was uncertain of how to market his new talent, so he started Gaye out singing backup and playing drums for several artists. Gaye's desire to sing romantic ballads prevailed, and he recorded his first album, *The Soulful Moods of Marvin Gaye*, in 1961. It was poorly received, and Gordy saw the failed recording as proof that the romantic content was not the way to go. Gaye was discouraged by what he saw as Motown's authoritarian and bureaucratic ways. He decided to work together with Gordy and another writer on a song with a more popular feel. The result was "Stubborn Kind of Fellow" in 1962; it became Gaye's first Top 10 R&B hit.

In the early days Gaye toured with other Motown hit makers, including the Vandellas, the Miracles, the Supremes, and Stevie Wonder. Nervous and self-conscious in live performance, he appeared very uncomfortable on stage. However, with each performance he became more at ease, eventually becoming a master at whipping his audience into a frenzy of excitement. He never completely overcame his stage fright and would later use drugs at

▼ *Marvin Gaye produced 26 albums in his 25-year career and sang on 18 Top 10 singles.*

As a young man, and throughout his career, Marvin Gaye admired the great "crooners," such as Nat King Cole, Sammy Davis, Jr., Frank Sinatra, and Jessie Belvin. He wanted to become known as a great balladeer. He was mentored and inspired by fellow Motown star Smokey Robinson and was inspired artistically by Sam Cooke. Gaye was also helped to develop his stage performances by Stevie Wonder early in his career. Many hip-hop and modern soul artists have sampled Gaye. Similarities are also easily seen in the work of modern artists such as D'Angelo and R. Kelly.

times to ease the anxiety. The problems caused by both the anxiety and the drug use would get worse toward the end of his life.

With several more hit singles and a promising future career, Gaye married Anna Gordy, Berry's sister, bought his parents a house in Washington, D.C., and had his first child, Marvin III. Berry Gordy paired Gaye with several female singers, but his collaboration with Tammi Terrell (1945–1970) was to prove his most successful. While Gaye had musical chemistry with all of his singing partners, he had a particularly close relationship with Terrell. When she collapsed during one of their performances in 1967, Gaye was devastated. When Terrell died of a brain tumor, Gaye did not perform or record for nearly two years.

What's Going On?

Shortly after Terrell's death Frankie Gaye returned from Vietnam with stories of bigotry and war atrocities, which greatly affected his brother Marvin. Influenced by this and the atmosphere of protest in the late 1960s and early 1970s, Gaye created the album *What's Going On?* It remains a decisive R&B work. However, Gordy did not think the protest themes were in keeping with Motown's image. The "What's Going On?" single had to be released without Gordy's knowledge. It sold 70,000 copies in its first week, and the album reached No. 1 on the R&B charts. Gaye appeared in a movie and a television production that year, and provided the music for the movie *Trouble Man* in 1972. Both *What's Going On?* and the *Trouble Man* score were nominated for Grammy Awards.

Late career

As his first marriage failed, Gaye adopted a new look that included his trademark skullcap and beard. He produced more popular work, including the 1977 disco hit "Got to Give It Up."

Gaye left Motown for CBS in 1976 and recorded four albums on the Columbia label. After spending time in Europe, Gaye returned to the United States in 1982. In 1983 he won two Grammy Awards for the single "Sexual Healing." He also delivered a soul-filled rendition of the national anthem at the NBA All-Star game that year.

A tour to promote Gaye's latest hits began well enough but rapidly deteriorated into a series of poor performances. The reasons for this were his worsening cocaine use and deep depression. He returned to his parents' home in Los Angeles. Nobody realized Gaye needed help, and he and his father began to argue. While many speculate about what happened, on April 1, 1984, Marvin, Sr., shot his son in the family home, and he died a few hours later.

KEY DATES	
1939	Born in Washington, D.C., on April 2.
1961	Releases first album, *The Soulful Moods of Marvin Gaye.*
1968	"I Heard It through the Grapevine" is his first No. 1 single.
1971	*What's Going On?* released and named one of Top 10 Albums of the Year.
1983	Wins two Grammy awards for "Sexual Healing."
1984	Killed by his father in Los Angeles, California, on April 1.
1987	Inducted into the Rock and Roll Hall of Fame.
1995	Inducted into the Soul Train Hall of Fame.
1996	Receives lifetime Achievement Award at the 38th Annual Grammy Awards.

See also: Cole, Nat King; Cooke, Sam; Davis, Sammy, Jr.; Diddley, Bo; Gordy, Berry, Jr.; Robinson, Smokey; Wonder, Stevie

Further reading: Dyson, Michael Eric. *Mercy, Mercy Me: The Art, Loves, and Demons of Marvin Gaye.* New York, NY: Basic Civitas Books, 2004.
http://www.vh1.com/artists/az/gaye_marvin/bio.jhtml (Biography and discography).

GEORGE, Zelma Watson
Diplomat, Singer

Remembered most for her role as a political adviser and diplomat during the 1950s and 1960s, Zelma Watson George was also a trained opera singer, musical researcher, and popular lecturer, and the first black woman to play a traditionally white role in an opera in New York.

Zelma Watson was born in 1903 in Texas, the eldest of six children. She was the daughter of a Baptist pastor, Samuel E. J. Watson, and his wife, Lena. Music was part of her life from an early age, both at home and in the church. During her childhood prominent black leaders often came to visit, preach in the church, and discuss political issues. They included W. E. B. DuBois, Booker T. Washington, and Mary B. Terrell. These discussions had a strong influence on Watson, making her proud of her heritage.

In 1917 the family was forced to move to Topeka, Kansas, when her father's work with black prisoners incurred local anger and threats from vigilantes. When Watson was refused permission to stay in a dormitory with white women for her studies at the University of Chicago, Illinois, the family moved again so that she could live at home. Following her graduation in 1924 with a BA in sociology, Watson went on to study voice at the American Conservatory of Music in Chicago from 1925 to 1927.

Civic work and music

Watson held posts as a social worker in Illinois, a probation officer in Chicago, and a dean at Tennessee State University, before moving to Los Angeles, California, in 1937. There she established the Avalon Community Center and remained its director until 1942.

In 1943 Watson received an MA from New York University. A grant from the Rockefeller Foundation enabled her to move to Cleveland, Ohio, to study for a doctoral thesis that cataloged about 12,000 compositions by African American composers. In 1944 she married attorney Clayborne George, whose name she took.

George's research inspired her to write a musical drama, *Chariot's A' Comin!*, which was televised in 1949. In 1950 George broke color barriers when she starred as Madame Flora (traditionally a white role) in *The Medium*, an opera by Gian Carlo Menotti. The opera transferred to New York and earned George the Merit Award of the National Association of Negro Musicians.

From music to politics

During the 1950s, although she continued to perform, George became more involved in national political issues. She was an adviser on several government committees on women and youth in the Dwight D. Eisenhower administration. From 1959 to 1961, as a member of the executive council of the American Society for African Culture, she went on an international lecture tour as a goodwill ambassador. In 1960 George was the only black member of the U.S. delegation to the United Nations.

In 1966 George became executive director of the Cleveland Job Corps Center for Women. On her retirement in 1974 she continued to lecture, write, and help run the Zelma George Shelter for homeless women and children, opened by the Interchurch Council of Cleveland in 1987.

Honors and awards

Recognized for the experience, knowledge, and passion that she brought to every task or role she took on, George was awarded numerous honors during her life, including the Dag Hammarskjöld Award for her contribution to international understanding in 1961, the Dahlberg Peace Award in 1969, and the Mary Bethune Gold Medallion in 1973. George died in Cleveland, Ohio, in 1994.

See also: DuBois, W. E. B.; Terrell, Mary B.; Washington, Booker T.

Further reading: Morton, Marian J. *Women in Cleveland: An Illustrated History.* Bloomington, IN: Indiana University Press, 1995.
http://www.umich.edu/~afroammu/standifer/george.html (University of Michigan African American Music Collection interview with George).

KEY DATES

1903	Born in Hearne, Texas, on December 8.
1949	Writes musical *Chariot's A' Comin!*
1960	Is only black member of U.S. delegation to the United Nations.
1966	Becomes director of Cleveland Job Corps for Women.
1994	Dies in Cleveland, Ohio, on July 3.

GERVIN, George
Basketball Player

George "The Iceman" Gervin is one of the 50 greatest players in National Basketball Association (NBA) history, recording a remarkable streak of scoring double figures in 407 consecutive games.

Gervin was born in Detroit, Michigan, in 1952. His interest in basketball showed at a young age. However, at the Martin Luther King High School in Detroit he found it difficult to make the school team. In a testimony to his tenacious character Gervin practiced shooting baskets alone in the school gymnasium at night. Staff allowed him to do this because he offered to sweep the floor afterward.

Moving up
Gervin eventually played high school basketball for four years and showed great skill, averaging 31 points and 20 rebounds a game in his senior year. Helped by his physical presence—he grew to 6 feet 7 inches (2.1m) tall—Gervin was named to All-American, All-Conference, and All-State teams. His power and style earned him the chance of a college basketball career. He attended Long Beach State University in California but left before the end of his first semester and joined Eastern Michigan University in 1971. Following a good performance in the 1971–1972 season, however, Gervin was thrown off the team after hitting an opposing player on court.

Opportunities to try out for Pan American and the U.S. Olympic teams were now lost, so Gervin found himself playing in the Eastern Basketball Association for the Pontiac Chaparrals. It was while playing there that he caught the attention of talent scouts. Soon after, Gervin took a professional position on the ABA Virginia Squires in 1972, being named to the All-ABA Rookie Team in 1973.

KEY DATES	
1952	Born in Detroit, Michigan, on April 27.
1972	Begins playing for the ABA Virginia Squires.
1974	Traded to the San Antonio Spurs.
1986	Retires from NBA basketball.
1992	Works for the San Antonio Spurs.
1996	Named to the Basketball Hall of Fame and the NBA 50th Anniversary All-Time Team.

▲ *George Gervin, a world-class basketball guard, was known as "The Iceman" for his on-court composure during hard-fought games.*

Gervin gave two years of solid scoring to the Squires before he was picked up by the San Antonio Spurs in 1974. With the Spurs Gervin began scoring an average of 23 points per game, and his playing kept improving when the Spurs joined the National Basketball Association (NBA) in 1976. Gervin began to rack up awards, including 12 ABA and NBA All-Star titles and the NBA All-Star Most Valuable Player in 1980. He also won four NBA scoring titles.

Retirement
Gervin was traded to the Chicago Bulls in 1985. The number 44 jersey he wore for the Spurs was retired when he left. Gervin retired from the NBA in 1986 with a career total of 26,595 points. He subsequently played briefly for Banco Roma in Italy and for the CBA Quad City Thunder team, but finally stopped playing in 1992, when once again he began working for the Spurs, first as community relations officer and later as assistant coach. In 1996 Gervin was named to the Basketball Hall of Fame and the NBA 50th Anniversary All-Time Team.

Further reading: McKissack, Fredrick, Jr. *Black Hoops: The History of African Americans in Basketball.* New York, NY: Scholastic, 1999.
http://www.nba.com/history/players/gervin_bio.html (Biography and NBA statistics).

GIBBS, Mifflin W.
Abolitionist, Lawyer

Mifflin Wistar Gibbs was a passionate abolitionist who became the first African American city judge in the United States, serving two years in the post.

Early life
Gibbs was born in 1823 in Philadelphia, Pennsylvania, to free parents. When his father died in 1831, Gibbs left grade school to help support his invalid mother and three siblings. At 16 he became an apprentice carpenter and then a journeyman contractor. During the 1940s he was a prominent member of the abolitionist movement and was closely involved with the Philadelphia stop on the Underground Railroad, a secret network that helped slaves escape from the South. In 1849 he joined fellow abolitionist Frederick Douglass on a speaking tour in western New York.

When gold was discovered in California in 1849, Gibbs headed west. Forced to give up carpentry in San Francisco because of white racism, he worked as a shoeshiner before opening a successful imported clothing store. In 1858 the lure of gold took Gibbs to British Columbia. There he made his money in real estate and other businesses, as well as studying law. Gibbs returned to the United States, married, and graduated from Oberlin College, Ohio, with a law degree in 1869.

An Arkansas lawyer
Gibbs moved to Little Rock, Arkansas, where he opened his own law practice. In 1873 he was appointed county attorney and later that year became the first African American municipal judge in the United States. Active in

▲ *Mifflin W. Gibbs had a varied and colorful life that included running several businesses, becoming a judge, and serving in the diplomatic service.*

the Republican Party, in 1877 he was made registrar of U.S. land in Arkansas, a position he held until 1886. In 1898 Gibbs was appointed consul to the Indian Ocean island of Madagascar. In 1901 he returned to Little Rock, where he continued to be involved in local affairs and civil rights.

In 1902 Gibbs published his autobiography, *Shadow and Light*. In 1903 he organized the Capital City Savings Bank and later the People's Mutual Aid Association, a health insurance company. In 1906, when President Theodore Roosevelt dismissed African American soldiers who had been accused of inciting a race riot in Texas, Gibbs switched his allegiance to the Democrats. In 1907 there was a nationwide economic panic and the Capital City Savings Bank closed. Gibbs died on July 11, 1915.

See also: Douglass, Frederick; Slavery

Further reading: Wheeler, B. Gordon. *Black California: The History of African-Americans in the Golden State*. New York, NY: Hippocrene Books, 1993.
http://www.arkansasblacklawyers.net/lawyers/mwgibbs.html
(Arkansas Black Lawyers page on Gibb).

KEY DATES	
1823	Born in Philadelphia, Pennsylvania, on April 17.
1849	Accompanies Frederick Douglass on speaking tour.
1869	Obtains law degree from Oberlin College.
1873	Appointed first African American judge.
1898	Serves as consul to Madagascar.
1902	Publishes autobiography, *Shadow and Light*.
1915	Dies in Little Rock, Arkansas, on July 11.

GIBSON, Althea
Tennis Player

In 1950 Althea Gibson became the first African American tennis player to compete in the U.S. Open championship in New York, and in 1957 the first black player to win the singles title at Wimbledon in England.

Gibson was born in the tiny community of Silver, South Carolina, in 1927. Her great-grandfather January Gibson, who farmed corn, cotton, and tobacco, was born into slavery. Althea's parents, Daniel and Annie Gibson, had inherited January's farm. However, as the Great Depression loomed and the farm's profits plummeted, the Gibson family looked north for opportunity. In 1930 the family moved to live in Harlem, New York, joining the northward migration of African Americans that occurred in the first half of the 20th century.

KEY DATES	
1927	Born in Silver, South Carolina, on August 25.
1956	Wins Wimbledon Doubles Championships between 1956 and 1958.
1957	During 1957 and 1958 wins Wimbledon and U.S. Open Singles Championships; is named Associated Press Female Athlete of the Year and Babe Zaharias Outstanding Woman Athlete.
1958	Publishes autobiography, *I Always Wanted to Be Somebody*, releases LP *Althea Gibson Sings*.
1968	Publishes memoir, *So Much to Live For*.
2003	Dies in East Orange, New Jersey, on September 18.

Sporting talent

Growing up, Gibson loved nothing more than playing games and running in the streets. She was a formidable basketball player and could play shuffleboard, volleyball, and badminton as well. She also had a reputation as a fierce fighter, who was very capable of defending herself and her family. She was so good that her father considered a career in boxing, imagining she might cash in on an interest in women boxers at that time.

For Gibson school was merely a place to get together with friends to plan the day's exploits. She enjoyed playing hooky and sometimes stayed away from home for days at a time with friends, at the movies or riding the subway. She and her friends discovered the Police Athletic League (PAL), an organization that sought to tackle delinquency by providing young people with sports equipment. PAL sports meets and tournaments were held in cordoned-off streets.

Gibson became PAL paddleball champion, and she began to learn to play tennis. At age 12 she drew spectators the first time she played on a tennis court. Gibson was discovered by a member of the Cosmopolitan Tennis Club, an elite black Harlem club where a well-known, one-armed tennis pro named Fred Johnson coached many black tennis champions. Along with another club member, Johnson contributed money to buy Gibson's first tennis racket.

With her aggressive personality and rambling lifestyle Gibson did not fit in with the club's members. She would often start a fight after losing a match. She dropped out of high school before reaching the 10th grade, taking on a series of odd jobs and living with an unofficial foster family in order to avoid reform school. In spite of her rough life, Gibson excelled at tennis, entering her first tournament only a year after her first lesson with Johnson.

Tennis career

Although she lost in her first national tournament, Gibson began to win in American Tennis Association (ATA; founded to increase opportunity for black athletes) tournaments in the mid-1940s, just as she was turning 18. She was introduced to boxer Sugar Ray Robinson, and he and his family provided an additional source of support for Gibson.

▼ *Althea Gibson with Jackie Robinson of the Brooklyn Dodgers in 1951.*

INFLUENCES AND INSPIRATION

Althea Gibson identified Babe Didrikson Zaharias (1914–1956) as one of her greatest inspirations. Mildred Ella Didriksen was born in Texas to Norwegian parents. Later she changed the spelling of her name and called herself "Babe" after baseball hero Babe Ruth. Like Gibson, Didrikson was a poor student and a tomboy who was frequently involved in fights. But she was also a talented athlete, perhaps the greatest woman athlete of all time. Her favorite sport was basketball, and her high

school team never lost a game when she played. In 1930 she began playing for the Casualty Insurance Company's team the Golden Cyclones in Dallas, leading them to the national championship in 1931. Didrikson also became a member of their track team and soon excelled. Between 1930 and 1932, she held American, Olympic, or world records in five different track-and-field events. On July 16, 1932, at an amateur track meet Didrikson won the national

championship on her own with 30 points; the runners up scored 22 points with 20 members. That afternoon she won six gold medals, broke four world records, and made the headlines of every sports page in the nation. The Associated Press voted her Woman Athlete of the Year, an award that she won five more times. In 1933 she began playing golf, in 1938 she married George Zaharias, and under his direction became one of the most successful women golfers in history.

Two black physicians, well-known in tennis circles, offered to put Gibson through college. However, when Hubert Eaton and R. Walter Johnson discovered that the young woman had dropped out of high school, they decided that she would complete school while living with the Eatons and spending summers with the Johnsons.

National competition

After completing high school at 21, Gibson jumped at the chance to attend Florida Agricultural and Mechanical College (A&M; now FAMU) on a basketball scholarship. At A&M she also played golf on the men's team. Supported by the ATA, Gibson was allowed to enter United States Lawn Tennis Association (now the USTA) tournaments and made a good showing.

To get to the top tournament, the U.S. Open at Forest Hills, Gibson would have to win invitational tournaments. However, she did not receive any invitations until the national tennis champion Alice Marble (1913–1990) accused the U.S. tennis community of racism. Following Marble's outburst, in August 1950 Gibson became the first black player at Forest Hills. She was on the verge of defeating then current Wimbledon champion Louise Brough, when a thunderstorm caused a delay. Brough managed to regain her composure and win the match.

International competition

In July 1957 Gibson won the singles title at Wimbledon, in London, England, making her the first black champion in the tournament's 80-year history. New York City responded with a ticker-tape parade, and Gibson scored her first

Forest Hills win shortly afterward. She was named Associated Press Female Athlete of the Year in 1957; the next year she became the first black woman on the cover of *Sports Illustrated* and successfully defended her titles at Wimbledon and Forest Hills.

After tennis

A multiply talented woman, Gibson followed her tennis successes with the release of an album of songs, a small role in the movie *The Horse Soldiers* (1959), and the publication of her autobiography, *I Always Wanted to Be Somebody*.

Following a failed tour as a tennis professional, Gibson took up golf, a sport she had played while at college. Although her strength and aggressive style of play provided a new model for the female golfer, some tournaments would not accept her because of her color.

In 1975 Gibson was named state commissioner of athletics in New Jersey, a first for a woman in the United States. Gibson used the position to make sports more accessible to young people, especially those in urban areas. In her later years Gibson suffered from strokes and heart problems; she died in 2003.

See also: Ashe, Arthur; Great Migration and Urbanization; Robinson, Jackie; Robinson, Sugar Ray

Further reading: Gray, Frances Clayton. *Born to Win: The Authorized Biography of Althea Gibson*. Hoboken, NJ: John Wiley & Sons, 2004.
www.altheagibson.com (Althea Gibson Foundation site).

GIBSON, Bob
Baseball Player

Bob Gibson is a towering figure in the history of the St. Louis Cardinals baseball team. He was a player primarily known for his scorching high-speed pitches. One commentator once quipped about Gibson: "He's the luckiest pitcher I ever saw. He always pitches when the other team doesn't score any runs."

Gibson was born Pack Robert Gibson in 1935 in Omaha, Nebraska. Although Gibson was destined to become an athlete, he was a sickly child who suffered from numerous complaints, including rickets (a softening of the bones caused by a poor diet), asthma, and a heart murmur resulting from a defective valve in his heart. Despite these handicaps and his family's poverty, Gibson became a talented school athlete, especially excelling in both baseball and basketball.

Choosing baseball

In the mid-1950s Gibson was awarded a basketball scholarship to Creighton University, a Catholic college in Nebraska. He also played varsity baseball for the college. He was soon spotted by major league talent scouts, and

▼ *Bob Gibson is one of the greatest baseball players of all time. He also played for a year with basketball entertainers the Harlem Globetrotters.*

in 1957 Gibson signed to play for the St. Louis Cardinals, although he did not begin playing for the team until 1958. Meanwhile, he fulfilled a childhood dream of playing basketball for the Harlem Globetrotters.

Baseball was to be Gibson's main sport, however. In 1959 he made his major league debut for the Cardinals. His initial performances were not spectacular, but in the 1960s he became a top player. His pitching took the Cardinals to victory over the Yankees in the 1964 World Series. That same year Gibson was awarded the National League Babe Ruth Award and the Major League Most Valuable Player (MVP) title. In 1967 Gibson showed further scorching talent in the World Series, during which he allowed only 14 hits and struck out 26 players in 27 innings. The following year Gibson had 22 victories and struck out 268 batters during the season, setting two World Series pitching records in the process.

Accolades

Before retiring in 1975, Gibson won numerous professional awards. They included three MVPs and two Cy Young Awards. His achievements came despite many injuries, including broken arms and legs. After retiring, Gibson became a pitching coach and radio sports commentator. In 1981 he was elected to the Baseball Hall of Fame.

KEY DATES	
1935	Born in Omaha, Nebraska, on November 9.
1957	Signs to play for the St. Louis Cardinals.
1959	Makes major league debut.
1964	Receives first MVP award.
1968	Strikes out 268 batters during the season.
1975	Retires from professional baseball.
1981	Elected to the Baseball Hall of Fame.

Further reading: Gibson, Bob. *Stranger to the Game*. New York, NY: Viking, 1994.
Gibson, Bob. *From Ghetto to Glory: The Story of Bob Gibson*. New York, NY: Prentice Hall, 2001.
http://www.baseballhalloffame.org/hofers_and_honorees/ hofer_bios/gibson_bob.htm (National Baseball Hall of Fame).

GIBSON, Josh
Baseball Player

Josh Gibson is a legend in African American baseball as one of the truly big hitters of the Negro Leagues. His reputation might have been even greater, but he died just as the major leagues began to field integrated teams.

Gibson was born in Buena Vista, Georgia, in 1911, and later moved to Pittsburgh, Pennsylvania. While at school in Pittsburgh, Gibson demonstrated physical power and speed in sports, primarily in track and baseball. In this second sport he showed great skill at both fielding and hitting. In 1927 Gibson turned semiprofessional and joined the Crawford Colored Giants.

Negro Leagues

During the 1920s and 1930s black baseball players competed within the Negro Leagues, organizations formed in the 19th century after blacks were banned from the white-dominated major leagues. In 1930 Gibson was spotted by Cum Posey (1891–1946), manager of the Homestead Grays of the Negro National League. He told Gibson to be ready to play for the Grays when he called. That call came when a Grays catcher, Buck Ewing (1903–1979), split his finger in a game, and Posey sent a cab for Gibson to come and join the team.

Gibson's addition helped make the Grays a powerhouse of Negro League baseball. His home-run totals and batting averages for his first season were as good as those of the best established names, and on one occasion Gibson hit a ball that flew more than 500 feet (152m) out of Yankee Stadium—the longest ball ever hit in the stadium.

In 1932 Gibson moved to the Pittsburgh Crawfords for a more lucrative contract. He continued his superb play with the new team, hitting 69 home runs in the 1934 season alone. Gibson became known for the awesome distance of his hits and attracted a huge public following. He traveled extensively, playing in Mexico and Cuba.

Poor health

Gibson returned to the Grays in 1936 and initially showed all his old talent. However, during the 1940s his health began to decline, his shoulder frequently popping out of joint. He also had problems with his mental health, being hospitalized for a nervous disorder in 1943. In 1947 Gibson suffered from a stroke while in a movie theater and died a few hours later. In 1972 he was inducted into the Baseball Hall of Fame.

▲ *Josh Gibson, playing for the East, is tagged out during the 12th annual East–West All Star Negro baseball game in 1944 at Comiskey Park, Chicago.*

KEY DATES	
1911	Born in Buena Vista, Georgia, on December 21.
1927	Begins playing semiprofessionally with the Crawford Colored Giants.
1930	Joins the Homestead Grays of the Negro National League.
1932	Moves to the Pittsburgh Crawfords.
1936	Moves back to the Homestead Grays.
1947	Dies in Pittsburgh, Pennsylvania, on January 20.
1972	Inducted into Baseball Hall of Fame.

See also: Color Bar and Professional Sports

Further reading: Brashler, William. *Josh Gibson: A Life in the Negro Leagues.* Chicago, IL: Ivan R. Dee, 2000.
http://www.baseballlibrary.com/baseballlibrary/ballplayers/G/Gibson_Josh.stm (Biography and statistics).

GIDDINGS, Paula
Writer, Academic

A noted journalist, historian, and feminist, Paula J. Giddings is best known for her pioneering historical study of African American women, *When and Where I Enter: The Impact of Black Women on Race and Sex in America* (1985). At the heart of her research is a determination to uncover the important role played by women in black political and social movements since the 19th century. In 2005 she was professor of African American studies at Smith College in Northampton, Massachusetts—a prestigious women's liberal arts college.

Early life
Giddings was born on November 16, 1947, in Yonkers, New York. Her mother, a school teacher in New York City, was an important influence who encouraged her to think freely and independently. After high school Giddings attended the historically black Howard University in Washington, D.C., from which she graduated in 1969. She began her career working in publishing, first at Random House and then at Howard University Press, before going on to become chief of the Paris, France, bureau for *Encore American and Worldwide News*. Meanwhile Giddings was also writing extensively for newspapers and magazines, such as the *New York Times Book Review*, the *Washington Post*, the *International Herald Tribune*, and the *Nation*.

Uncovering forgotten histories
In 1985 Giddings published *When and Where I Enter*, the first in-depth modern study of African American women's history, which brought to light the achievements of often-overlooked figures such as educator Anna Julia Cooper and antilynching campaigner Ida B. Wells. Drawing on speeches, diaries, letters, and other original documents, Giddings demonstrated how black women have overcome racist and sexist attitudes. The book had an immense impact on African American studies, opening up a feminist perspective in an area that had previously been largely the preserve of black male academics and concerned mainly with the achievements of black men.

Academic success
The book's success enabled Giddings to launch her own academic career. Her appointments have included teaching at Spelman College, where she was United Negro College Fund Distinguished Scholar (1986); the New Jersey Laurie Chair in Women's Studies at Douglass College, Rutgers University (1989–1981); and professor of women's and African American studies at Duke University (1996–2001). In 1993 Giddings was named a fellow of the John Simon Guggenheim Foundation, one of the nation's highest academic honors. She is the recipient of the Candace Award from the National Coalition of 100 Black Women and the Anna Julia Cooper Award from *Sage*, a scholarly journal about black women.

In addition Giddings has been a judge for the National Book Awards, served on the council of the Author's Guild of America, been a member of the advisory board of the Global Women's Studies Program at Hunter College, New York, and served on the governor's advisory committee on black affairs in New York.

Ongoing writing career
Giddings has continued to publish articles and studies in her field. Her 1988 book *In Search of Sisterhood: Delta Sigma Theta and the Challenge of the Black Sorority Movement* marked the 75th anniversary of the largest black women's organization in the nation. It comprises mainly professional and upper-class women who see their role as agents of change in a variety of social and political issues. Giddings's 2005 book *Ida: A Sword Among Lions: Ida B. Wells and the Campaign Against Lynching*, tells the story of journalist Ida B. Wells-Barnett, who became co-owner and editor of a newspaper and used her editorials to mount an international campaign against lynching.

KEY DATES	
1947	Born in Yonkers, New York, on November 16.
1969	Graduates from Howard University, Washington, D.C.
1985	Publishes *When and Where I Enter: The Impact of Black Women on Race and Sex in America*.

See also: Cooper, Anna. J; Wells-Barnett, Ida B.

Further reading: Giddings, Paula J. *When and Where I Enter: The Impact of Black Women on Race and Sex in America*. New York, NY: Amistad, 1996.
www.mastermediaspeakers.com/paulagiddings (Biography).

GILLESPIE, Dizzy
Musician, Composer

Dizzy Gillespie was one of the giants of jazz; he is credited, together with Charlie Parker, with having created bebop, the rhythmically and harmonically complex style that initiated the modern jazz era. His influence as a trumpet player has been compared to that of Louis Armstrong and Miles Davis.

John Birks Gillespie was born in South Carolina in 1917, the youngest of nine children. He began to play music at an early age, first piano, then trombone, and by age 12, trumpet. By the age of 15 Gillespie had taught himself well enough to earn a music scholarship at a small agricultural school, the Laurinburg Institute, North Carolina, where he studied for two years.

In 1935 Gillespie joined his family in Philadelphia and began to play in bands, earning the nickname "Dizzy" for his comic stage antics. He moved to New York City in 1937 and played in several big bands, including those of Cab Calloway, Ella Fitzgerald, Benny Carter, and Billy Eckstine.

▼ **Dizzy Gillespie began to dream of playing the trumpet in a jazz band at age 13 when he heard a radio broadcast of Roy Eldridge playing trumpet.**

During the 1940s Gillespie, together with other musicians such as Charlie Parker, Kenny Clarke, Thelonious Monk, and Charlie Christian started playing in the style known as bebop. Gillespie formed his own band in 1945 and created his first compositions. Along with Cuban percussionist Chano Pozo, Gillespie pioneered the integration of Latin music with jazz.

In 1953 Gillespie began to play his trademark trumpet with an upturned horn, specially commissioned by him after experiments with an accidentally damaged trumpet. He led an increasingly busy career touring, recording, leading small and big bands, and being a guest soloist.

Gillespie benefited from a stable private life and disregard for drugs; his high profile gave bebop credibility. By the 1980s he had become a great statesman of jazz and was the recipient of many awards: the United States National Medal of the Arts, the French Commandeur d'Ordre des Arts et Lettres, and 14 honorary doctorates.

Although Gillespie is known mostly as a trumpet player, some of his compositions, such as "Bebop," "A Night in Tunisia," and "Manteca," entered the standard jazz repertoire. In 1966 his compositions were compiled and published as *Dizzy Gillespie: a Jazz Master*. In 1979 Gillespie published his autobiography, *To Be or Not to Bop*. He died in 1993 of pancreatic cancer.

KEY DATES	
1917	Born in Cheraw, South Carolina, on October 21.
1945	Forms his own band.
1956	Tours internationally with sponsorship from the State Department.
1979	Publishes biography, *To Be or Not to Bop*.
1993	Dies in Englewood, New Jersey, on January 6.

See also: Armstrong, Louis; Calloway, Cab; Carter, Benny; Davis, Miles; Eldridge, Roy; Fitzgerald, Ella; Monk, Thelonious; Parker, Charlie

Further reading: Shipton, Alyn. *Groovin' High: The Life of Dizzy Gillespie*. New York, NY: Oxford University Press, 1999. http://www.pbs.org/jazz/biography/artist_id_gillespie_dizzy.htm (Biography).

GILLIAM, Dorothy
Journalist

Dorothy Gilliam is a distinguished journalist who worked for the *Washington Post* for more than 30 years and served as president of the National Association of Black Journalists between 1993 and 1995.

Early life

Dorothy Butler was born in 1936, the eighth of ten children, in Memphis, Tennessee. Her father, an African Methodist Episcopal minister, moved the family to Louisville, Kentucky, to a new church when Gilliam was four. Growing up in the segregated South made a deep impression on Gilliam. The family moved again, to rural Kentucky, when her father was taken ill. He died in 1951, when Gilliam was 14. She graduated from Lincoln Institute high school and then received a scholarship to attend Ursuline College in Louisville for two years. In her freshman year she began working for the *Louisville Defender*, sparking off an interest in journalism.

Between 1955 and 1957 Gilliam studied at Lincoln University, where she came under the guidance of Armistead S. Pride, the head of the School of Journalism. After graduation she worked for *Jet* and *Ebony* magazines in Chicago before embarking on a master's degree at Columbia Graduate School of Journalism in 1960.

The Washington Post

In 1961 Gilliam joined the *Washington Post*, beginning an association with the newspaper that lasted for more than 30 years. She was the first African American woman hired as a full-time reporter at the paper and one of only three black reporters. In 1962 she married artist Sam Gilliam. The couple had three children, but later divorced.

Gilliam left the *Post* in 1965 when pregnant with her second child, but returned in 1972 to work as assistant editor on the "Style" section. In 1976 her book *Paul Robeson—All American* was published. In 1979, after seven years with the "Style" section, she asked for a transfer and moved to the "Metro" section. Gilliam started to write a twice-weekly column on education, politics, race, and her own experiences. She also continued to work as a reporter and editor.

In 1985 Gilliam became chair of the Institute for Journalism Education, a multiracial organization that pushed training for minorities. In 1993 she was appointed president of the National Association of Black Journalists,

KEY DATES

1936	Born in Memphis, Tennessee, on November 24.
1957	Graduates from Lincoln University.
1961	Graduates from Columbia Graduate School of Journalism.
1961	Joins the *Washington Post*.
1993	Becomes president of the National Association of Black Journalists.
1997	Becomes director of the Young Journalists Development Program.
2003	Receives Shapiro Fellowship.

a position she held until 1995. She lobbied for the controversial move to include Hispanic, Asian, and Native American journalists in the African American journalists' fight to end racism.

Helping others

In 1997 Gilliam became director of the Young Journalists Development Program, an in-house program run by the *Post* to educate and encourage young people interested in journalism and to increase the number of minorities employed in newsrooms. One of her main concerns was to improve the poor standard of many of the nation's high school newspapers, particularly in schools that had a large number of minority students. The *Post*'s staff participate in the program and the *Post* also provides equipment.

Gilliam received the Shapiro Fellowship from the George Washington University School of Media and Public Affairs for the academic year 2003–2004. At George Washington Gilliam lectured and developed a program for minority students.

See also: Robeson, Paul

Further reading: Gilliam, Dorothy Butler. *Paul Robeson—All American*. Washington, D.C.: New Republic Books, 1978.
www.lumoalumni-washdc.org/Gilliam.htm (Site for alumni of Lincoln University).
http://npc.press.org/wpforal/gill.htm (Washington Press Club interviews with Gilliam).

GIOVANNI, Nikki
Poet, Educator

Outspoken poet, orator, critic, educator, publisher, and political activist Nikki Giovanni is dedicated to civil rights and equality, focusing on the ability that every individual possesses to make a difference.

An emerging voice
Yolande Cornelia Giovanni was born in Knoxville, Tennessee, in 1943. She moved shortly after her birth to Cincinnati, Ohio, home of her father's family. The daughter of two teachers, Giovanni was renamed Nikki by her older sister before she was three. Aged 15, she went to live with her maternal grandparents in Knoxville, where her grandmother began to exert a powerful influence on the teenager, emphasizing the necessity of helping others and fighting against inequality.

Encouraged by two of her high school teachers, Giovanni applied as an early entrant to Fisk University, Tennessee, in 1960. Graduating in 1967, she published her first book of poetry in 1968, *Black Feeling, Black Talk,* urging African Americans to appreciate their individuality and to understand how their environment was heavily influenced by white American culture.

▼ *Nikki Giovanni in her office in 1973. Her poems range from revolutionary battlecries to family memoirs and children's rhymes.*

Award-winning work
Giovanni was quickly recognized as a leading figure in black poetry, and her collections of poems, *Black Judgment* (1968) and *Re: Creation* (1970), expressed her militant approach to securing civil rights.

In her other collections, such as *The Women and the Men* (1975), Giovanni's poetry explores her family and personal relationships. She has also written several books of poetry for children, including *Spin a Soft Black Song* (1971) and *Ego-Tripping* (1973).

Giovanni is also celebrated for her recordings, both of her own work, such as her Grammy-nominated *The Nikki Giovanni Poetry Collection* (2003), and of her conversations with the eminent African American writers Margaret Walker and James Baldwin.

Since 1987 Giovanni has taught writing and literature at Virginia Tech, where she is a University Distinguished Professor. Her continuing importance to African American literature was demonstrated when she won National Association for the Advancement of Colored People (NAACP) Image Awards for three volumes of her poetry, *Love Poems* (1998), *Blues: For All the Changes* (2000), and *Quilting the Black-Eyed Pea* (2003).

See also: Baldwin, James; Walker, Margaret

Further reading: Josephson, Judith Pinkerton. *Nikki Giovanni, Poet of the People.* Berkeley Heights, NJ: Enslow Publishers, 2003.
http://nikki-giovanni.com/ (Giovanni's official site).

GLOVER, Savion
Dancer, Choreographer

One of the most talented tap dancers working today, Savion Glover is celebrated for his energetic, inventive dance style. Through his strong urban image and innovative use of contemporary popular music Glover has helped bring tap to a new young and multiracial audience.

A child prodigy

Born in 1973 in Newark, New Jersey, Glover was bought up by his mother and grandmother in a bustling, crowded family home. He showed his talents from an early age, tapping out rhythms on the household furniture, and started taking drum lessons at age four.

A year later he won a scholarship to study at the Newark Community School of the Arts and, at age seven, began taking tap lessons at the Broadway Dance Center. He soon showed dancing abilities that were way beyond his years. By 1984 his gifts had won him the starring role in the Broadway show *The Tap Dance Kid*.

After further training Glover returned to Broadway in the 1986 revue *Black and Blue*, for which he won a Tony Award nomination. In the same year he also appeared in the motion picture *Tap*, alongside renowned African American tap dancers Sammy Davis, Jr., and Gregory Hines.

Shows and appearances

By this time Glover was developing his own distinctive style of tap. It featured fast-paced, pounding footwork, or "hitting," and complex, improvised rhythms. It was this robust style that Glover brought to Broadway in 1996 in the hip-hop show *Bring in 'da Noise, Bring in 'da Funk*. Playing to full houses for three months, the show won Glover a Tony Award for best choreography (the creation and arrangement of dances).

In 1997 Glover performed for President Bill Clinton in a televized show called *Savion Glover's Stomp, Slide, and Swing: In Performance at the White House.* In 2000 he was

▲ *As well as winning awards for his performances on stage, Savion Glover has appeared on television, including several seasons of* **Sesame Street,** *and in a P. Diddy music video.*

the star of Spike Lee's controversial comedy drama *Bamboozled*. Another high point in Glover's career was headlining the closing ceremony of the 2002 Winter Olympics in Salt Lake City, Utah.

Glover continues to choreograph and tour with numerous shows. He is known for experiments that partner tap-dancing techniques with unexpected musical styles and other art forms. One of his most celebrated innovations was including a string quartet in his 2005 Off-Broadway hit *Classic Savion*.

See also: Combs, Sean; Davis, Sammy, Jr.; Hines, Gregory; Lee, Spike

---

Further reading: Glover, Savion, and Bruce Weber. *Savion!: My Life in Tap*. New York, NY: HarperCollins, 2000.
http://www.savionglover.com (Glover's official site).

KEY DATES	
1973	Born in Newark, New Jersey, on November 19.
1984	Makes his Broadway debut aged 11 in *The Tap Dance Kid*.
1996	Performs in acclaimed Broadway revue *Bring in 'da Noise, Bring in 'da Funk*.

GOLDBERG, Whoopi
Actor, Comedian

Whoopi Goldberg is one of the most successful African Americans working in television, movies, and theater. She has received more than 40 awards, including nine National Association for the Advancement of Colored People (NAACP) Image Awards.

Early life
Goldberg was born Caryn Elaine Johnson in 1955. Her father left when she was young. Goldberg suffered from dyslexia, a reading disability, and had little interest in school. At the age of eight she began to study at the Hudson Guild in Helena Rubinstein's Children's Theater. At age 14 Goldberg left school to act full time.

Goldberg appeared in several Broadway shows but suffered from severe insecurity about her looks. She developed a dependency on drugs in the early 1970s, but she sought treatment for her addiction and in 1973 married her drug counsellor. The couple had a daughter, but they later separated.

▼ **Whoopi Goldberg has hosted the Academy Awards ceremony four times, the only black woman to do so.**

Goldberg moved to San Diego, California, with her child, and worked different jobs while still performing with local theater groups. She decided to take a new name, Whoopi Cushion, but in the late 1970s she changed her surname to Goldberg.

Success
In 1982 Goldberg developed a one-woman show called *The Spook Show*, which featured characters based on Goldberg's own experiences. In 1985 she won awards for another show, named simply *Whoopi Goldberg*. In the same year she received an Oscar nomination and Golden Globe Award for her performance in the Steven Spielberg movie adaptation of Alice Walker's novel *The Color Purple*.

In the second half of the 1980s Goldberg appeared in many films, including several comedies such as *Jumpin' Jack Flash* (1986). In 1988 she was offered a role in *Star Trek: The Next Generation*. As a fan of the original 1960s cult series, Goldberg leapt at the chance.

In 1990 Goldberg became the second African American woman to win a supporting actress Oscar for her role as a medium in *Ghost*. She also won a second Golden Globe Award for *Made in America* (1993). Other successes in the 1990s included the musical comedy *Sister Act* in 1992. Goldberg published a memoir *Book* in 1997, produced and starred in the Emmy-winning show *Hollywood Squares* between 1998 and 2002, and in 2003 she appeared in her own television show entitled *Whoopi*.

KEY DATES	
1955	Born in New York on November 13.
1982	Develops *The Spook Show*; wins several awards.
1985	Appears in *The Color Purple*; nominated for an Oscar and wins a Golden Globe Award.
1990	Wins Oscar for her performance in the romantic drama *Ghost* with Demi Moore and Patrick Swayze.

See also: Walker, Alice

Further reading: Gaines, Ann. *Whoopi Goldberg*. Philadelphia, PA: Chelsea House, 1999.
http://www.imdb.com/name/nm0000155/ (IMDB page on Goldberg).

GOODE, Sarah E.
Inventor

Sarah E. Goode was one of the first African American women to be granted a U.S. patent. A patent gives the inventor the right to exclude others from making, using, offering for sale, or selling the invention in the United States or importing the invention into the United States.

Goode's invention was the cabinet bed. It was a writing desk that unfolded into a bed when it was time to sleep. She had the idea after seeing the cramped conditions many people endured in American cities during the late 19th century. In 1885 Goode's designs were accepted by the U.S. Patent and Trademark Office, and her invention was protected by U.S. patent no. 322,177.

From slavery to making history

Although her exact birth date and place is unknown, Sarah E. Goode was probably born in 1850. She was born into slavery.

At the end of the Civil War (1861–1865), when slavery came to an end in the United States, Goode was freed. She moved to Chicago, and as a talented businesswoman she looked around for opportunities to make money. She opened a furniture shop, figuring that there would be a large demand for furniture from all the people moving to the city to seek their fortune after the end of the war.

Space-saving idea

Goode worked hard to make her business successful, selling a range of conventional furniture. Like all entrepreneurs, she also kept an eye out for new business ventures.

As she had predicted, the population of Chicago continued to grow very fast, and the new arrivals all needed somewhere to stay. This had the effect of pushing up the cost of rented accommodations across the city. As a result, Chicago's thousands of new citizens had to make do with living in tiny apartments since they could not afford any more space. The demands on space were even more pressured following Chicago's Great Fire of 1871, in which more than 200 people died and about 18,000 buildings were destroyed. The pressure on housing became so extreme that many people even lacked the room for a bed and were forced to sleep in chairs or on the floor.

While the population boom in Chicago would soon fuel the birth of the skyscraper and high-rise living, Goode saw a business opportunity. She began to think of designs for space-saving furniture that would meet the needs of her customers. She had an idea for a bed that could be stored away. The result was the "folding cabinet bed."

The hideaway bed

Goode's invention was both stylish and practical. It became the predecessor of the popular hideaway bed. Complete with a mattress and spring support, the cabinet bed had a folding construction, with hinged sections that could easily be raised or lowered. When not in use as a bed, Goode's invention folded away into a writing desk. The desk included shelves, a roll-top cover, extendable tabletop surface, and compartments for stationery and writing materials. Goode received her patent for the bed design on July 14, 1885.

Was she the first?

Although Goode is considered by many people to be the first black woman to receive a patent, it is likely that another African American woman inventor beat her to it. The United States Patent and Trademark Office has a record from 1884 of a patent for a hand-operated machine for kneading and rolling dough. The inventor could not write, and so the patent was signed with a cross. Although the evidence is far from conclusive, sources suggest that the owner of this patent, no. 305,474, granted on September 23 the year before Goode's, was Judy W. Reede, an African American from Washington, D.C.

KEY DATES

1850 Born at about this date.

1865 Freed at the end of the Civil War, Goode moves to Chicago and opens a furniture shop.

1885 Invents the cabinet bed; receives patent on July 14.

Further reading: Sullivan, Otha Richard, and Jim Haskins (eds.). *Black Stars: African American Women Scientists and Inventors.* New York, NY: John Wiley, 2002.
http://www.blackinventions101.com (Museum of Black Innovations and Inventions).
http://www.blackinventor.com (The Black Inventor Online Museum).

GOODE, W. Wilson
Politician, Preacher

A committed philanthropist, politician, preacher, and writer, W. Wilson Goode became the first African American to be elected mayor of Philadelphia.

Born to a family of migrant farmers in 1938, Woodrow Wilson Goode attended 11 different schools before graduating from John Bartman High School. Inspired by a teacher who told him he could "be somebody in life," Goode was accepted at Morgan State University, Baltimore, Maryland, becoming the first member of his family to go to college. He graduated with a BA in history and political science in 1961.

Following graduation, Goode found work as an insurance claims adjustor, a probation officer, and a building maintenance supervisor, before enlisting with the Army in 1962. He returned to college in 1966, attending the University of Pennsylvania's Wharton School of Business, from which he graduated with a master's degree in governmental administration.

▼ **Wilson Goode held public office for more than 20 years, including two terms as mayor of Philadelphia.**

Public service
Goode was appointed executive director of the Philadelphia Council for Community Advancement in 1969. It was an organization aiming to rejuvenate poorer communities, providing them with affordable housing. As he launched a number of education, employment, and economic programs, Goode quickly became known for his leadership skills. In 1979 Philadelphia's mayor selected Goode to be head of the Pennsylvania Public Utilities Commission. One of his first tasks was to investigate the March 28 accident at Pennsylvania's Three Mile Island nuclear power plant, when a large part of the core melted, and the system became dangerously radioactive.

The following year Goode won widespread support and broke down racial barriers when he became the first African American to be named city manager of Philadelphia. In 1983 Goode was elected as the first black mayor of Philadelphia, serving two terms.

After leaving office in 1992, Goode published his autobiography, *In Goode Faith*. In 1996 he entered the Eastern Baptist Theological Seminary and was awarded a PhD in ministry in 2000. Goode's contribution to public life has been rewarded with honors from more than 2,000 organizations, and he has been presented with 14 honorary degrees. In 2005 he was the senior adviser on Faith Based Initiatives for Public-Private Ventures and chair of several organizations, including the Free Library of Philadelphia.

KEY DATES	
1938	Born in Seaboard, North Carolina, on August 19.
1962	Serves tour of duty in the Army.
1969	Appointed executive director of the Philadelphia Council for Community Advancement.
1983	Elected mayor of Philadelphia.
2000	Receives his PhD in ministry.

Further reading: Goode, Wilson W., and Joann Stevens. *In Goode Faith*. Valley Forge, PA: Judson Press, 1992.
http://www.thehistorymakers.com/biography/biography.asp?bioindex=320&category=politicalMakers (HistoryMakers biography).

GOODING, Cuba, Jr.
Actor

Versatile actor and producer Cuba Gooding, Jr., is famed for his energetic and varied performances. The son of two singers, Gooding was born in 1968. He moved with his family from the Bronx, New York, to Los Angeles, California, at age four. After his parents separated when he was six, the Gooding family moved repeatedly, and Cuba attended four different high schools.

His changing circumstances did not affect his achievement, however. He was class president in three of his high schools and won the Drama Teachers' Association of Southern California Drama Festival competition with a monologue from Shakespeare's *Twelfth Night*.

After performing as a break-dancer with Lionel Richie at the 1984 Los Angeles Olympics at age 16, Gooding began appearing regularly in commercials before being cast in a small role in the *Hill Street Blues* television series. Determined to develop his craft, Gooding attended drama workshops and in 1988 made his film debut in the Eddie Murphy film *Coming to America*.

Hitting the big time

In 1991 Gooding demonstrated his A-list potential, delivering an acclaimed performance as Tre Styles in *Boyz N the Hood*. He continued to work consistently, landing sizable film roles, including *A Few Good Men* (1992). His star turn, however, was as Rod Tidwell in the comedy drama *Jerry Maguire*. Gooding turned in a scene-stealing performance as the self-centered football player, earning him the Oscar for Best Supporting Actor in the process.

Gooding's success continued through the late 1990s and into the new millennium, with significant roles in a string of high-profile films, including *As Good as It Gets* (1997), *What Dreams May Come* (1998), *Instinct* (1999), *Men of Honor* (2000), and *Pearl Harbor* (2001).

▲ *Cuba Gooding, Jr., is perhaps best known for shouting the catchphrase "Show me the money!" at Tom Cruise in the movie* **Jerry Maguire.**

In 1999 Gooding produced and starred in the crime thriller *The Murder of Crows*. Later he pursued more light-hearted projects, starring in the comedy *Rat Race* (2001) and the musical *The Fighting Temptations* (2003), and supplying his voice for the Disney animated film *Home on the Range* (2004).

See also: Murphy, Eddie; Richie, Lionel

Further reading: Edelson, Paula. *Cuba Gooding, Jr.: Black Americans of Achievement.* Langhorne, PA: Chelsea House Publications, 2000.
http://www.imdb.com/name/nm0000421/ (IMDB page on Gooding).

KEY DATES	
1968	Born in the Bronx, New York, on January 2.
1972	Moves with his family to Los Angeles.
1991	First major role in *Boyz N the Hood*.
1996	Wins Best Supporting Actor Academy Award for his role in *Jerry Maguire*.
2002	Is honored with a star on Hollywood Walk of Fame.

GORDON, Dexter
Musician

Dexter Keith Gordon was one of the outstanding saxophonists in the history of jazz. He was a leading figure in the bebop genre, a style of jazz in which Gordon was the first great tenor player. He had a uniquely relaxed sense of musical phrasing, always playing slightly behind the beat.

Early life
Born in 1923, Gordon started to play the clarinet at age 13. He also had lessons on the alto saxophone, moving to the tenor saxophone in his late teens. He was taught by Lloyd Reese, who also tutored Charles Mingus and many other successful jazz artists.

In 1940 Gordon began playing in Lionel Hampton's (1908–2002) touring band. After leaving the band in 1943, Gordon began recording music. Recordings survive of his classic work with Nat King Cole, Fletcher Henderson, and the jazz legend Louis Armstrong.

▼ *Dexter Gordon was 6 feet 5 inches (1.96m) tall and was known as Long Tall Dex.*

Gordon came to prominence as a soloist when he played in the orchestra of Billy Eckstine (1914–1993) between 1944 and 1946 and with different groups in New York and on the West Coast. The recordings of his saxophone duels with Wardell Gray (1921–1955) now have historical importance, charting the emergence of new ways of playing tenor saxophone.

Comeback
Gordon's career was interrupted during the 1950s by problems with drug addiction, but he made a comeback in the 1960s. Following a very successful tour of Europe in 1962, Gordon decided to remain there. At first he based himself in Paris, France, but later moved to Copenhagen, Denmark. There he led a life of teaching, performing, and recording. Again, some of his surviving sessions are highlights in the history of jazz.

Gordon returned to the United States in 1977, but his career was again disrupted by alcoholism. In 1986 he made another comeback by starring in the film *Round Midnight*, which portrayed the life of an expatriate alcoholic saxophonist in Paris loosely based on his own experiences. Gordon's performance won him an Oscar nomination.

While never quite seen as a revolutionary jazz artist, Gordon's unique style influenced the next generation of saxophonists, such as Sonny Rollins (1930–) and John Coltrane. In his final years Gordon was influenced in turn by Coltrane and took up the soprano saxophone.

See also: Armstrong, Louis; Cole, Nat King; Coltrane, John; Henderson, Fletcher; Mingus, Charles

Further reading: Britt, Stan. *Dexter Gordon: A Musical Biography*. New York, NY: Da Capo Press, 1989.
http://www.pbs.org/jazz/biography/
artist_id_gordon_dexter.htm (Biography).

GORDY, Berry, Jr.
Entrepreneur

Founder and owner of the Tamla–Motown record labels, Berry Gordy, Jr., created one of the most impressive stables of songwriters, producers, and musicians in pop history. In 1994 Gordy said, "We were black-owned, but interracial. Blacks, whites, Arabs, and Jews all working together, when that wasn't common."

Gordy was born in Detroit, Michigan, in 1929. His family was middle class, but they were hard hit by the Great Depression of the 1930s and for a time relied on welfare. They went to church regularly, where Gordy was exposed to Negro spirituals and spiritual music, styles that would indelibly influence his musical career. He also developed a love of jazz. Gordy was good at sports and he dropped out of school in 11th grade to become a professional boxer. In 1951 he was drafted into the Army to serve in the Korean War (1951–1953).

▼ **Berry Gordy liked to stay in the background but remain in total control of his businesses.**

The start of a musical career

In 1953 Gordy opened the 3-D Record Mart: House of Jazz with financial backing from his family, but the store closed in 1955. Gordy took a number of jobs, and in his spare time he wrote songs.

Gordy's break came when his sisters and brothers, who ran a photograph concession in the Flame Show Bar, which showcased African American performers, put Gordy in touch with club owner Al Green. Green asked Gordy to write songs for the artists he managed, including Jackie Wilson, for whom Gordy wrote the song "Reet Petite."

In 1958 Gordy met the Matadors and became friendly with lead singer Smokey Robinson. The band changed its name to the Miracles, and Gordy became the manager. He produced their 1958 single "Got a Job" on the End Records label, but realized that he would make more money and have more control if he set up his own label. He created Tamla Records and established a music publishing company named Jobete.

Gordy's family loaned him the $800 he needed to rent office space. He created "Hitsville USA," the headquarters of the recording company, where he lived with Raymona "Miss Ray" Liles, his second wife. Liles helped Gordy write many hit songs and to establish Motown, the company named for "Motor Town" Detroit. Together they also set up Rayber Voices, a studio group that provided backing on most of Motown's early recordings.

Tamla Records initially recorded rhythm-and-blues (R&B) artists. Its first release, R&B singer Marv Johnson's

KEY DATES	
1929	Born in Detroit, Michigan, on November 28.
1953	Opens jazz store, which folds two years later.
1957	Jackie Wilson records Gordy's song "Reet Petite."
1959	Opens "Hitsville, USA," the first Motown HQ.
1972	Moves Motown to Los Angeles, California.
1988	Sells Motown Records to MCA and Boston Ventures.
1990	Inducted into Rock and Roll Hall of Fame.
2001	Sets up Gwendolyn B. Gordy Fund to help less-fortunate Motown artists.

INFLUENCES AND INSPIRATION

The studio-based Funk Brothers were instrumental in creating the Motown sound. Working in a dimly lit, dingy room called the "Snakepit" or at Millie's Chit Chat Lounge, this group of musicians helped turn numerous Motown singers into stars over the 14 years that they played together. Largely unrecognized by the public, the group featured Earl "Chunk of Funk" Van Dyke, a jazz pianist, as leader, drummer Benny Benjamin, and bassist James Jamerson.

Together with a handful of other talented Detroit musicians, these men created the trademark sound of Motown and influenced the development of post-1960s pop music. The Funk Brothers usually recorded in three-hour sessions every day, sometimes more than four songs a session. They were paid $10 a song until Gordy approved the track.

In 2003 former Supremes star Mary Wilson argued that the Funk Brothers "made music that the people of the world could enjoy and no longer have to hide that they listened to rhythm and blues. They made it pop. They took one ethnic genre and created a uniquely American genre: the Motown sound." Their talent was recognized in the award-winning 2003 documentary *Standing in the Shadows of Motown: The Best Kept Secret in the History of Pop Music*, and in 2004, when they were awarded a Grammy for Lifetime Achievement.

"Come To Me," was a minor hit. Gordy found that he could not keep up with the demands of national production and distribution, however, and leased Johnson to United Artists. In 1959 Gordy released "Bad Girl" by Smokey Robinson and the Miracles; distributed by Chess Records, the single reached No. 93 on the pop charts.

Taking control

Robinson convinced Gordy to take control of distribution. This paid off when Motown distributed Robinson's 1960 song "Shop Around," which reached No. 1; it was key to establishing Motown as an important independent label. Also in 1960 Gordy acquired the contract of singer Marvin Gaye, who had a series of moderate hits in the 1960s but in the 1970s became one of Motown's biggest stars.

Mary Wells, another early Motown discovery, had her first Top 10 R&B hit in 1960 with "Bye, Bye, Baby." Girl bands were also important to the emerging label. In 1961 Gordy signed a young trio of singers and renamed them the Supremes; they would become one of his greatest successes. The Marvalettes had Motown's first No. 1 with "Please Mister Postman" (1961). Their success encouraged Gordy to sign Martha and the Vandellas, who went on to have a string of hits.

In the early 1960s Gordy signed a blind, 11-year-old pianist, whom he renamed "Little Stevie Wonder." With the addition of the Four Tops, who had previously recorded for Chess Records, it seemed that Motown could do no wrong. The songwriting team of Brian Holland, Lamont Dozier, and Eddie Holland, who started working together in 1962, wrote the hugely successful "Where Did Our Love Go," which became a prototype for other Motown songs in what

Gordy established as a "production line" approach to music. Along with the songwriting trio, the Funk Brothers—the musicians who created the core Motown sound and played on practically every track—helped give the label its distinctive sound (*see box*).

Gordy wanted Motown to appeal to mainstream white audiences. He employed Maxine Powell, the owner of a modeling school, and choreographer Cholly Atkins to create a Motown "package": sophisticated and polished singers who behaved well and sang and danced beautifully. The move paid off: Between 1964 and 1967 Motown had 14 No. 1 pop singles and 20 No. 1 R&B chart hits. By 1966 Motown was releasing about 75 percent of the records that made the national charts.

But there were squabbles and jealousies in-house. Holland-Dozier-Holland quit after a bitter argument over royalties. In 1971 Gordy moved Motown to Hollywood, California. At the beginning of the 1970s, the label still had major stars such as Diana Ross and the Jackson 5, but as the decade went on it lost key talent. In 1988 Gordy sold Motown for over $60 million to MCA and Boston Ventures; the company was later acquired by Polygram for over $3 million in 1993.

See also: Dozier, Lamont; Gaye, Marvin; Jackson 5; Robinson, Smokey; Ross, Diana; Wonder, Stevie

Further reading: Gordy, Berry. *To Be Loved: The Music, the Magic, the Memories of Motown*. New York, NY: Time Warner, 1994.
http://www.history-of-rock.com/motown_records.htm (History of Motown with links to performers).

GOSSETT, Louis, Jr.
Actor

An Academy Award-winning actor and veteran of stage, screen, and television, Louis Gossett, Jr., is renowned for his versatile performances. Born in 1936 in Brooklyn, New York, Gossett was a success academically as well as on the basketball court of his high school.

When a leg injury left him temporarily unable to play basketball, Gossett turned his talents to acting. At his first Broadway audition at age 16, he beat out 400 other hopefuls to the lead in *Take a Giant Step.* His mature performance won him the Donaldson Award for best newcomer in 1953.

Gossett entered New York University on a basketball scholarship and, upon graduation, played briefly for the New York Knicks before devoting himself to acting. Cast in the historic Broadway production of *A Raisin in the Sun*, opposite Sidney Poitier in 1959, Gossett delivered a critically acclaimed performance, which he recreated for the 1961 film adaptation. He received a steady supply of work from then on, appearing in a range of films, including *Travels with My Aunt* (1972), *The River Niger* (1976), and *The Deep* (1977).

Awarded for good work

In 1977 Gossett became world famous for his role in the historical slave drama *Roots*. His performance won him an Emmy. Securing his status as an exceptional character actor in 1982, Gossett won both a Golden Globe and the Oscar for Best Supporting Actor for his role as a drill sergeant in *An Officer and a Gentleman*. Gossett continued his successful film career with roles in the *Iron Eagle* series of action films (1985, 1986, 1992, 1995) and *Toy Soldiers* (1991). He won a second Golden Globe for *The Josephine*

▲ **Louis Gossett, Jr., shows off his 1982 Oscar for his role in** An Officer and a Gentleman.

Baker Story (1992) and in 1998 a National Association for the Advancement of Colored People (NAACP) Image Award and a further Emmy for his role in the popular TV series *Touched by an Angel*.

Gossett supports several charities, such as the Family Tree and the Muscular Dystrophy Association. He has been given many social-justice awards for his work, including the Martin Luther King, Jr., Alumni Award and Senator Carolina Mosby's Above and Beyond Award.

See also: Baker, Josephine; Poitier, Sidney

Further reading: Mapp, Edward. *African Americans and the Oscar: Seven Decades of Struggle and Achievement.* Lanham, MD: Scarecrow Press, 2003.
http://www.louisgossett.info (Official site).

KEY DATES	
1936	Born in Brooklyn, New York, on May 27.
1953	Wins lead role in Broadway production of *Take a Giant Step*; wins Donaldson Award.
1958	Plays briefly for the New York Knicks.
1977	Wins Outstanding Lead Actor Emmy for *Roots*.
1982	Wins Academy Award and Golden Globe for Best Supporting Actor for *An Officer and a Gentleman.*
1998	Receives NAACP Image Award.

GRACE, Charles Emmanuel
Religious Leader

The charismatic and flamboyant Charles Emmanuel Grace, known to his thousands of followers as "Sweet Daddy" and "Daddy Grace," headed up a phenomenally successful church that brought him great personal wealth. To this day his church continues to thrive.

Marceline Manoel de Graca was born in the Cape Verde islands off western Africa on January 25, 1881, to parents of Portuguese and African descent. In about 1908 Grace emigrated to New Bedford, Massachusetts, where he did menial jobs. It is thought that he established his first church in West Waltham in 1919. In the mid-1920s he held evangelical meetings that attracted more than 10,000 followers in Charlotte, North Carolina.

The United House of Prayer

In 1926 Grace incorporated his church, the United House of Prayer for All People of the Church on the Rock of the Apostolic Faith, in Washington, D.C. He included "all people" in the title because his church made a point of taking in poor people and those who were not welcome at other churches. Grace's churches were very popular, with as many as half a million members, 100 congregations, and 70 churches along the East Coast. Nearly all the members were African Americans.

Grace had many detractors. His success brought him enormous wealth; he owned some 40 residences, including a unit in the luxurious El Dorado on Central Park West in New York City. He lived in an 85-room mansion in Los Angeles, California. His flamboyant appearance—with long hair; 6-inch (15-cm) fingernails painted red, white, and blue; and extravagant clothes—added to people's

▲ *The extragavant lifestyle of "Sweet Daddy" Grace—here with his chauffeur—brought him much criticism.*

suspicions. His followers, however, were grateful for his generosity. He provided them not only with churches but also with apartments, pensions, retirement homes, burial plans, and free food in his church cafeterias.

Grace's income came from many schemes. He sold soap, vitamins, hair products, and ice cream that were considered divine by his followers. When Grace died in 1960 his finances were in chaos and the Internal Revenue Service claimed $6 million in back taxes. About 5,000 people attended his funeral service at which Grace delivered his own eulogy on tape. He had once said, "I never said I was God but you cannot prove to me I'm not."

See also: Religion and African Americans

Further reading: Halter, Marilyn. *Between Race and Ethnicity: Cape Verdean American Immigrants, 1860–1965.* Urbana, IL: University of Illinois Press, 1993.
www.soulofamerica.com/cityfldr/charlotte14.html (Biography).

KEY DATES	
1881	Born in the Cape Verde Islands on January 25.
1919	Establishes his first church in West Waltham, Massachusetts, at about this time.
1920s	Attracts 10,000 followers at meetings in Charlotte, North Carolina.
1926	Incorporates the United House of Prayer for All People of the Church on the Rock of the Apostolic Faith.
1960	Dies in Los Angeles, California, on January 12.
1961	Tax irregularities settled

GRANDMASTER Flash

DJ, Entrepreneur

Many of the aspects of rap music that are familiar today can be traced back to the innovations introduced by the disc jockey Grandmaster Flash. Flash also released *The Message*, one of the first rap albums to be internationally successful.

Grandmaster Flash was born Joseph Saddler on January 1, 1958, in Barbados. His family emigrated to the United States when he was a child, and Flash grew up in the Bronx, New York City. He showed a love of music at an early age. By listening to his father's varied music collection, the young man introduced himself to a wide range of musical styles, from jazz to funk to heavy metal.

Block parties

In the mid-1970s New York was home to a vibrant party scene with DJs playing at block parties. They were often held in local parks, and the DJs used their own amplifiers and loudspeakers, which together were known as soundsystems. The idea of soundsystems had been brought to New York by immigrants from the West Indies, chiefly Jamaica, where they have been used to entertain crowds since the 1950s.

From age 16 Flash played music at these free parties. Many of the DJs who played at such events were local celebrities. One of them, Kool DJ Herc (*see box on p. 124*), was particularly influential on the young Flash and the history of hip-hop. Kool DJ Herc used two turntables with his soundsystem, which allowed him to switch between two records, playing the best selections of each. Grandmaster Flash took Herc's approach, and refined it to create the basis of a new musical style called hip-hop. While Herc's DJ style was innovative, it was also haphazard; Flash began to work at a smoother style in which one tune would mix seamlessly into another.

Mixing music

By the late 1970s Flash was studying electronics at the Samuel Gompers Vocational and Technical High School, and the knowledge he gained enabled him to produce a mixer that helped him blend music together. Flash practiced his DJ style at home and refined a number of techniques that would later become central to rap music. One such technique was "cutting," which involved moving a record forward or back manually on the turntable to repeat a section of the music, creating a scratching sound

in the process. Another technique was "punch phrasing," which involved a particular section of music or lyrics from one record being inserted over another.

Grandmaster Flash and the Furious Five

Flash's remarkable skills as a DJ soon began to draw huge crowds. In the late 1970s he broadened his appeal by appearing on stage with MCs (master of ceremonies). MCs had been part of soundsystem culture for some time. Originally, they had just shouted out short phrases, exhorting the crowd to dance. Gradually, however, MCs had begun to use the long intricate rhymes known as raps. After working with a number of MCs, including Kurtis Blow (1959–), Flash eventually assembled a stable team, the Furious Five. They were Melle Mel

▼ *Grandmaster Flash was given his nickname because of his remarkable skills at the turntables.*

INFLUENCES AND INSPIRATION

One of the greatest influences on Grandmaster Flash (and rap music in general) was Kool DJ Herc. Born Clive Campbell in 1955, Herc was a Jamaican immigrant whose block parties were famous throughout the Bronx in the early 1970s. Herc was known for the sheer volume of noise that his soundsystem produced and also for his innovative approach to DJing. Herc used two turntables (or decks) and would often have the same record playing on each. He would play the instrumental section in the middle of the song (known as the "break") on one turntable and then play the same section on the second turntable. He could create a continuous loop of sound by going back and forth between the turntables. Herc's approach was copied not just by Grandmaster Flash but by virtually every hip-hop DJ in New York. Herc, however, was not destined to reap much financial reward for his contribution to music. He drifted out of music after being stabbed at one of his own parties and never released a record of his own.

(Melvin Glover), Cowboy (Keith Wiggins), Kidd Creole (Nathaniel Glover), Scorpio (Eddie Morris), and Raheim (Guy Williams).

In 1979 "Rapper's Delight" by the Sugar Hill Gang became the first rap record to cross over to a mainstream audience. In response the Furious Five released a single of their own, "We Rap More Mellow," which was put out under the name the Younger Generation. It was followed later in 1979 by "Superappin'," the first record to be released under the name Grandmaster Flash and the Furious Five. The group then signed with Sugar Hill Records, for whom they recorded "Freedom," a Top 20 hit on the national rhythm-and-blues (R&B) chart in 1980.

However, the single that really put Flash's name on the map was "The Adventures of Grandmaster Flash on the Wheels of Steel" (1981). The track was a showcase for Flash's virtuoso DJ skills, a collage of sound made up of excerpts of songs from other artists, including such seemingly unlikely sources as white rock acts Blondie and Queen. The following single, "The Message," released in July 1982, made even more of a mark. This time MC Melle Mel took center stage. His lyrics detailed the harsh realities of trying to survive in the black ghettos of New York City. "The Message" achieved platinum status, selling one million copies in a month. It was the first single to show that rap could deliver a social commentary, and it introduced hip-hop to an international audience.

"The Message" proved to be the high point of Grandmaster Flash's career. In 1983 Flash took Sugar Hill Records to court, believing that he was not receiving his fair share of royalties. The court case led to a split in the Furious Five. Kidd Creole and Raheim stayed with Flash, while Melle Mel, Scorpio, and Cowboy recorded under the name Grandmaster and Melle Mel, finding success with the anticocaine track "White Lines."

Grandmaster Flash himself would spend much of the 1980s battling cocaine addiction. Flash had a few minor hits but never again enjoyed widespread commercial success. His 1980s albums *They Said It Couldn't Be Done*, (1985), *The Source* (1986), and *Ba Dop Boom Bang* (1987) sold relatively poorly and generally disappointed his fans.

The Furious Five reunited sporadically in the 1980s and 1990s, and for a while Flash hosted a show on the New York radio station Hot 97. He resurfaced again in 2002, when he released *The Official Adventures of Grandmaster Flash*, a compilation album of the songs that he used to play in his now legendary 1970s block parties. In the spring of 2004 Flash began a tour of schools and colleges, talking about his contribution to music. Later that year Grandmaster Flash was nominated to join the Rock and Roll Hall of Fame, the first rap star so recognized. The fact that he was not elected was a source of considerable controversy.

KEY DATES	
1958	Born in Barbados on January 1.
1979	"Superappin'" is the Furious Five's first single.
1982	"The Message" hits the Billboard chart in July.
1983	The Furious Five splits after a court battle.
2004	Grandmaster Flash is the first rapper to be nominated to join the Rock and Roll Hall of Fame.

See also: Music and African Americans

Further reading: Fernando, S.H., Jr. *The New Beats*. New York, NY: Doubleday, 1994.
http://www.grandmasterflash.com (Official site).

GRANT, George F.
Inventor, Dentist

One of the first African Americans to graduate from Harvard Dental School, George F. Grant was a successful dentist, an imaginative inventor, and, perhaps above all, an enthusiastic golfer. He is credited with inventing the golf tee.

Education

George Franklin Grant was born in 1847 in Oswego, New York, to former slaves. As a boy he ran errands for his local dentist before being promoted to dental assistant.

Aged 19, Grant resolved to establish himself independently and moved to Boston, Massachusetts, to train as a dentist. At first he was an apprentice to a dentist in the city, but then he decided to go to Harvard Dental School. He was one of just two African Americans in the class, the first to ever study at the school. Grant graduated with honors in 1870.

Dental innovator

In 1871 Grant became Harvard Dental School's first African American faculty member when he was appointed to the department of mechanical dentistry. He remained a member of the faculty for 19 years.

Determined to help people born with cleft palates, which are both disfiguring and prevent sufferers from speaking properly, Grant began to develop a prosthetic insert, called the oblate palate, which could be put in the mouth to help the patient talk and eat.

Grant won national and international recognition for this innovative treatment and became a world authority in the field of mechanical dentistry. A founding member and later president of the Harvard Odontological Society, Grant was elected president of the Harvard Dental Alumni Association in 1881.

Golf problems

Grant was a passionate golfer and landscaped his very own golf course in an open meadow near his Massachusetts home. At the time, golfers formed a pyramid of damp sand or dirt whenever they needed to tee off, or begin hitting the ball toward the putting green and the hole. The ball was placed on the mound to allow players to hit it very hard without damaging the ground or clubs.

However, the process produced a lot of debris on golf courses, and players were often dissatisfied with the unpredictable results of the system. Grant's dissatisfaction drove him to devise an alternative solution. He set out to create a device that supported the ball high enough off the ground but did not interfere with a golfer's swing and follow-through.

Invention

In 1899 Grant patented his design for a pointed wooden peg with a rubber head. The ball, which was made of rubber at that time, was held by the head. This invention, which Grant named a tee, gave a golfer greater control when driving the ball up the fairway.

Grant asked a local firm to manufacture his invention on a small scale. He never publicized his invention or tried to market it, although he gave numerous tees to his friends.

Following Grant's death in 1910, his idea was forgotten until the early 1920s, when New Jersey dentist William Lowell patented a tee that would eventually become standard: a wooden peg with a funnel-shaped head, concave top surface, and narrow stem. The "Reddy Tee" was cheap to mass produce, but most importantly Lowell marketed it aggressively. Because of its success it was assumed that Lowell had invented the golf tee. It was only in 1991 that the United States Golf Association acknowledged Grant's significant contribution to golf.

KEY DATES	
1847	Born in Oswego, New York.
1870	Graduates from Harvard Dental School.
1881	Elected president of the Harvard Dental Alumni Association.
1899	Receives U.S. patent no. 638,920 for an improved golf tee.
1910	Dies in New Hampshire.
1991	United States Golf Association recognizes Grant as inventor of the golf tee.

Further reading: Burt, McKinley. *African-American Inventors.* Portland, OR: National Book Company, 2000.
http://www.ourgolf.com/history/georgegrant.html (Grant biography and patent description).

GRAVES, Earl G.
Businessman

Earl Gilbert Graves was born in 1935, the son of a West Indian garment worker, and was raised in the Bedford Stuyvesant area of New York. He went to Morgan State University, Maryland, as a scholarship student, and while there operated several campus businesses.

Graves graduated in 1958 with a BA degree in economics and then served two years in the Army, where he rose to captain with the Green Berets. In 1962 he worked as a narcotics agent with the Treasury, and then went on to sell and develop real estate in Brooklyn. In 1966 he was hired as an assistant to Senator Robert F. Kennedy (1925–1968). After Kennedy's assassination, Graves set up Earl G. Graves Associates, a management-consulting firm advising corporations on urban affairs and economic development.

Business in mind

Graves wanted to contribute to the economic development of black Americans, and in 1970 he launched *Black Enterprise* magazine, the first publication for African Americans interested in business. The magazine is still regarded as the ultimate resource for African American business professionals and policymakers.

Throughout his career, Graves has been a passionate promoter of higher education and is committed to creating opportunities for young people to learn about business. In 1995 Morgan State University renamed its school of business and management, the Earl G. Graves School of Business and Management in recognition of his support.

Graves has also been active in the Boy Scouts of America, and became the second National Commissioner of the Boy Scouts of America and the first African American to hold the position.

▲ **Earl G. Graves (right) and basketball player Magic Johnson (center) clasp hands with Pepsi-Cola President Craig E. Weatherup after the pair bought a large soda-bottling company in 1990.**

In 1997 Graves wrote a book called *How to Succeed in Business Without Being White*, which records the success stories of African Americans who have made it in the business world. The book made both the *New York Times* and the *Wall Street Journal* Business bestsellers lists.

In 1999 Graves received the National Association for the Advancement of Colored People (NAACP) Spingarn Medal, the highest achievement award for African Americans. Graves was named by *Fortune Magazine* as one of the 50 most powerful and influential African Americans in corporate America in 2002 and was also appointed to serve on the Presidential Commission for the National Museum of African American History and Culture.

In 2005 Graves was president and CEO of Earl G. Graves, Ltd., which publishes *Black Enterprise*. He also served as a director of several corporations, including American Airlines and DaimlerChrysler.

See also: Johnson, Earvin "Magic"

Further reading: Graves, Earl G. *How to Succeed in Business Without Being White: Straight Talk on Making It in America*. New York, NY: Harper Business, 1998.
http://www.aetna.com/foundation/aahcalendar/1995graves.html (African American History Calendar).

KEY DATES	
1935	Born in Brooklyn, New York, on January 9.
1966	Hired as an administrative assistant on the staff of Senator Robert F. Kennedy.
1970	Launches *Black Enterprise* magazine.
1997	*How to Succeed in Business Without Being White* is released and reaches the *New York Times* and the *Wall Street Journal* Business bestsellers lists.
1999	Receives the NAACP Spingarn Medal.

THE GREAT MIGRATION AND URBANIZATION

The Great Migration is the name given to the movement of millions of African Americans from the rural South to the cities of the North, particularly in the early decades of the 20th century. The migrants were looking to escape the problems of racism in the South and felt they could find better jobs and enjoy a better quality of life in the North. It is estimated that more than a million individuals participated in the first wave of migration, which started around 1916. Between that date and 1970 some six million black Southerners moved to cities in the North and West of the country. The unprecedented social movement transformed the cultural and political landscape.

The first wave

The first wave of the Great Migration occurred during World War I (1914–1918) and the 1920s.

KEY DATES

1900s Boll weavil attacks cotton crops.

1905 Robert Abbott founds the *Chicago Defender*.

1916 Approximate start of the first wave of the Great Migration.

1917 United States enters World War I.

1922 International Harvester introduces the row tractor.

1929 Stock market crash brings an end to the first wave of migration.

1931 John D. and Mack Rust invent the first spindle cotton picker, which picks one bale a day; by 1933 it picks five bales a day; by 1953 over 15,000 cotton pickers are at work.

1940 Second wave of migration begins.

1970 Population begins to drift away from cities.

It created the first large, urban black communities in the North, where the black population rose about 20 percent between 1910 and 1930. Cities such as Chicago, Detroit, New York, and Cleveland saw some of the largest numbers of new arrivals. Between 1910 and 1920, for example, Chicago's African American population rose by 65,000, or

Black migrant farm workers prepare to move to move from North Carolina to seek work in the North in the 1920s.

148.2 percent. In Detroit, where car-making plants offered opportunities for jobs, the population rose in the same period by over 610 percent.

During the early 1900s African Americans were overwhelmingly rural and Southern. Fifty years later blacks were mainly an urban population: Almost three-quarters of black Americans had migrated to Northern cities. Blacks fled the South for many reasons. Some wanted to escape discriminatory Jim Crow laws, which excluded blacks in the South from many of the rights enjoyed by their white contemporaries. Others moved to seek work, largely because of a decline in agricultural work (*see box on p. 128*).

Patterns of migration

Until 1916 black Southerners had primarily moved within the South,

A steelworker and his family in Pittsburgh, Pennsylvania, in 1935. The city's thriving iron and steel industries attracted black workers.

North that provided a cheap and ample supply of labor for flourishing industries.

That situation changed with the outbreak of World War I in Europe in 1914. European immigration into the United States slowed to a trickle, while millions of American workers eventually left their jobs to serve in the military. Soon Northern employers needed additional workers to meet the demands of war production. They looked to the South for laborers, and particularly to its African Americans.

Among the industries worst hit were the railroads, which were nearly crippled by the loss of workers to the military. The railroads were so desperate for help that some offered to pay travel expenses to encourage African Americans to relocate from the South to the North. The Pennsylvania and Lake Erie Railroad recruited between 75,000 and 100,000 Southern

searching for better land or more favorable terms of sharecropping. The North was an attractive destination for them—it promised relief from Jim Crow laws and other forms of racial oppression that dominated the South—but for most Southern blacks moving

was impracticable. There was a shortage of jobs for African Americans outside of the South. Not only did many Northern employers have their own racial prejudices; there were also large numbers of European immigrants flowing into the cities of the

TURNING POINT

The first wave of African American migration to the North was partly fueled by a decline in agriculture in the South. Since the civil war many black sharecroppers had worked long hours for little money in a exploitative system that tied them to white landowners. In some ways sharecropping was little better than slavery.

In the early 1920s, however, conditions for Southern blacks

deteriorated further when the cotton harvest on which they depended was hit by an infestation of the boll weevil. The insect's young fed on the fibers in the cotton bolls. The pest wiped out the crops of thousands of farmers and sharecroppers, forcing them to seek other means of income. One planter called the boll weevil "a billion dollar bug that got behind the Southern Negro

and chased him across Mason and Dixon's line."

Meanwhile the introduction of agricultural machines such as the row tractor (1922) greatly reduced the South's need for field laborers, most of whom were African Americans. The labor surplus meant that landowners could pay workers as little as 75 cents per day. In contrast, Northern industries paid between $3 and $5 per day.

blacks. Meanwhile other labor representatives traveled around the South encouraging blacks to migrate North. In 1917 a steel company in Pittsburgh, Pennsylvania, hired a train to move 200 workers north from Alabama. In 1923 another Pittsburgh company was hiring about a thousand black migrants every month.

Influence of the press

Southern blacks were also encouraged to move by the African American press. Founded in 1905 by Robert Abbott, the weekly *Chicago Defender* was the largest and most influential black-owned newspaper in the United States. It was widely read by African Americans in the South. The paper crusaded against white Southerners and actively encouraged blacks to move to Chicago and the North. The paper was so critical of the South and helped draw so many blacks North that many Southern towns banned it from sale. In 1918 its circulation was 125,000: Roughly two-third of its readers lived outside Chicago.

In response, Southern newspapers argued that black Americans belonged south of the Mason–Dixon Line. It was clear to some commentators, however, that the only way to ensure African Americans stayed in the South was to improve their conditions. The South Carolina *Columbia State* newspaper observed in 1916, "If the Southern people would have the Negroes remain, they must treat the Negroes justly." Some Southern employers did indeed try to prevent the outflow of labor by promising better pay and work conditions, although there were

Angry whites gather along a street in an affluent Northern residential area in this 1950s demonstration against integrated housing.

also some who attacked black passengers on northbound trains, trying to force them to remain in the South. Nevertheless, economic opportunity in the North and political oppression in the South ensured that the northward flow continued until the Great Depression of the 1930s ended the North's demand for workers.

Conditions in the North

Initially the North—and later the West—did seem to offer blacks the chance to live with greater dignity and hope. Northern cities offered access to political, economic, cultural, social and educational institutions, few of which were available to African Americans in the South. Despite the jobs and housing available in the North, however, life for many African Americans remained difficult. Many remained poor and lived in the worst parts of town. Many also found it difficult to adjust to the conditions of urban living. The

arrival of large numbers of African Americans amid other immigrant groups also produced significant racial tension and occasional race riots (*see box on p. 130*).

Blacks also faced informal forms of racial discrimination, including residential segregation, discrimination in hiring, and limits on advancement in the workplace. Incomes could be unstable: In times of economic slowdown, black workers tended to be the first to be laid off by employers. By the end of the 1920s some blacks had given up on their dream of a better future in the North: Increasing numbers of migrants made the return journey back to the South to attempt to improve conditions there.

Nevertheless, many migrants did find significant improvements in living conditions in the North. A black clergyman, while admitting that prejudice toward the migrants was widespread, added that, "The color bar isn't drawn in their faces at every turn as it is in the South."

In the North most African Americans no longer had to live with the constant threat of

The arrival of large numbers of African Americans in northern cities, where they tended to settle in separate communities, aroused hostility among some whites. Whites saw the new arrivals as a threat to their jobs; their suspicion was intensified when employers used black migrants as strikebreakers. In 1917 the hostility led to race riots. They broke out first in East St. Louis in Illinois, where blacks had found jobs as strikebreakers in the meatpacking business. White gangs attacked blacks and their homes, killing at least 39 people, and wounding many more. Further riots broke out in Pennsylvania and New Jersey.

In 1919 another wave of race riots swept the North. They started in Washington, D.C., where soldiers and sailors demobilized at the end of World War I turned on blacks after newspapers printed sensational accounts of black men assaulting white women. In Chicago, meanwhile, a black boy drowned in Lake Michigan after he was stoned by whites for swimming in a part of the lake used exclusively by whites. When police refused to arrest anyone for the incident, rioting spread across the city. In the next three days 38 people died in the violence, 23 of whom were black. Some 535 people were injured and a thousand mainly black families left homeless.

In 1921 a race riot that broke out in Tulsa, Oklahoma, escalated when both sides armed themselves. The violence left about 75 African Americans and about 10 whites dead; white rioters had burned the African American part of the city to the ground.

violence. Their homes were sturdier and better equipped than those they had left. Black children went to school for a full year and had high schools available to them; adults could (and did) go to night school. One black migrant wrote to his family back in the South, "I should have been here twenty years ago. I just begin to feel like a man. My children are going to the same school with the whites and I don't have to humble to no one."

Meanwhile, political recognition (if not real power) provided African American communities with a sense of importance and dignity. Factory wages were adequate in good times to provide for consumer goods that were unaffordable to most black Southerners.

In Chicago, for example, well-paid jobs in packinghouses, steel mills, garment factories, and a variety of other industries were often unionized and offered a stable income. Black migrants like William Levi Dawson (1888–1970) rose to political power. Born and raised in Albany, Georgia, Dawson migrated to Chicago after graduating from Tuskegee Institute and studied law at Northwestern University. He then entered local politics, becoming an alderman on the city council, and was eventually elected to Congress in 1942. Chicago's South Side housed an energetic and vibrant black community, known to some as Bronzeville, similar to Harlem in New York City.

Second wave

Between 1940 and 1970 a "Second Great Migration" took place from the South to the North and West. It involved even more people than the first wave—at least four million. The participants in this second wave left the South mainly because ongoing mechanization of the cotton process, such as the introduction of the mechanical cotton picker, was putting manual laborers out of work.

This wave of migration had a different character from the earlier one. By 1940 African American communities were well established in nearly all Northern cities, and family and community networks linked North and South. Later migrants usually followed paths established by family members who had gone before. Whole church congregations sometimes relocated together, or in stages. Ties between the migrants and the communities they left behind were kept alive through letters and journals.

Meanwhile, jobs in the North became increasingly stable as factories grew more unionized or became unionized for the first time. The West also became far

Floyd McKissick, national director of the Congress of Racial Equality, joins a picket line in Harlem, New York City, in 1966, to protest the drafting of African Americans to fight in the Vietnam War.

more significant as a potential destination. It had many shipyards and docks that were busy with war production, and which were desperate for workers.

Industrialization and urbanization
As the Second Great Migration continued, however, so some of the conditions faced by African Americans declined. Schools by now were entirely segregated and slums were more evident. Many black Americans had been disillusioned by the racial hostility they discovered in the North. The illusion that race relations in the North were better or more tolerable than those in the South increasingly seemed simplistic and inaccurate.

As migration continued into the 1950s and 1960s, so the experiences of newcomers and earlier migrants were increasingly shaped by deindustrialization and the appearance of high-rise housing projects. Service sectors such as banking and insurance began to replace industry in terms of economic importance. Like other industrial workers, African Americans suffered as the industrial boom began to deteriorate in the late 1960s and early 1970s and unemployment rose.

The deindustrialization process undermined the prosperity of great industrial urban centers such as Detroit, Chicago, Cleveland, New York, and Los Angeles. The resulting economic decline devastated the infrastructure of once thriving cities. As jobs disappeared and incomes fell, state and local governments were unable to raise as much tax to pay for the provision of local facilities. African American areas of cities suffered particularly, due in part to a combination of systematic neglect and institutional racism. Living conditions declined and whole districts became virtual slums.

Black protest
Declining conditions led to mounting political radicalism among urban African Americans, and a rejection of the nonviolence of the civil rights movement. The black power movement, for example, emerged to promote an ideology of self-definition, self-love, and active resistance to racism in all forms. Disillusion with the slow pace of racial change, the deterioration of urban communities heavily populated by African Americans, and the renewed popularity of black nationalism led to a black awakening and a new political self-assurance.

Since the 1970s a small but noticeable migration has seen African Americans leave central cities to move back to the South or to working-class and middle-class suburbs. By the start of the 21st century Southern cities such as Atlanta, Charlotte, Houston, and Nashville were seeing the return of a record number of blacks seeking better housing and jobs.

See also: Abbott, Robert; Dawson, William L.; Civil Rights; Discrimination; McKissick, Floyd; Political Movements

Further reading: Lehman, Nicholas. *The Promised Land: The Great Black Migration and How It Changed America.* New York, NY: Vintage, 1992. Harrison, Alferdteen. *Black Exodus: The Great Migration from the American South.* Jackson, MS: University Press of Mississippi, 1991. http://www.loc.gov/exhibits/african/afam008.html (Library of Congress site with maps and graphs).

GREAVES, William
Fillmmaker, Actor

William Greaves is an independent African American filmmaker, actor, director, producer, dancer, and writer. William Sloan, of New York's Museum of Modern Art, called him "the leading black documentary filmmaker in the United States today."

Greaves was born on October 8, 1925, in Harlem, New York. From a young age Greaves showed a talent in drawing, and he won several medals for his work. At age 14, he was considered to be one of the top 75 best artists in the state of New York.

His father convinced Greaves to go to Stuyvesant High School, which was a prestigious science-based school. Greaves excelled in his courses and went on to study engineering at City College. He also took dance classes while in college, and in 1944 he decided to drop out to pursue a career in the performing arts. He soon joined the

American Negro Theater, where his performances were critically acclaimed. He went on to appear on Broadway alongside actors such as Sidney Poitier and Anthony Quinn. His first movie role was in the all-black cast of *Miracle in Harlem*. A year later he was cast in *The Fight Never Ends*, starring as heavyweight fighter Joe Louis.

▼*William Greaves has been an important figure in the history of African American cinema.*

Changing attitudes

In the 1950s Greaves became increasingly frustrated by the negative way in which African Americans were presented in the media. He began to study film production and took courses in African history. In 1964 he started his own company, William Greaves Production, Inc.

Greaves has produced more than 200 documentary films, many of them about important African American historical figures such as Ralphe Bunche, Booker T. Washington, Frederick Douglass, and Malcolm X. He says that documentaries interest him because of their "role in consciousness-raising and as an advocacy instrument."

Greaves also produced four feature films, including *Bustin' Loose*, with actors Richard Pryor and Cicely Tyson. His work has won more than 70 awards, including an Emmy, an Image award from the National Association for the Advancement of Colored People (NAACP), and a Life Achievement award from the Association of Independent Video and Filmmakers.

See also: Bunche, Ralph; Douglass, Frederick; Louis, Joe; Malcolm X; Poitier, Sidney; Pryor, Richard; Tyson, Cicely; Washington, Booker T.

Further reading: Bahn-Coblans, Sonja. *William Greaves, Just Doin' It: An Analysis.* Trier, Germany: Wissenschaftlicher Verlag, 1997.
http://www.williamgreaves.com (William Greaves Productions).

GREENE, Joe
Football Player

Joe Greene was the toughest member of one of the stingiest defensive units in the history of the National Football League (NFL), the Pittsburgh Steelers' so-called Steel Curtain. "Mean Joe" Greene led Pittsburgh to four Super Bowl titles in the 1970s. He was voted a record 10 times to the Pro Bowl and twice named NFL Defensive Player of the Year.

College football

Born in 1946, Charles Edward Greene was raised in Temple, Texas. Already a formidable force on his high school football field, Greene won a football scholarship to North Texas State College, majoring in physical education. Here Greene showed himself to be a natural leader and captained the college team to a three-year record. It was at this early stage in his career that the left tackle earned his nickname "Mean Joe" for his daunting defensive play. "Mean Joe" became a national star when he was named Consensus All-American in his senior year. On graduating in 1969, Greene was the number-one draft choice of the Pittsburgh Steelers and was voted NFL Rookie of the Year at the end of the season.

Playing for the Pittsburgh Steelers

Greene played 13 seasons with the Steelers, leading the team's defense. Renowned for his fearless and aggressive defense style, Greene helped the team win four Super Bowl titles in six years and reach six AFC championship games in eight years. Greene won the George Halas Award for his defensive abilities and was named NFL Defensive Player of the Year in 1972 and 1974. He was elected to the Team of the Decade for the 1970s.

▲ *"Mean Joe" Greene was one of the toughest of all players, missing only nine pro games owing to injury.*

In 1980 Greene was asked to appear in an ad for Coca-Cola. The ad won two Clio awards (which honor the advertising industry), including best male performance for Greene, and was voted seventh best commercial of all time by *TV Guide.* As a result Greene was invited to make a number of television and film appearances.

Retiring as a professional player in 1981, Greene tried his hand at several new jobs, including CBS announcer and restaurant owner. In 1987 he was inducted into the Professional Football Hall of Fame and became a defensive line coach, first for the Pittsburgh Steelers, and then the Miami Dolphins and Arizona Cardinals. In 2004 Greene returned to the Pittsburgh Steelers to work as a scout.

Further reading: Burchard, S. H. *Mean Joe Greene.* New York, NY: Harcourt Brace Jovanovich, 1976.
Fox, Larry. *Mean Joe Greene and the Steelers' Front Four.* New York, NY: Dodd, 1975.
http://www.profootballhof.com/hof/member.jsp?player_id=80 (Pro Football Hall of Fame biography).

KEY DATES	
1946	Born in Temple, Texas, on September 24.
1969	Drafted to the Pittsburgh Steelers.
1972	Wins NFL Defensive Player of the Year award.
1974	Wins Associated Press and NFL Defensive Player of the Year awards.
1981	Retires from professional football.
1987	Elected to the Professional Football Hall of Fame.

GREENER, Richard
Educator, Lawyer

Richard Greener was the first African American to graduate from Harvard University. A lawyer by training, he was a strong advocate for the resettlement of freed slaves to the western states and territories.

Richard Theodore Greener was born in 1844 in Philadelphia, Pennsylvania, but grew up principally in Boston and Cambridge, Massachusetts. When Greener was 12, his father, a seaman, walked out, and Greener quit school to help support his mother. With help from his different employers he was able to continue his studies.

One of his employers, Augustus E. Bachelder, offered financial support so that Greener could attend Oberlin College in Ohio in 1862. After experiencing racism there, Greener returned to New England, where he graduated from Phillips Academy in Andover, Massachusetts, in 1865. He was then accepted at Harvard College by its president,

▼ *A lawyer and civil servant, Richard Greener also worked as a professor at several universities.*

Thomas Hill, who wanted to experiment by educating an African American. Greener's education to date had been patchy, and he had to repeat his first year. After that his academic advances were spectacular.

Greener graduated from Harvard in 1870, the first African American to do so, and started to teach. While teaching, he studied for a law degree and passed the South Carolina Bar in 1876. Greener moved to Washington, D.C., the following year with his wife.

Political activity
Greener was an enthusiastic supporter of resettling in western states freed African American slaves. After arriving in Washington, D.C., he made speeches and lobbied on behalf of such settlers.

He started his own law firm in 1881. Between 1885 and 1892 he served as secretary of the Grant Monument Association and from 1885 to 1890 as a civil servant. A staunch supporter of the Republican Party, he worked as head of the Colored Bureau of the party for the 1896 election. In 1898 he was appointed to diplomatic positions in India, Russia, and China. In 1905 he returned to the United States and settled in Chicago, where he worked as a lawyer and insurance agent until his death in 1922.

Further reading: Sollors, Werner, et al. (eds.). *Blacks at Harvard: A Documentary History of African American Experience at Harvard and Radcliffe.* New York, NY: New York University Press, 1993.
http://www.massmoments.org/index.cfm?mid=35
(Massachusetts Foundation for the Humanities biography).

SET INDEX

Set Index

Set Index

Set Index